SMALLTALK, OBJECTS, AND DESIGN

Smalltalk, Objects, and Design

Chamond Liu

toExcel

San Jose   New York   Shanghai

Smalltalk, Objects, and Design

Reprinted from the original 1996 edition with minor corrections

Published by toExcel, an imprint of iUniverse.com, Inc.

For information address:
iUniverse.com, Inc.
620 North 48th St., Suite 201
Lincoln, NE 68504
www.iUniverse.com

ISBN 1-58348-490-6
Printed in the United States of America

"My good friend, every profession requires effort and devotion and practice."

— advice to the young Perceval
[de Troyes 1190]

Contents

Acknowledgments

This book derives from two activities—developing and teaching courses, and developing software. But the real sources are the people I've encountered along the way. Many of them have profoundly shaped my thinking about software—Dave Collins, Peter Deutsch, Amarjeet Garewal, Steve Goetze, Ralph Johnson, Doug Lea, Bertrand Meyer, Tom Morgan, Dave Thomas, Rebecca Wirfs-Brock, and Kirk Wolf—and many others have left smaller but chaotically important impressions: Bruce Anderson, Marilyn Bates, Katherine Betz, Desmond D'Souza, Phil Hartley, Richard Helm, Felix Laura, and John Vlissides. From here the list is too long to enumerate, for it includes individuals with whom I sweated over their businesses' real object-oriented design and programming problems, plus all the students and instructors through the years from whom I learned about teaching objects and Smalltalk and C++.

I am grateful to the many people who were kind enough to share their opinions on draft manuscripts. Bruce Anderson assailed hackneyed expressions and examples; Kent Beck made me rethink my pedagogical approach; Katherine Betz streamlined discussions; Michele Choate caught stylistic slips; Eric Clayberg taught me new things about Smalltalk; Dave Collins, a closet historian, set chronologies straight; Ken Cooper pointed out awkward transitions; Lisa Goetze suggested improvements to the exercises; Steve Goetze was a sounding board for impetuous ideas and, sensitive to the zeitgeist, warned me off gratuitous soapboxes; Ralph Johnson's enthusiasm and tact kept me going when there was still no end in sight; Doug Lea urged technical respectability where there was none; Ruth Liu distinguished what I actually said from what I meant to say; Tom Morgan flushed out structural and conceptual flaws; Larry Smith was the conscience of the IBM Smalltalk product; Dave Thomas alerted me to trends from the ANSI standardization effort; Michael Tsuji painstakingly and repeatedly dissected the entire manuscript from the standpoint of someone who professed to be ignorant of objects, and so highlighted innumerable spots where readers would have gone astray; and Kirk Wolf's razor-sharp sensibilities caught sloppy assertions about objects. Kim Arthur, David Bernstein, Wai-Mee Ching, Bill Creager, Amarjeet Garewal, John Granlund, and Greg Lee also provided helpful comments. For felicitous anecdotal tidbits, I am grateful to Kent Beck, Roy Campbell, Dave Collins, Erich Gamma, Tami Kinsey, Hal Lorin, and Kirk Wolf.

Thanks also to the unsung heroes of the publishing world: Tommy Barker, Steve Brill, Lee Fitzpatrick, Leslie Haimes, Ted Kennedy, Mary Piergies, and especially Marjan Bace for his guidance on the care and feeding of a book; Dave Lynch for his illuminating and provocative copyediting; and Sheila Carlisle for the care and precision with which she transformed the raw manuscript into an attractive form. I also thank IBM for giving me time to begin this project. Neither they nor I imagined it would take so long.

Everything owes something to root causes (had it not been for such-and-such, this-and-that would never have happened). Thus I, and every practicing object-oriented programmer, am indebted to Alan Kay and his associates at the Learning Research Group at Xerox PARC for inventing Smalltalk, and Bjarne Stroustrup for giving us the C++ counterpoint. The dialectic between these schools of thought inspires much of what follows.

CHAMOND LIU
Clarity Computing

Preface

This book is about Smalltalk and objects, in more or less balanced measure. By this I mean that there is ample Smalltalk to expose and crystallize in the reader's mind all the important object-oriented design ideas, and not so much as to distract from them. Smalltalk is an excellent vehicle for this task because it is small and simple enough that learning about it intrudes as little as possible on learning about design. Yet it is rich enough to precisely clarify what can otherwise degenerate into academic discussions.

By no means is this an advanced book, on either Smalltalk or objects. I have strived to stick to the matters that seasoned Smalltalk developers are fully aware of but consider too obvious to explain. These matters range from what today would be deemed elementary ("What do I mean by an object?") to sophisticated ("Can I reuse a pattern of objects?"), but mostly reside somewhere in the middle ground. I think back to how long (too long) it took me to internalize all these "obvious" matters and imagine that some well-placed explanations along the way could have saved me a good bit of trouble. I hope to save some of you that trouble.

One can't talk about objects and Smalltalk without also talking in practically the same breath about design. "Design" is a word that all computer people know, yet many still disagree about its meaning, or what it produces, or when it begins and ends. For the purposes of this book, to design is to discover alternatives, weigh them, and consciously choose among them. Design, like life, is all about striking the right balance. In this sense of design, we are liable to be designing even at moments when our job description says we are doing something else entirely: we may discover design alternatives and weigh or reject them while we are doing object analysis or modeling, writing code, or peeling carrots.

The goal is to design more like veteran software developers do. They choose among alternatives quickly and subconsciously, drawing upon years of experience, something like chess grandmasters choosing among moves. Lacking this experience, novices have a hard time discovering plausible alternatives, and an impossible time discovering subtle ones. For their sake then, I often argue alternatives and the trade-offs between them, so that they will have an outside chance of considering the same design alternatives that the veterans do.

The approach is not encyclopedic. Absent are systematic tours through class libraries, discussions of the visual programming or collaborative development tools that are available for Smalltalk environments, and discourses about notations and methodologies. Notations are as capable of obscuring ideas as they are of elucidating them, so the few that appear are deferred until they become indispensable to the presentation. If it is not already clear, let me also issue the explicit disclaimer that this is not a catalog of Smalltalk tricks and techniques.

Smalltalk is not the only way to think about object-oriented software. C++, the most widespread object-oriented language, contrasts sharply with Smalltalk in so many ways that awareness of C++ enriches the overall object-oriented experience. Therefore I include remarks about C++ whenever they may enhance your appreciation of objects.

For those new to objects, reading the chapters in order will make most sense. On the other hand, because of my own weakness for selectively reading portions of books, many chapters are relatively independent and accessible without having to digest everything that comes before. Thus, you can pick chapters and sections according to your background and goals, and if you encounter some you can't (or don't want to) crack, leave them and return later. It is even plausible to plunge immediately into Smalltalk (Chapter 3), referring to the first two chapters only as needed.

The examples are all as simple as possible, because the simplest things form the clearest and most surprising lessons. Exercises appear irregularly, whenever understanding the topic at hand demands active participation. There is a blend of design exercises and programming exercises that require a Smalltalk workstation. Solutions accompany the meatier design exercises, but of course even for exercises with solutions I recommend you try them first on your own.

The programming exercises are written on an IBM Smalltalk base. You can work them on either the Professional or Standard version of IBM Smalltalk or VisualAge. Most of them are generic enough that they, or variations of them, can be made to work for other dialects of Smalltalk, but only ambitious readers should attempt to do so. A few small hints for such readers appear in the Appendix. The exercises on windowing are a notable exception: interpreting them into other dialects will be beyond the means of even the most determined reader. Every dialect has its own event and windowing protocols, so building windows in other dialects is a wholly different experience.

Learning occurs differently in different people. That is why diversions—I call them "commentaries"—are separated out for some readers to blow by and others to dive into, according to their fancy. These diversions are variously technical (like comparisons with other ways of doing objects, particularly C++), historical, or philosophical.

When you finish the book, I hope you will be able to think about software problems in some of the ways that the veterans do, and be able to implement your thoughts in Smalltalk. Not expertly, however. Mastery of both object-oriented design and Smalltalk comes only with actual practice. Of course, these are truisms for any activities, from driving a car to playing the piano. But Smalltalk, more than most software tools, requires you to plunge in and abandon yourself to the language and environment. A taste for adventure definitely helps, more than in learning how to drive a car.

Notes on the organization

This is not an orthodox book. Much of its structure derives from my experiences in sustaining the eagerness and momentum of typical Smalltalk beginners for thirty-six or so hours a week, making sure that they learn some really important things. For example, polymorphism does not appear as a formal topic until Chapter 14, not because it is the fourteenth most important topic, but because students have matured enough by then to get an adrenaline rush from it.

You will not find a predictable or monotonous rhythm. People learn best when they sometimes sweat and program in the depths of Smalltalk proper, and at other times sit back and reflect on how ideas interconnect. One chapter (4) consists entirely of hands-on exercises, but on balance the book is weighted more toward thinking than coding.

Here, then, are a few alerts about the content.

The first fifteen chapters cover the basics, material that every practicing developer absolutely must know about objects in Smalltalk. The first two chapters establish a groundwork of objects, classes, and inheritance in a way that is meant to be completely reassuring. All nuances, paradoxes, and the like are reserved for later.

Chapter 3 is practically the only "language" exposition in the book. It covers probably 95 percent of the Smalltalk language and also forewarns readers of common gotchas. Chapter 4 is a concentrated opportunity to practice the lessons of Chapter 3 as well as many more essentials. You should surface from it with a sound intuition of what it's like to live in a Smalltalk programming environment. The orthodox approach is to spread this material around at least a little, but Smalltalk has so few facts and laws that it is feasible to get the bulk of them out of the way in this one fell swoop.

Chapters 5 and 6 begin the assault on major object-oriented conceptual matters, namely abstract classes, containers, and object identity. The next two chapters, 7 and 8, pause to tackle the nuts and bolts of designing and implementing a basic application. Chapters 9 and 10 resume the discussion of ideas essential to the sound practice of objects. This material questions, among other things, when inheritance produces the right design.

The next three chapters, 11 through 13, form a unit on the topic of user interfaces. They begin with an obligatory discussion of model-view-controller, continue with Motif programming (which is specific to the IBM dialect of Smalltalk), and conclude with how not to make a mess of the user interface. This final chapter in the unit is unusual for a book on objects. It is an attempt to emphasize the connection between objects and user interfaces and confront heads-down programmers with the moral obligation to do it justice.

Chapters 14 and 15 expound on polymorphism from several angles, enough to browbeat everyone into internalizing its value and applicability. These chapters fittingly conclude coverage of the essentials, the omission of any of which would be a major embarrassment for me and you.

Chapter 16 demystifies the workings of method dispatch, storage management, and the like, mostly emphasizing Smalltalk, but contrasting with C++ for the sake of perspective. The purpose is not so much academic as to demonstrate how these contrasting workings influence the development gestalt of an object-oriented language.

Chapter 17 should raise your consciousness about the two distinct rationales for inheriting, which I call beauty and the beast. Sensitivity to this issue is an earmark of mature object-oriented designers. The chapter includes a lengthy discussion of consistency (page 201), bordering on the philosophical, which is probably the headiest section in the book.

Chapter 18 covers some favorite design patterns, and how to realize them in Smalltalk. Because it ties together so many ideas, it should reassure you that you have actually learned something, because you will understand the patterns if and only if you've been conscientious about all the programming and thinking that have gone before.

Chapter 19 illustrates what object-oriented frameworks are and why they matter by way of one concrete client/server framework.

Chapter 20 is another demystifying chapter, and the most optional one in the book. I discuss the basics of metaclasses (a class's class) from the standpoint of what they buy the programmer, as well as the extraordinary lengths to which Smalltalk goes to preserve a uniform view of objects. Metaclasses are the final technical topic in the book, and are positioned last because the reader needs to have thoroughly internalized Smalltalk's conceptual underpinnings before appreciating them.

The book concludes with a subjective assessment (Chapter 21) of what is wrong and right with typical object-oriented development efforts.

Typographical conventions

Boldface type, as in **MyClass**, indicates Smalltalk names and code. Italics indicate emphasis and also special instructions, like picking the *Display* menu item. Text that would appear on a computer screen is in bold italics, as in ***Here is the result.***

In keeping with a spirit of candor, no attempt has been made to homogenize the appearance of screen shots of Smalltalk browsers. Browsers vary from dialect to dialect, of course, but also within a dialect (e.g., the standard and Trailblazer browsers in IBM Smalltalk). For that matter, they can even be customized to display or suppress information, according to the whims of the programmer. Rather than present a façade of consistency, the browsers you will see are the ones that I happened to be using at the time.

CHAPTER 1

Objects

The central idea in object-oriented programming is, of course, the programming object. This opening chapter explores this idea, and along the way introduces just a little Smalltalk. But don't get caught up in the details of the Smalltalk fragments here; their purpose is to illustrate concepts.

1.1 Objects

A programming object has some operations plus some information. We often portray programming objects as "doughnuts," as in this drawing of a bank account object on the left. If you—a "client"—want to use this object, you are aware of three operations that it ought to be able to do: tell you its balance, withdraw some money, or deposit some money. That's it. In fact, you don't even get to know that $150 are ensconced within the object. That information is held *privately* within the object, inaccessible to your prying eyes. Thus a more accurate picture of your point of view is as shown below.

We can define a programming object as having an outside, consisting of the operations you can ask of it, plus an inside, concealing information from you that may nevertheless be used by the object's operations. You can see the outside, but not the inside. The software engineering term for this idea is *encapsulation*: the inside of the object is encapsulated

1

by the object's operations. As a rule, data are inside and operations are outside. (We will see occasions when this rule is not what we want, but for the time being it is a good rule of thumb.)

If it happens that you really want to know about the inside of an object, like the account's balance, you can hope to get it only indirectly, by using one of the object's operations. In this example, one hopes that, by invoking the **balance** operation, the object will respond by announcing that it contains $150. Notice the notational quirk: **deposit:** and **withdraw:** are followed by colons, but **balance** is not. This is a Smalltalk idiosyncrasy. It's a convenient way to indicate that an operation requires an argument—when you deposit or withdraw money from an account, you specify an amount; when you ask for the balance, you don't.

Another way to conceptualize a programming object is to think of it as a little person: You can ask this little person, this *homunculus* (from the Latin, *man + little*), to perform any of his operations, but you haven't any idea how he actually implements them, or what he uses from his own insides to do them. When you're designing an object's operations, you should not be embarrassed to think of the object as a little person and wonder, "What ought a smart little account object be capable of?"

This blatantly anthropomorphic question sounds like a cheap trick. But metaphor—I include imagery and simile and analogy—is a powerful cognitive tool. Metaphors let you use what you already know about one domain (like people) to clarify your thoughts about a less familiar domain (like banking software). This device encourages you to say things like, "An account ought to be smart enough to hand out money or tell me how much money he has." As a matter of fact, the idea of a programming object in the original Smalltalk, Smalltalk-72, was a metaphor for a biological cell [Kay 1988]. Imagery like this may not measure up to, "Shall I compare thee to a summer's day?" but you get the idea [Shakespeare 1609].

Now that you understand what objects are, let's develop some ways to think about using them. When you "ask" an object to perform one of its operations, you send it a *message*. Now, everyone cavalierly assumes they understand what a message is, which is a sign that they haven't thought much about it. The trouble is that "message" connotes many ideas. (An e-mail message? A whisper? The thing on my answering machine? A Post-it? A TCP/IP packet?) "Message" is too abstract a word. A better word is *telegram*. A "telegram" is tangible: I can touch it, I can see the information it carries, and I can picture the moment it arrives at the door of its addressee. It is not some vague electronic-sounding thing like a "message." Therefore, I encourage you to think of an old-fashioned telegram whenever you see the term "message."

A message has a bundle of information, consisting of the operation's name and any arguments it needs. For example, to withdraw $50 from the account object, you'd send a message (or telegram)—**withdraw: 50**—to it.

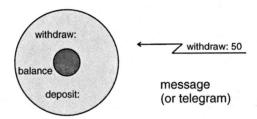

The account object, which has been dormant, awakens and promptly starts executing its **withdraw:** operation. All kinds of interesting things could now happen, producing all kinds of effects. For instance, the account object could in turn send messages to other objects, perhaps with the effect of appending to a report for the bank's auditors. Or, maybe nothing much interesting happens, other than that the $150 concealed within the account object drops to $100. Eventually, though, the account object finishes executing **withdraw:**, and returns an object to you. Maybe it's a receipt object. Whatever it is, it's what you've been waiting for. You sent the message, and you expected some result, and now that you've got it, you're ready to do something else.

To reiterate: in Smalltalk, the normal result of your firing a message is always that some object is returned to you. The returned object may even be uninteresting to you, but you always get one, whether you need it or not. You should think of the consequences of any message as twofold: first, something happens—the operation has an effect—and second, at the end of execution, some object is returned. Remember, an *effect* plus a *return*.

Here are some pretty straightforward candidates for programming objects:

- A bank account, as we've just seen, with operations for depositing, withdrawing, and querying the balance.

- A dictionary, with operations to add or remove entries, or update them.

- A window in a user interface, with operations for displaying, resizing, moving, and so on.

(Some languages from the early 1980s have special syntaxes for defining programming objects like these. For example, one could use a *package* in Ada or *module* in Modula-2.)

A more unusual prospect for a programming object is an integer, like 7. Smalltalk embraces a principle: "Everything is an object." So Smalltalk, unlike other object-oriented languages, insists that integers are objects, too. This statement may sound harmless enough, but it will challenge our customary understanding of arithmetic.

Consider an expression like:

7 + 4

We expect a result of **11**, and we expect that reversing the order thus:

4 + 7

produces the same result. We've been trained since elementary school to expect this expression to behave in this symmetric fashion. Some of us recited slogans like "addition is commutative" to describe this symmetry. We were studying *addition*, and we concentrated on the plus sign.

The object point of view has a different emphasis. That is, if the integer 7 is to be an object, then the focus is going to shift; 7 will be much more interesting and the plus sign much less so. Here's what happens:

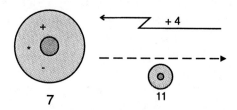

The message, + 4, strikes the 7 object, whereupon the plus operation executes and eventually returns **11**, another integer object. Note that the symmetrical feeling you had in elementary school is absent. Instead, the 7 object plays a leading role. It's a homunculus that's clever enough to respond to messages, such as the one labeled + 4. It recognizes + as one of its operations, and it also expects the + to be accompanied by an argument, which in this case is 4. It executes the operation, and eventually returns the object 11 to whomever sent the message. Fortunately, this is the same answer we got in elementary school. But the line of reasoning we used to get it is unlike anything we learned in elementary school. The symmetry is gone, and the center of attention has shifted from the operation (+) to the object (7).

A lot of people find this model of arithmetic distasteful. One of my outspoken friends, who isn't a Smalltalk programmer, denounces schemes like this as conspiracies from the "lunatic fringe" (a label Smalltalk's critics in the early 1970s also used). The only redeeming virtue seems to be consistency: integers, along with bank accounts and dictonaries, are just another kind of object, activated by messages just like the rest. As you hear more about Smalltalk, you'll recognize that Smalltalk is one of the most stubbornly consistent software systems around, whether one likes it or not. Everything will be an object.

Before leaving this lunatic-fringe discussion, what about the argument 4? I mentioned that the 11 that's returned is also an (integer) object; is the argument also an object? Yes, absolutely. Arguments as well as return values are objects in Smalltalk. Everything is an object.

Now, there is one conceptual distinction between an object like an integer and an object like a bank account. Think about the inside of the 7 object. Should it change after the telegram + 4, as the balance inside a bank account changes after the telegram **withdraw: 50**? For that matter, what *is* inside an integer object? Well, think of the inside as a special *7-ness* quality—the precise bits and bytes don't matter. This quality is what makes 7 respond to + 4 with 11 rather than, say, 13. No one else has such a quality. This 7-ness never changes; later on if we send 7 the telegram + 19, we trust that it will respond with 26. Objects like integers are *immutable*—they never change—in contrast with *mutable* objects like accounts, whose insides may change.

1.2 Examples of Smalltalk messages (telegrams)

In Smalltalk, the usual rule of thumb is to parse expressions from left to right. Consider:

```
9 talk
```

This syntax differs from that of most programming languages. It means that I'm firing a message named **talk** to the object 9. Parsing from left to right, the object comes first, followed by the message that it receives. What happens next depends entirely on whether and how integers have been programmed to respond to requests to talk. For example, in my demonstration Smalltalk system, the result of *executing* 9 **talk** is the following text on my screen: *Hello, I am one more than 8*. Another example with the same syntax is:

```
4 factorial
```

From left to right, I'm asking the 4 object to calculate its factorial, that is, 4*3*2*1. If I ask Smalltalk to *display* the result, I'll get *24*. (I'll discuss the distinction between *executing* and *displaying* in the next section.)

This example should be familiar from the discussion of the preceding section:

```
6 * 7
```

From left to right, 6 receives the message * 7. If I ask Smalltalk to *display* the result, we will see *42*. This left-to-right rule can cause surprises; about half of Smalltalk novices guess the wrong answer to:

```
5 + 6 * 2
```

The correct answer is 22, not 17. Why? Proceed from left to right. The 5 object receives a request for its + operation, namely the + 6 message. The result, which is the 11 object, in its turn (left-to-right), receives a request for its * operation, namely the * 2 message. And it (the 11 object) responds with the final result, the 22 object. For the first time we have an example of something in Smalltalk that differs plainly from what we learned in school. Like it or not, that's how Smalltalk works. Of course, if I really want to get the answer 17, I can use parentheses to change the precedence of Smalltalk's parse:

```
5 + (6 * 2)
```

The next example requires a little guesswork:

```
'turnip' reversed
```

Proceeding from left to right, the first element, **'turnip'**, is the object that receives the message. Because of the single quotes, it is reasonable to surmise that it is a character string. The message apparently asks it to reverse itself. If we ask Smalltalk to *display* the result, Smalltalk will display the characters of the original string spelled out in reverse order: *'pinrut'*.

This one has a different form than the others:

```
HomeBudget spend: 229 on: 'VCR'
```

The object on the left appears to be something that manages home accounting and inventory. The message is less obvious. A colon, you recall, signals the presence of an argument. But two colons? Smalltalk's parsing rule for this situation is to treat all the colons and their arguments together as a single message. Thus, **spend: 229 on: 'VCR'** is a complex bundle of information packaged in one telegram aimed at **HomeBudget**. Evidently, the telegram (message) informs the object of a purchase of a new VCR for $229. In my system, if I ask Smalltalk to *execute* this expression, Smalltalk responds with: ***You bought a VCR and you are poorer by 229 dollars.***

1.3   Pitfall: the effect versus the return

Notice the distinction between what an operation does—its *effect*—and the object it chooses to return to its invoker. Depending on the situation, you may care more about one than the other. Sometimes the name of an operation suggests that it's the effect that matters:

```
7 storeOn: someFile
```

This expression looks like it has the effect of placing the 7 object out on a disk, in a file the argument **someFile** refers to. This effect is apparently the purpose of the message;

what the object returns to the sender is irrelevant. Sometimes, part of the effect is to explicitly display feedback to the screen, as in the example, **9 talk**, in the previous section. We don't care what object **9 talk** returns; whatever object it is is irrelevant.

On the other hand, the opposite may be true. In:

    7 factorial

we don't care about the effects that occur while **factorial** does its calculation. We're much more interested in the object it flings back at us when it's done, which happens to be **5040**. In this case we want to see the *return*, not the *effect*.

You can specify whether you want Smalltalk to display the return or not. That's the finicky distinction between *displaying* and *executing* in the preceding section. If you *display* an expression, the effect occurs *and* Smalltalk displays the returned object on the screen. If you just *execute* the expression, the effect occurs but Smalltalk ignores the returned object. For the examples so far, you have to trust my choices of *displaying* or *executing* because you haven't seen the code that implements each operation. The names of operations may suggest what their effects and returns are, but the only way to be sure is to read their code. In Chapter 4, you'll work through exercises that will help keep the distinction straight.

1.4   Why objects matter

When all the rhetoric is set aside—the rhetoric about reusability and productivity and so on—the salient characteristic of objects is that they reduce translation. That is, objects promote a common vocabulary: everyone, whether a software professional or not, has some intuitive understanding of what an object is. Thus we can understand one another more easily when we use objects to describe our thinking. Objects, then, promote mutual understanding—between users, analysts, executives, designers, programmers, testers.... They reduce the effort of translating one person's thoughts to another's, and therefore reduce misunderstandings as an idea passes from one person to the next.

As for reuse and productivity, they are nothing more than side effects of better understanding. It is more important to concentrate on clear objects than on the side effects; unless the objects are clearly understood, they will be neither productive nor reusable. Concentrate on clear objects and you will eventually produce reusable ones; concentrate on reusable objects and you will produce muddled ones. In this light, the goal of this book is to clarify and deepen your understanding of objects, which in the end will deepen your ability to understand and be understood by other people in the software enterprise. And that is the source of the economic value of objects.

1.5   Recap: objects

Programming objects appeal to different people for quite different reasons. Right brain, intuitive individuals appreciate their metaphorical power. For example, the object-oriented customer-information system at Brooklyn Union Gas Company[1] has gas meter and bill objects, exactly analogous to gas meters and bills in the company's real problem domain. To design gas meter software, developers imagine real gas meters. This expedient helps them reason about programming objects in ways they are already familiar with from their everyday experience; it reduces the gap between the problem (billing for gas service) and the solution (programming). This cognitive economy—breaching the gap between two domains—is the essence of metaphor.

Meanwhile, left-brain, analytic individuals are drawn to the software engineering benefits of objects. If software consists of objects, which are by definition encapsulated, then their insides can be improved without affecting their outsides, and therefore without affecting the rest of the system. Problems are more easily isolated to specific objects and fixed, and the system is generally more tolerant of change, more malleable. In short, modularity in software is desirable, and objects provide a level of modularity beyond traditional structuring techniques.

One other inherent characteristic of objects deserves mention. Traditional software structuring techniques concentrate first on *function*—the function of a program, its sub-functions, their sub-sub-functions.... But human cognition often works the other way, recognizing *things* first, and the functions that connect them afterward. For example, upon hearing that the neighbor's dog bit the mail carrier, I conjure up a picture of the two antagonists first, then a moment later, the dog's jaws closing on the victim's leg. I don't conjure up an abstract bite first. Since our minds are naturally practiced at thinking about *things* in the everyday world, why not parlay that practice into the software world? This is what objects do for us programmers.

To summarize the machinery available so far: if I have programming objects, I can build software out of them, as shown in the diagram on the right. Unfortunately, this software doesn't have much structure—it's just a chaotic bunch of communicating objects. In the next chapter we'll enrich the picture by way of structuring principles—classes and inheritance.

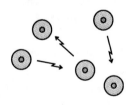

---

[1] This landmark project, deployed in 1990 under the leadership of Tom Morgan, is noteworthy for being the first large-scale object-oriented mainframe application. See [Davis and Morgan 1993].

1.6   Exercise: warmup (the image)

Generally, the *image* is the file that contains all the objects you use and create, as well as other critical Smalltalk objects. By starting Smalltalk you activate the image, and all these objects, of which there are tens or hundreds of thousands, spring to life, ready to work when asked. In IBM Smalltalk, the default name for the image file is simply *image*.

❑ Once you have installed Smalltalk, make some provision for disaster recovery. The minimal provision is to copy your image file to a backup file of your choosing.

❑ Start Smalltalk by double-clicking on the icon for Smalltalk or VisualAge. If you've never used a cut-and-paste editor, take a few minutes to practice with Smalltalk's. Type a line of text in the *System Transcript* window and figure out how to:

  • Split it and rejoin it. (Hint: try the <enter> and <backspace> keys.)

  • Copy a portion of it to another place in the same window.

  • Move a portion and delete a portion.

❑ In the transcript, type the following lines, highlight them one at a time, and *display* the resulting object:

```
4 factorial
6 * 7
5 + 6 * 2
5 + (6 * 2)
'turnip' reverse
```

You are now operating with objects in the image.

1.7   Commentary: perspectives on objects

The metaphorical character of a programming object (page 2) dates back at least to the pioneering work of Alan Kay at Xerox PARC (Palo Alto Research Center) in the early 1970s. Not everyone agrees that metaphor is valuable in programming. In a 1989 paper, the eminent computer scientist Edsger Dijkstra, father of structured programming (or at the very least, executioner of the GOTO statement), ridiculed the use of analogy and metaphor and advocated purely formal thinking in their stead. His paper set off a firestorm of impassioned rejoinders [Dijkstra et al. 1989].

Research on invention and creativity suggests that imagery, not formal reasoning, fuels the creative process. The study by mathematician Jacques Hadamard includes a response from Albert Einstein that makes this point clearly [Hadamard 1954].

Having found an apt metaphor, one must take care not to let it limit the imagination, either: although the spreadsheet was inspired by an accountant's ledger sheet, it transcended the capabilities of a real ledger sheet. Alan Kay calls this step the "magic" of going beyond a metaphor [Kay 1990]. For the use of metaphor and magic in user interfaces, see Chapter 13.

A complementary property of objects, even a corollary of the anthropomorphic view, is their *autonomy* [de Champeaux et al. 1993; Collins 1995]. Autonomy implies that objects are likely to act independently, which in turn implies that they may act concurrently. Concurrently executing objects are also a natural consequence of the biological metaphor of cells acting concurrently by the billion [Kay 1988]. Although some languages mix concurrency and objects, no consensus exists on a proper model for the two. In practice one usually builds concurrent objects on top of the same facilities that non-object systems use—semaphores or other low-level operating system services. For samplings of research approaches to the problem, see [Yonezawa and Tokoro 1987; Agha et al. 1989; Agha et al. 1991; Briot 1992; CACM 1993].

The contrast between function on the one hand and data on the other leads to two polar approaches to software design, namely, traditional functional decomposition (dating from the 1960s) and data-driven or entity-relationship decomposition (dating from the 1970s). Objects occupy a middle ground; they have the tangibility and data content of an entity, but their outsides are defined by their function or behavior. This synthesis of data and function is what differentiates object-driven approaches from the others.

CHAPTER 2

Classes and inheritance

The previous chapter hinted at the cognitive and programming potential of objects. To fulfill this potential, we need to organize them in our minds. We need two structuring principles: classes and inheritance.

2.1 Classes

How do you create objects? In some languages you have to build them one at a time, but it's more convenient to have a mechanism that produces them for you. This mechanism is called a *class*.

You can think of a class as a factory that can produce programming objects. Each factory makes just one kind of object, or product. For example, we could have a **BankAccount** class, from which we produce bank accounts, a **Menu** class, from which we produce menus for a user interface, or a **Dictionary** class, from which we produce objects that behave like real dictionaries.

In Smalltalk, here's how you might use a **Dictionary** class:

```
Dictionary new
```

Left to right, **Dictionary** receives the message named **new**. Because **Dictionary** is a class or factory, it responds to **new** by creating a brand-new dictionary object. What happens to this object from now on is up to you. Being a dictionary, it may have operations like **add:** that would permit you to add a new entry to it. You could gradually add to it and make it into any kind of dictionary you liked.

Realistically, if we want to continue to use this dictionary object, we should establish a handle by which we could refer to it. That is, we would use a variable name, like **X**:

```
X := Dictionary new
```

The := is Smalltalk's assignment. It means that we want to assign the result of **Dictionary new** into the variable **X**. Assignment is an exception to the left-to-right rule. First, Smalltalk does what's to the right of the assignment (**Dictionary new**), then it assigns that result into the variable to the left (**X**).

We can now add things to the dictionary by referring to it as **X**:

```
X add: ...an entry...
```

and

```
X add: ...another entry...
```

If we need another dictionary, we can just *execute*:

```
Y := Dictionary new
```

X and **Y** refer to two distinct dictionary objects, but they come from the same class, namely **Dictionary**. And having come from the same class, or factory, they behave similarly. They both support operations appropriate for dictionaries, like adding, looking up, or removing entries. We can use these operations to grow them in much different ways—**X** into a Danish dictionary, perhaps, and **Y** into a Portuguese one.

In object-oriented systems, dictionary objects are widely used to associate one kind of information with another. Many dictionaries are present in Smalltalk (that is, in Smalltalk's image—page 9) before you even begin to use it; you won't even be aware of most of them. One of them, the *system dictionary*, is Smalltalk's central object. It records associations between variables and the objects they refer to. For instance, after Smalltalk executes:

```
X := Whale new
```

the system dictionary contains an entry for **X** associating it to the actual whale object. There are hundreds of other dictionaries in a live Smalltalk image; they hold all sorts of associations—character names to their numeric values (like **'XKunderscore'** to **95**), mouse events to window system event numbers (like **'WmButton1down'** to **113**), and so on. These dictionaries are crucial to running Smalltalk, but mostly operate unbeknownst to you.

In a language like Smalltalk that has classes, objects are not individualistic. Those from the same class have the same operations—their behavior is the same. We can indicate that objects are from the same class by enclosing them in a box. This representation is less chaotic than our picture of objects at the end of Chapter 1 (page 8); the software is more organized. We will soon give it even more organization, when we discuss inheritance.

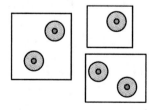

2.2 The word "class"

"Class" is a misleaning word because it has meanings that predate object-oriented programming. Schoolchildren are commonly taught to use "class" as a synonym for "set." Mathematicians, on the other hand, use "class" to refer to collections that were found nearly a century ago to be too large to be treated as sets. (An example of such a collection is the "class of all sets.")

Of course, both the schoolchild and the mathematician have at the back of their mind some notion of a collection of entities. For object-oriented developers, however, the better conceptual model for a "class" is a *factory* rather than a *collection*. (Not that it's a crime to lapse into convenient expressions like "this object belongs to that class," so long as you remain aware that you really mean that "this object was created by that class.") Inexperienced designers who think of class **Onion** as the collection of all onions run into trouble when they have to partition onions into those on the grocer's shelf versus those in a shopping basket; they attempt to invent more classes (**Shelf-Onion, BasketOnion,...**) when what they really need are containers (shelves, shopping baskets,...) to hold their onions. More on containers in Chapter 6.

Another word that is often confused with "class" is "type." To casual object-oriented programmers, they are synonymous. Indeed, for many discussions, there is no harm in using the words interchangeably. But in fact types are *not* classes, and we will see later (Chapter 17) why it is perilous to assume they are. Until then, it would be pedantic to fuss over the distinction, and we will suffer little harm by occasionally saying **Onion** is a "type" instead of a "class." (The terms *abstract data type* or *data type* also occur in software-engineering discussions. They are synonyms or near-synonyms of "type," but they and their nuances won't concern us at all in this book.)

2.3 Inheritance

Inheritance, our second structuring principle, means that you may specify in your programming language that a class is a special kind of another class. It's a notion that we all studied in school. The picture at the right meant that an insect is a special kind ("specialization") of animal, that a butterfly is a special kind of insect, and so on. We called the study of hier-

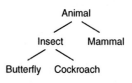

archical pictures like this *taxonomy*. Object-oriented programmers say that the picture depicts a hierarchy of classes in which **Butterfly** is a *subclass* of **Insect**, or equivalently, **Insect** a *superclass* of **Butterfly**. They also commonly say that **Butterfly** *inherits* from

Insect. People who work in artificial intelligence sometimes call this relationship *AKO*—A-Kind-Of. **Butterfly** is AKO **Insect**. Whatever the terminology, the underlying idea is the one we learned in school, that of classifying things by increasing degrees of specialization.

The botanist Carl von Linné, better known as Linnaeus, popularized this way of thinking about plants (as well as animals) in the eighteenth century. Nowadays, children take the idea for granted; they think the taxonomy of plants and animals is just a tedious academic exercise. But back then, the idea extended the very way in which people could think about the world. For example, if I connect butterflies with insects, I establish a mental crutch that helps me *reuse* knowledge I already have about insects. Everything I know to be true of insects automatically applies to butterflies—six legs, egg-laying, metamorphose, breathe through holes in their bodies.... All I had to do was stipulate that a butterfly is a kind of insect (or say "inherits from" or "is a subclass of"). That's a lot of cognition to get free, or for the small price of stipulating an AKO relationship.

Now let's apply this idea to Smalltalk. Part of Smalltalk's inheritance hierarchy looks like this:

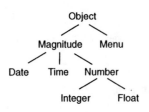

Class **Float** (floating point numbers) is a special kind of **Number**. So too is class **Integer**. Everything that's true of a **Number** object (we can add them, multiply them, and so on) is also true of a **Float** or **Integer** object. It's the same idea as the Linnaean biological taxonomy, only this is a taxonomy of classes in Smalltalk.

Class **Object**, the highest class in the diagram, is analogous to class **Animal**. Just as everything in the Linnaean picture is a kind of **Animal**, everything in Smalltalk is a kind of **Object**. This diagram legitimizes the expression, "In Smalltalk, everything is an object." And just as **Animal** is quite abstract, with few specific qualities, **Object** is similarly abstract.

The other classes in the diagram all have intuitive meanings, with one exception. What role does class **Magnitude** have? Start by thinking about its subclasses. Whatever is true of **Magnitude** objects must also be true of **Date**, **Number**, and **Time** objects. In other words, to imagine what **Magnitude** objects do, you should look for whatever behavior dates, numbers, and times have in common. Try not to think about the insides of these objects. Think about behavior—the outside of the object—rather than the internal, private way in which the object's data happen to be stored. Remember that behavior, the outside, is what matters to users of an object. What behavior do dates, numbers, and times all have?

Here are some bad guesses: multiplication and addition. Although it's reasonable to multiply two numbers together, it's unreasonable to try to multiply two dates, like **July 4, 1776** and **October 14, 1066**. Similarly, addition makes sense for numbers, but we aren't interested in adding **3 o'clock** and **2 o'clock**, or **July 4** and **October 14**.

Nevertheless, something about dates, numbers, and times is similar. What? Not arithmetic, as we've just determined. What about the sense of order? Dates are ordered, as are numbers and times. But we would have to express this idea in terms of behavior, or operations. How? Why not comparison operations, like > (greater than) or <= (less than or equal to)? A date may be greater than another date, a number greater than another number, or a time greater than another time. These comparisons then are the operations that the subclasses have in common. We'll simply place them in the **Magnitude** class, instead of replicating them in all three subclasses. The subclasses then inherit them. Instant code savings.

It's a great, Linnaean idea, but in real object-oriented systems, there's sometimes a catch. The subclasses might still have to have their own version of some of the operations, because the code for the operations is likely to depend on how the data inside the object are represented, and this representation could well be different for different subclasses. For example, because the bit conventions used to store floating point numbers are different from those for dates, the code that compares them must be different too. We will deal later with this situation. For now, staying at a conceptual level, let's just celebrate having factored the concept of comparison out of the three subclasses and into their **Magnitude** superclass.

This discussion illustrates a simple guideline about taxonomy, hence about object-oriented design. Whenever you sense commonalities between classes of objects, consider defining a superclass and "factoring" the commonality out of the subclasses and into the superclass. That's what the Smalltalk-80 designers did late in the 1970s to **Date**, **Number**, and **Time**, and their decision has proved so durable that the design occurs today in all commercial Smalltalk systems.

The little hierarchy under **Object** and **Magnitude** is just a part of Smalltalk's class hierarchy. The full class hierarchy includes classes for windowing, the compiler, graphics, text, operating system services, and much more. All told, a fresh VisualSmalltalk (formerly Smalltalk/V) image arrives with about 700 classes, a fresh VisualWorks (Smalltalk-80) image arrives with about 1400, and a fresh VisualAge (IBM Smalltalk) image arrives with about 2000. Here's a view of some IBM Smalltalk classes, with help from a tool known as a browser:

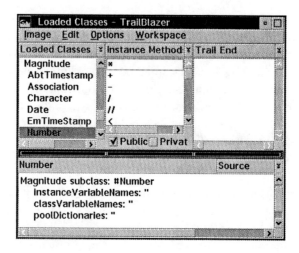

The upper-left windowpane focuses on subclasses of class **Magnitude**; it can be scrolled to reveal many more classes. Since class **Number** is highlighted, the list of operations you see in the middle windowpane, namely *, +, −, and so on, are the ones that numbers understand. In other words, these operations correspond to the telegrams that you can send to **Number** objects. You can see that numbers understand the usual arithmetic operations. And you could see many more by scrolling the windowpane. Don't forget that because of inheritance, you can also use operations that are defined in any superclasses of **Number**. By highlighting **Magnitude**:

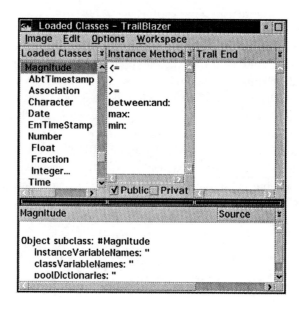

you can see operations that **Number** inherits from **Magnitude**, and they're exactly the comparison operations we suspected earlier, plus a few others. I've elongated the window to show more of **Magnitude's** subclasses. Compare the hierarchy implied by this screen shot with the diagram of Smalltalk's hierarchy on page 14. (The three dots following **Integer** mean that there are subclasses of **Integer**, presently concealed by the browser. To toggle between revealing and concealing these classes, one double-clicks the mouse over **Integer**.)

It is also worth glancing at the lower windowpane. Don't get distracted by syntactic peculiarities or the last three lines; the first line is the most significant. It is the Smalltalk code that makes class **Magnitude** a subclass of class **Object**. Similarly, in the preceding screen shot you can see the code that makes class **Number** a subclass of class **Magnitude**.

Class browsers are standard tools in all Smalltalk products, although their form varies from product to product. Even within one product, there are alternate browsers. The browser above is particularly adept at suppressing superfluous information; other browsers show more information, sometimes more than you care to see. Browsers are the most common way for a programmer to navigate through Smalltalk's code libraries. As you'll see, you can also use browsers to write or change and compile code. (Similar tools, often less nimble, are available in good C++ environments as well.)

One use of inheritance is incremental programming. If you can find a class that comes close to fulfilling your need, but doesn't quite do it, you can create a subclass from it and simply write the relatively small amount of code that distinguishes what you need from what the class already provides. Before you plunge pell-mell into this style of programming, understand that, when practiced imprudently, it can produce obscure and arbitrary designs. In later chapters we'll discuss the challenges of crafting high-quality inheritance hierarchies. For now, think of inheritance as Pandora's box, releasing prospects for hope as well as disaster.

We can picture the inheritance relation between two classes by nesting the rectangles of our earlier schematic (page 12). In Smalltalk, the outermost rectangle represents class **Object**. Since this rectangle contains all the objects, "everything is an object." The nested rectangles on the right could indicate that **SavingsAccount** and **CheckingAccount** are two subclasses of **BankAccount**, or that **Integer** and **Float** are two 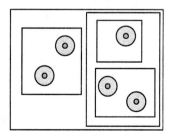 subclasses of class **Number**. Keep in mind that this schematic notation is just that—a notation. Remember to resist the temptation to think of objects as *literally* being inside their class. It is better to think of objects as being *created* from their class—the class is a factory for producing new objects.

One fundamental point. You should implant in your mind an intuition that objects of a subclass have *more* qualities than objects of its superclass. A butterfly has all the qualities of an insect, and then some. A savings account object has all the qualities of a bank account, plus more. The same goes for a date object and a magnitude object. When you subclass, you enrich your objects. This is an essential intuition, even though the time will come later on when we must challenge it.

2.4   Terminology

It's time to deal with terminology—the technical jargon that you need to communicate clearly with other object programmers. The following terms arise from the Smalltalk community, but they are accepted by the broader community of C++ and other object programmers too.

- Objects are also called *instances*.

- The data inside an object are described by *instance variables*. In other words, these are the variables that belong to an instance.

- An object's operations are called *methods*.

- Invocations of methods are called *messages*, as you already know.

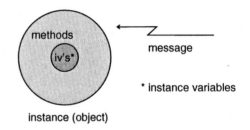

A message arrives at an object, where it activates a method. The message is like a telegram, and the method represents whatever the object does in response to the telegram. Some simple examples:

Class	Instance	Message	Effect or Return
Account	MySavings	MySavings withdraw: 230	Processes a withdrawal
Integer	134	134 - 95	Returns **39**
String	'hello'	'hello' size	Returns **5**
Set	MySet	MySet add: 'hello'	Puts one more object, namely the string **'hello'**, into **MySet**

You will sometimes encounter alternative terms. An object's outside, consisting of the "names" of all the methods that a user of the object can see, is known as its:

- *protocol*
- *behavior*
- *interface*
- *services*
- *public member functions* (a C++ term)

Instance variables, an object's inside, are also sometimes called the object's:

- *attributes*
- *characteristics*
- *memory*
- *state*
- *private member data* (a C++ term)

To be historically precise, **MySet add: 'hello'**, not just **add: 'hello'**, is a message. In other words, messages include their receiver object. Nevertheless, the term "message" is commonly used in both ways, with or without the receiver object. The distinction rarely matters in conversation.

Technical aside: Because "everything is an object," Smalltalk messages are themselves first-class objects, too. In other words, telegrams have behavior in their own right. (We'll exploit this feature in the ghost design pattern on page 226.) IBM Smalltalk goes even further, by explicitly observing the distinction above: a "message" without a receiver object is an instance of class **Message**, and a "message" with a receiver object is an instance of class **DirectedMessage**.

Many readers will have correctly noticed a jarring similarity between messages and function (or procedure) calls in conventional languages. Both are invocations of operations. Moreover, although the term "message" may conjure images of simultaneous events, messages are no more simultaneous than calls; rather, both calls and messages are *synchronous*: while the method or procedure executes, nothing else happens; the sender or caller *blocks*. In other words, a telegram's sender waits for a response.

There is a key distinction between messages and function calls, however. A message always has a distinguished "argument," namely the receiver object, who is responsible for responding to the call; a conventional call treats all its arguments as peers.

Method usually means the operation, *including* all the code that goes into its implementation. But sometimes we want to refer to a method without also referring to all this code; we want to refer only to its "name." The Smalltalk term for a method's name is *selector* (or *message selector*). In the following picture, the method, shown only in part, is a substantial body of code that you are probably not prepared to read yet, but the selector is simply **add:**.

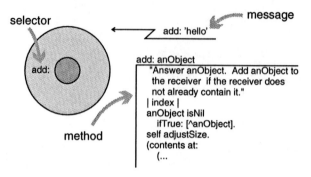

To make matters worse, you'll hear C++ programmers say *signature* instead of *selector*, and *function* instead of *method*. In casual conversation, most object programmers aren't too careful about all these distinctions. They say *method* when they mean *selector*, or *message* when they mean *method*. Don't let terminology discourage you. Just retain a firm grasp on the imagery: a telegram (message) arrives at an object (instance), the object recognizes it (the selector) and executes the appropriate body of code (method).

Some data-driven development methodologies, not customarily favored by Smalltalk developers, reserve the word *attribute* for only the most primitive kinds of things inside objects—things like integers and characters—but not for complex objects within objects. Thus some people would say that my bicycle's color is an attribute, but its rear wheel is too complicated to be an attribute. But a Smalltalk philosopher insists on evenhandedness to the extreme, and so treats both color and wheel in the same way. They are peer instance variables, one of which happens to be more complicated than the other.

Finally, a really substantive distinction: you must carefully distinguish between a *variable* and the *object* that is its value. In Smalltalk, it's a good idea to think of a variable as a *pointer* to an object. For example,

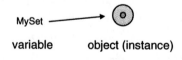

in this diagram **MySet** is a *variable* that points to an actual set *object* (*instance*). All variables, including instance variables, should be thought of as pointers to objects. Thus, a **wheel** or **color** instance variable inside a bicycle object points to an actual instance of a class like **Wheel** or **Color.**

2.5   Exercise: hierarchies

Here are four hierarchies to practice with. For each one, decide whether it may reasonably represent inheritance.

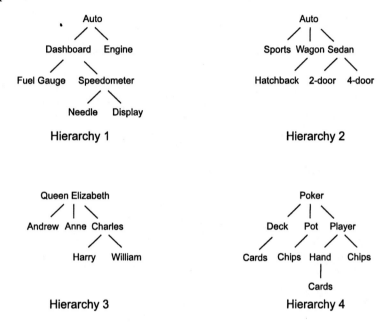

2.6   Solution and discussion: Aggregation hierarchies

Hierarchy 1 is definitely not inheritance. Engines are not special kinds of cars. Nevertheless, this kind of hierarchy is important. It describes a hierarchy of parts, and goes by various names: *part-of, aggregation, assembly, whole-part, composite,* or *has-a* (an auto "has-a" dashboard). In fact, aggregation hierarchies are even more fundamental than inheritance ones. Children realize that things are made up of other things—her hand "has-a" thumb—long before they think about specialization of classes. Aggregation hierarchies have been essential in programming, long before the popularization of inheritance. Some authorities elevate them to one of their defining object-oriented principles [Booch 1994; Collins 1995]. There isn't much hope for your software if you can't do a good job of putting little things together to make big ones.

Hierarchy 2 is a fine example of inheritance. It's reasonable to think of **Hatchback** as a special kind of **Station Wagon**, or **Sedan** as a special kind of **Automobile**.

If you think hierarchy 3 is inheritance, you are saying that Charles is a special *kind* of Queen Elizabeth. That's an odd statement. Moreover, an inheritance tree should always depict classes, not individual instances of a class. In what way can we interpret Charles as a class (a factory for producing objects)? We are more likely to think of him as an individual instance of some class, perhaps the class **Person**, or perhaps **Royalty**. Interpreting hierarchy 3 as inheritance therefore gets us into trouble.

Nevertheless, one could argue that "inheritance" is applicable to hierarchy 3. After all, Charles inherits hair color, blood type, even money from the Queen. The problem is that the vernacular usage of "inheritance" isn't the same as the object-oriented programmer's usage. It's just a case of one word taking on different meanings in different contexts. If we wanted terminology for this kind of hierarchy, we might call it *genealogical, family-tree*, or *genetic*. (The vernacular meaning aligns neatly with a language called SELF. SELF is an alternative approach to object-oriented programming, in which instances (Charles) rely on other instances (Elizabeth) for behavior, rather than on classes.)

Hierarchy 4 is also not a likely inheritance hierarchy. It again exemplifies aggregation—important but not the same as inheritance. It also demonstrates something common in aggregations, namely that a node may appear more than once in the hierarchy. Both **Chips** and **Cards** appear twice here. You will never see that in an inheritance hierarchy. We will revisit this whole matter of aggregation versus inheritance plus some notable connections between them in Chapter 9.

When dealing with aggregation, watch for some subtle distinctions: the automobile aggregation, consisting of its engine and so on, differs qualitatively from the relationship between a pot and its chips. An engine is more tightly coupled to its car than chips are to the pot. Object-oriented designers sometimes call the loose relationship between a pot and its chips a *container*, instead of an aggregation. Pots contain chips and (an earlier example) baskets contain onions. We'll discuss container classes more fully in Chapter 6. Another distinction is sharing. A sub-object in an aggregation may or may not be shareable. My arm is mine alone, but a word-processing document has sub-objects (like graphics or spreadsheets) that are sometimes shared by other document objects.[1]

2.7   Example: aggregation plus inheritance

You may remember from our snapshots of a class hierarchy browser that defining a subclass in Smalltalk has this unwieldy form:

---

[1] For a lengthier treatment of these nuances, see [Civello 1993].

```
Number subclass: #Fraction
instanceVariableNames: 'numerator denominator'
...
```

This code specifies an inheritance relationship between fractions and numbers and also defines instance variables to represent the numerator and denominator of a fraction. On the right is a pictorial representation of the fraction object **3/4**, where I've embellished the sketch with some of the methods that a fraction ought to have. The instance variables are, in effect, parts of the fraction. Since they should represent the integer objects **3** and **4**, respectively, I'll add those objects to the sketch below.

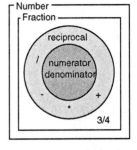

Again, I've embellished the integers with some of the methods they ought to have. This final sketch demonstrates the interplay between aggregation and inheritance: **3** and **4** are parts of **3/4** (aggregation) and at the same time both **Fraction** and **Integer** are subclasses of **Number** (inheritance). In object-oriented software, you don't get far without both aggregation and inheritance.

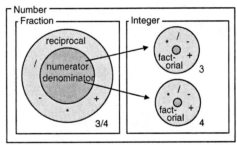

2.8 Syntaxes for inheritance

Here is the syntax for specifying inheritance in seven object-oriented languages. The first is the Smalltalk syntax you just saw:

Inheritance Syntax	Language
`Insect subclass: #Butterfly ...`	Smalltalk
`Insect Class Butterfly (...`	Simula-67
`class BUTTERFLY inherit INSECT ...`	Eiffel
`@implementation Butterfly : Insect {...`	Objective-C
`class Butterfly extends Insect { ...`	Java
`type Butterfly = object(Insect) ...`	Object Pascal
`class Butterfly : public Insect { ...`	C++

For sheer clarity of expression, it's hard to beat Eiffel or Java. But the real point of the table is that every object-oriented language has a direct way to express inheritance.

2.9   Example: inheritance in Smalltalk

Suppose I ask Smalltalk to *execute*:

```
Whale new talk
```

Left to right, **Whale** is a class, **new** creates a new instance of the class, in other words a whale object, and this instance then receives the **talk** message. In my demonstration system, Smalltalk would respond with: *I am pretty quiet*. In which class is the **talk** method that executed?

One begins of course by looking in class **Whale**. If we don't find **talk** there, we'll keep looking up the class hierarchy until we do. Here are two browsers with class **Whale** and its superclass **Mammal** highlighted:

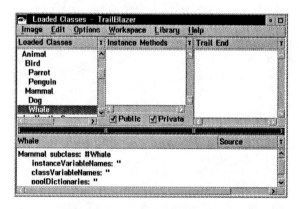

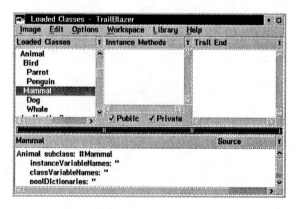

Neither browser shows any instance methods at all defined in these two classes. We surmise that the **talk** method must be inherited from still higher in the hierarchy, and so we examine class **Animal**:

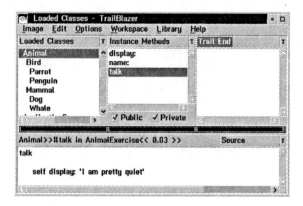

This time we see not only the **talk** selector, but its code in the lower pane. Moreover, this code contains the string of characters we sought—**'I am pretty quiet'**. Evidently this is the method that executed.

Now suppose I want whale instances to talk in a way that is appropriate for whales, but I don't want to affect the way in which other animals talk. I had better not modify the talk method in the animal class. Instead, I'll write *another* talk method, in the whale class. In this method I'll replace **'I am pretty quiet'** with a string more suitable for whales:

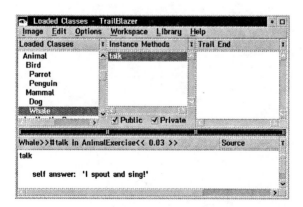

Now if I again *execute*:

```
Whale new talk
```

Smalltalk will display: *I spout and sing!*. I've altered the behavior of only the intended objects, whales, without perturbing the rest of the system. If I *execute*:

```
Animal new talk
```

Smalltalk will still display: *I am pretty quiet.*

Inheritance lets us reuse default behavior from superclasses when we want it (*I am pretty quiet*), but also lets us override and alter the behavior when we want that (*I spout and sing!*).

Summary: Whenever two or more methods with the same selector (**talk**) could respond, Smalltalk executes the first one it finds as it goes up the class hierarchy. In other words, same-named methods lower in the hierarchy override or eclipse those above them. (We'll discuss a small exception (page 54), when we talk about the special variable **super**.)

2.10   Exercise: building a class hierarchy

In IBM Smalltalk or VisualAge, any code you write must belong to an *Application*. An application generally contains several classes and their methods.[2]

❑ Create an application:

  1 From the transcript, drop down the *Smalltalk tools* menu, and pick *Manage Applications.*

  2 From the Application Manager, pick *Applications > Create > Application*. (For prerequisites, the defaults will do.)[3]

  3 Select your new application, then pick *Applications > Browse Application.*

❑ Build the class hierarchy shown on the right, popularized by Digitalk in its Smalltalk/V tutorials. Start by making **Animal** a new subclass of **Object**. To define a new class, select its proposed superclass and pick the *Add Subclass*

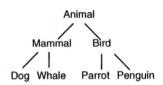

---

[2] There are situations in which some of a class's methods may belong to one application, and some to others, but we won't worry about them in this book.

[3] This sequence of menu selections is just a guide; the actual sequence you need will vary between versions of the product.

menu option. (In the dialogue box that pops up, select *subclass*.) When you finish this step, you should have an application browser that resembles this one:

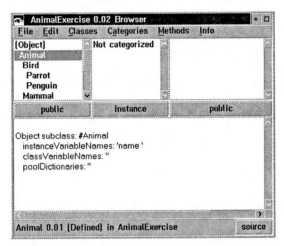

❑ Finally, give all your animals the ability to have a name, by defining an instance variable **name** in class **Animal**. Do so by editing the text for **Animal**, as the browser above shows, and picking the *Save* menu option.

2.11   Commentary: what is object-oriented programming?

In the mid-1980s, there wasn't much consensus on what constituted "object-oriented programming." Although everyone agreed that Smalltalk and C++ were object-oriented, some also said Ada and Modula-2 were object-oriented, and a few people said they had been doing object-oriented programming in C and Pascal. In those days, a lot of unproductive disputes were incited by people who were naturally reluctant to acknowledge that their favorite programming style or language was deficient in some way.

To move beyond these disputes, the community needed a stake in the ground. Happily, in 1987, Peter Wegner proposed a definition for object-oriented languages [Wegner 1987]. Definitions act like benchmarks; they are arbitrary points of reference, and hence nothing is intrinsically right or wrong about them. We gauge them by their usefulness—how they help us understand the world around us. Wegner's definition was deemed useful; people embraced it as a plausible benchmark, and in so doing got back to the business of discussing substantive software matters instead of defending their prejudices about their favorite programming languages.

Wegner's definition had three elements, essentially the three principles we have discussed. For a programming language to be *object-oriented*, he required that it:

- Be *object-based*, meaning that you can easily make encapsulated programming objects in it.

- Be *class-based*, meaning that every object belongs to (is manufactured from) a class.

- Support *inheritance*, meaning that classes may be arranged in a subclass–superclass hierarchy.

He depicted his definition this way:

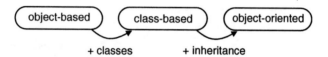

The three principles—objects, classes, and inheritance—are a starting point for discussing object-oriented development. Most authorities add *late* or *dynamic binding* to their definitions, something we'll discuss in the chapter on *polymorphism*, Chapter 14. Whether there should be still other defining characteristics of the object-oriented paradigm depends on the authority. As we discussed earlier, some add *aggregation* to the definition. [Meyer 1988] insists on *garbage collection* and *multiple inheritance*, important topics that we'll discuss in Chapters 9 and 16. Again, there is no such thing as a "correct" definition. It is more important to understand what the ideas are and how they affect software development than to lapse into disputing what ought to be part of the definition.

By the way, there are also languages that everyone agrees are object-oriented, but that *don't* comply with the Wegner requirements. The most significant of these is the research language SELF, which displaces classes and inheritance with *delegation*. Delegation lets one object delegate to another object whatever behavior the first cannot handle. Instead of a chain of superclasses, each object relies on a chain of delegates. See [Chambers 1989] for SELF, and [Lieberman 1986; Lalonde 1986] for other discussions of delegation.

Wegner's three object-oriented programming principles are already part of everyone's experience. When you adjust your refrigerator or drive a car, you're using encapsulated objects; you needn't be aware of their inner workings. When you think of the notion of a dog, you think of the features shared among normal dogs—the dog class. And when you think of successive levels of specialization, like furniture then sofas, you're subclassing or inheriting. None of these ideas is new; we are just transporting them into the realm of progamming.

2.12 Commentary: other languages

Here's a lineup of languages against the three principles:

	Objects	Classes	Inheritance
Ada	+		
APL			
C			
CLOS	+	+	+
CLU	+	+	
COBOL			
C++	+	+	+
Eiffel	+	+	+
FORTRAN			
Java	+	+	+
Modula-2	+		
Objective-C	+	+	+
Pascal			
Prolog			
Simula-67	+	+	+
Smalltalk	+	+	+

Whether a language has one of the characteristics (objects, classes, or inheritance) can be a matter of opinion; you could reasonably challenge some entries in the table. For example, in both Ada and Modula-2, it's not too much of a stretch to define classes as well as objects.[4] Also, variants of many standard non–object-oriented languages are object-oriented. Examples include Borland's Pascal products and Apple's Object Pascal, as well as Ada95 (known earlier as Ada9X) and versions of COBOL and FORTRAN.

There are also some unreasonable challenges: one could argue that a language like C is object-based, because it is possible, with work, to build objects in C. One could

---

[4] Nevertheless, Wegner classified them only as object-based. That's because Ada and Modula-2 objects do not *necessarily* come from classes; indeed, they generally don't, and so software built from those languages often lacks the structural coherence of the drawing on page 12.

even argue that all languages are object-oriented! After all, they are all computationally complete, which is a technical way to say that any task that can be done by any one of them can be done by all of them. For example, you could theoretically use any of them to write a C++ compiler. Therefore, they can all support objects, classes, and inheritance. This generous interpretation of what it means to support objects (or classes or inheritance) is plainly unproductive. We want to know that a language has constructs that make it effortless to use objects, not that objects may be used through some circuitous route.

2.13   Commentary: history

Plato postulated a theory of "forms," wherein an ideal form of a bed is the basis for all the ordinary beds in the world [Plato 375 B.C.]. His forms prefigured Smalltalk's classes, a historical debt that was explicitly acknowledged in an article on Smalltalk-72 [Shoch 1979]. However, Plato's emphasis is the opposite of an object-oriented programmer's: Plato argues that the ordinary beds are less significant than the ideal bed.

Linnaeus's classification of plants [Linnaeus 1753] became an international standard. Although he was first to apply inheritance systematically on a wide scale, the intellectual roots of inheritance go all the way back to Plato's successor Aristotle, who wrote, "If we do speak of the animals severally, it is plain that we shall often be saying the same things about many of them" [Aristotle 330 B.C.]. Thus if two classes have common features, Aristotle suggests that we can save our breath by ascribing those features instead to what we could today call a superclass.

Inheritance and object-oriented programming have been around since the mid-1960s. Smalltalk itself evolved at Xerox PARC during the 1970s. That work culminated with Smalltalk-80, the first commercial Smalltalk. See [Kay 1993] for the fullest account of its history. Smalltalk-80 later evolved into ParcPlace's Objectworks\Smalltalk and VisualWorks (which includes visual-programming tools) but is still commonly called Smalltalk-80. The Digitalk Smalltalk/V family originated in the mid-1980s and is now known as VisualSmalltalk, and IBM Smalltalk (often bundled in VisualAge) appeared in 1994. In 1995, ParcPlace and Digitalk joined into one company, ParcPlace-Digitalk, which is now combining the two families of products (VisualSmalltalk and VisualWorks) into one dialect. Other less-prominent Smalltalks are also available commercially today.

An ANSI committee is defining a Smalltalk standard that will consist of a core body of classes and methods. However, because this core will be only a small proportion of any one dialect, the standard will not be able to ensure portability of whole Smalltalk applications.

The following family tree shows some of the milestones in the history of object-oriented languages. (Object-oriented languages are in boldface type.)

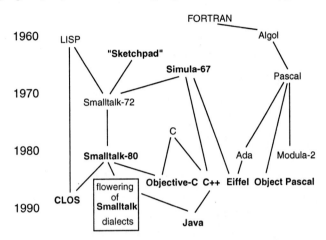

Two early landmarks were Sketchpad and Simula-67. Sketchpad, a direct manipulation graphics system developed at MIT by Ivan Sutherland, evinced the principles we've discussed but was not a programming language. Thus, people regard Simula-67 as the first object-oriented programming language. Between Smalltalk-72 and Smalltalk-80 were Smalltalks -74, -76, and -78; inheritance first appeared in Smalltalk-76. CLOS (Common Lisp Object System) is part of the Common Lisp standard.

CHAPTER 3

Smalltalk introduction

Smalltalk's *language* is tiny. You will learn almost all of it from this chapter alone. And much of the chapter reviews what you've already seen in the first two chapters. Not that Smalltalk itself is tiny. A typical Smalltalk system out of the box includes a library of thousands of classes. And in Smalltalk you can't do *anything* without classes, even, as you'll soon see, something as ordinary as a conditional or a loop. Though it is a quick matter to learn the language, learning "Smalltalk" is a heftier challenge. To become effective you will have to learn many (but by no means all) of the classes. Moreover, using them *wisely* really amounts to doing good object-oriented design. This mastery takes months of practice—getting in there with your own fingers and snooping through the system and writing and stumbling through your own applications. A modicum of curiosity and daring helps.

3.1 Elementary objects

A few elementary Smalltalk objects merit their own special notations. Here are some examples:

Sample Instance	Its Class
37	**Integer** (really the subclass **SmallInteger**)
'To be or not to be'	**String**
2.71828	**Float**
$p (the character *p*)	**Character**
true	**Boolean** (really the subclass **True**)
false	**Boolean** (really the subclass **False**)

One of the by-products of these notations is that you do not issue the customary messages **Float new** or **Integer new** to produce a number object. Instead, the expression **2.71828** by itself produces a reference to a floating point object. In fact, *executing* or *displaying* **Float new** or **Integer new** results in an error or walkback window.[1] Smalltalk disables the **new** message for numeric classes.

3.2   Messages and their precedences

Smalltalk has exactly three kinds of messages: *unary*, *binary*, and *keyword*. *Keyword messages* are messages that contain colons. The message:

```
HomeBudget spend: 229 on: 'VCR'
```

is an example. It's the keyword message whose selector is **spend:on:**.

Note that this selector consists of two keywords that are smashed together. Each of them expects an argument. Hence this message includes two argument objects, namely **229** and **'VCR'**. A keyword message can have any number of keywords (i.e., colons), and it must have one argument following each colon.

Now, another way to mentally parse the message above is:

```
(HomeBudget spend: 229) on: 'VCR'
```

that is, in the form of one message following another, for a grand total of two messages. This is an alternative, but it is not the way Smalltalk works. The original expression had no parentheses, so Smalltalk interprets it in just one way, as a single message that happens to have two arguments riding on it. If you want instead to indicate two separate messages, you must explicitly use the parentheses.

Binary messages are the simplest to recognize. They're denoted by special symbols, such as **+ - * / < <= > >=.**

```
17 <= 14
```

is a binary message. Its selector is **<=** and the object it returns is the **false** object.

The comma is a surprising example of a binary message. You use it most often to concatenate two **String** objects:

```
'Let them eat ' , 'cake.'
```

If you ask Smalltalk to *display* the result, Smalltalk displays: *'Let them eat cake.'* Commas and comparisons and arithmetic symbols aren't the only binary selectors. You can define a binary message using any one or two of the symbols **+ - * / \ ~ > < = @ % | & ?,**

---

[1] These windows are known as *walkbacks* in Smalltalk, because, as you will see in Chapter 4, they let you "walk back" through the code that executed just before the error.

as a selector. Not that you should. The selector @\ is perfectly valid, but it is hard to imagine a good use for it.

All other messages—those whose selectors neither are special symbols nor have colons—must be *unary messages*. The selector for a unary message consists of a single word. Examples are:

```
'smart' reversed
```

whose selector is **reversed**, and:

```
4 factorial
```

whose selector is **factorial**.

When faced with a more complicated expression, comprising more than one kind of message, Smalltalk's *precedence rule* is unary, then binary, then keyword. For example,

```
12 between: 7 and: 9 + 2
```

contains a keyword message and a binary message. Since binary has higher precedence than keyword, 9 + 2 executes first, resulting in 11. Next, **12 between: 7 and: 11** executes, which is a keyword message (with two arguments) asking **12**, "Are you between 7 and 11?" to which **12** finally responds with the **false** object.

What happens if we alter the expression by inserting parentheses?

```
(12 between: 7 and: 9) + 2
```

The parentheses change the precedence; in this case the result will be an error window (walkback). Here's why. The parenthesized expression executes first, resulting in the **false** object. Then **false + 2** executes, which asks the **false** object to add 2. Because the Smalltalk **false** object doesn't understand addition, it pops up the walkback window, announcing an error. As in any other language, parentheses make a big difference.

3.3   Pitfalls: basic Smalltalk gotchas

The first simple pitfall is that Smalltalk is case-sensitive, which means that you can't write **whale** instead of **Whale** and expect your code to work the same. We'll discuss Smalltalk's capitalization conventions in the upcoming section on variables (page 39).

Another pitfall is that Smalltalk assignments are *not* messages.[2] Assignment is an exception to the left-to-right rule. Smalltalk processes the right-hand side of the := first, then puts the resulting object in the variable on the left-hand side. For example,

---

[2] In a twisted sort of way, you can think of an assignment as a peculiar kind of message, of lower precedence than the other kinds, and where the receiver is the object that "owns" the variable being assigned to. For example, an assignment to an instance variable can be interpreted as a message to the instance of the form **instVarAt:put:**. But it is neither customary nor linguistically illuminating to view assignments in this way.

```
X := 12 between: 7 and: 9 + 2
```

doesn't mean that **X** refers to the **12** object. It means that the entire expression on the right of the assignment executes, resulting in the **false** object, only after which does assignment occur. In the end, **X** refers to the **false** object, not the integer **12**.

More insidious pitfalls surround the differences between instances of **Character, String, Symbol,** and **Array**. But before telling you about the differences, I want to highlight a similarity. Along with numbers such as **19** or **2.71828**, these objects are often called *literals*. In IBM Smalltalk, literals are immutable—they are read-only objects and cannot be modified. (Literal strings and literal arrays are mutable in other dialects.) Here is how you indicate literal objects:

Smalltalk	Meaning
19 and 2.71828	Numbers (aSmallInteger and aFloat)
$b	The single character **b**
'rosebud'	aString
#rosebud	aSymbol (explained below)
#(5 'rosebud' 7)	anArray

(It's a Smalltalk tradition to ram words together and use just an uppercase letter to mark the boundary, as in *aString*.)

An instance of **Symbol** is a sequence of 1 or more characters beginning with a number sign (#). Aside from cosmetic differences between symbols and strings, they differ in one profound respect: Two strings may have the same character sequence, but no two symbols may have the same character sequence. Even if the symbol **#rosebud** occurs more than once, Smalltalk construes all occurrences as referring to one and the same underlying object. As a by-product, copying a symbol results in ... the same symbol! This behavior of symbols plays a role in matters of *object identity*, which we will discuss in Chapter 6.

An instance of **String** is a sequence of 0 or more characters delimited by single quotation marks. Note that although '' has no characters and 'b' has one character, both denote legitimate instances of **String**. And don't confuse the string 'b' with the character $b; they are instances of entirely different classes. As in many other languages, a quote within a string must be doubled: 'Alice''s Restaurant'.

Again, a Smalltalk system may contain many instances of the string 'rosebud', but at most one instance of the symbol **#rosebud**. In Smalltalk, it so happens that **Symbol** is a subclass of **String**. Thus, you can think of a symbol as a special kind of string in which the meaning of "sameness" or identity differs.

Notice that by putting parentheses after #, instead of characters, you no longer get a symbol. Instead, you get an array. The array #(5 'rosebud' 7) has three elements: first the integer 5, then the string 'rosebud', and finally the integer 7. You can nest literals inside a literal array. As examples, #(5 #rosebud 7) has three elements, the second of which is a symbol, and #(5 #(2 11 13) 7) also has three elements, the second of which is another array. (In these last two examples, odd as it may seem, the inner # is optional in IBM Smalltalk.)

Finally, quotation marks delimit comments, and are ignored by Smalltalk. Thus, "rosebud" is a comment. You can use comments freely anywhere white space occurs in your code.

3.4   Examples

What do you expect will be returned from each of these expressions?

```
3 - 5 * 2
Integer superclass
#(me you they) at: 2
```

The answers should be -4, **Number**, and **#you**. The first consists of two consecutive binary messages, processed left to right. The second is a unary message sent to **Integer**, asking this class to tell us its superclass. The last is a keyword message with a single argument, **2**, asking the array object to reply with its second element; this second element is the symbol **#you**.

What do you expect to be the effect of each of these messages? Don't think about the return, just the effect.

```
#zero at: 1 put: $h
'zero' at: 1 put: $h
'zero' copy at: 1 put: $h
#zero copy at: 1 put: $h
```

The first two messages should fail (!) because literals are immutable. The third one works fine; copying the literal string produces another string, which is not a literal. This copy's first letter is replaced, so that the copied string becomes **'hero'**. The final message again fails. That's because the copy has the same sequence of characters as the original symbol, and for symbols the copy must then *be* the same as the original, which we know to be immutable.

3.5   Exercise: a hypothetical method

The code below is an entire, hypothetical Smalltalk method named **replaceLastBy:**. It introduces several elements of the language. Look it over and try to answer these two questions:

❑ What does the method do?

❑ What is a class for which it would make sense?

   Here is the code:

```
replaceLastBy: anObject
        |last|
        last := self size.
        self at: last put: anObject.
```

You will need explanations for several things you are seeing for the first time:

- The first line just has the selector—the keyword **replaceLastBy:**—plus a dummy name the method will use for the argument. I've chosen **anObject** for this name, which represents a healthy, orthodox Smalltalk coding style, but in theory any name is equally legal.

- The next line (after the comment) declares a local variable between the vertical bars; its name is **last**, although again it could be anything we like. You can use local variables throughout the method to refer to objects. And you can declare any number of them between the bars, separating them by blanks.

- To understand **self**, which appears in the final two lines, it helps to think anthropomorphically. Imagine that *I* am the object for which the method is executing. **self** is a special Smalltalk variable that refers to *me*. (But you may not know who *I* am yet because that's the second question in this exercise.)

- Finally, notice the periods at the ends of lines; they separate Smalltalk statements. Because periods are separators, the final period is optional.

   As a final hint before attacking the two questions above, imagine a concrete situation. Imagine that some object has several elements within it and receives the message **replaceLastBy: $e.**

3.6   Solution and discussion

What does the method do? Imagine that *I* have, say, 4 elements. In other words, imagine that I am some sort of collection. Then **self size** calculates my size, which is **4**. And **self at: 4 put: anObject** substitutes **anObject** for whatever my 4th element is. For instance, suppose that I am a string containing the characters **b**, **l**, **u**, and **r**, and a variable **Me** refers to me. If I receive the message (or telegram):

```
Me replaceLastBy: $e
```

then I am being asked to replace my last element with the character **e**. The method thus transforms me into a string with characters **b**, **l**, **u**, and **e**. In general, no matter what object **Me** refers to, the method will attempt to replace that object's last element.

As for the second question, what is a likely class for **Me**? An obvious candidate is **String**, because **'blur'** is a string. Others? Perhaps **Array**, or any class whose instances have an indexed ordering on them. **String** and **Array** are the two most obvious, but you will encounter others as you learn more about Smalltalk.

Another language element that appears often in methods is the caret, **^**. **^xyz** means that the method should return **xyz** to whoever invoked it and stop executing. If there's a complicated expression to the right of the **^**, the whole expression executes, then the method returns to the invoker whatever the expression produced and stops executing. Thus, the statement:

```
^5 + 6 * 2
```

in a method would terminate the method and return **22** to its invoker. Or,

```
^self
```

would terminate the method and return "me" to the invoker.

Now, if a method, like the one in this exercise, contains no carets, Smalltalk still insists that the method return something—Smalltalk methods always return some object. This default return object is always **self**. Therefore the method could have been written equivalently as follows:

```
replaceLastBy: anObject
    |last|
    last := self size.
    self at: last put: anObject.
    ^self
```

3.7   Kinds of variables

Variables may be spelled with any letters. Whether the first letter of the variable is uppercase or lowercase is a matter of preference in some Smalltalks (IBM Smalltalk and VisualWorks), but is strictly enforced in others (Smalltalk/V). Although IBM Smalltalk offers consderable latitude in this regard, I recommend you use the common conventions (which are the same as the Smalltalk/V rules). Your Smalltalk code will then resemble other Smalltalk code, which fosters mutual readability. Here are the conventions:

Begin variables like **anObject** or **last**, which are visible to only one object, with a lowercase letter. The most common kinds of these variables are:

- *formal arguments* like **anObject**, declared along with the selector at the top of the method.

- *local or temporary variables* like **last**, declared within vertical bars.

- *instance variables* like **numerator**, declared along with its class **Fraction** (page 23).

We'll come to another kind of variable when discussing *blocks* on page 55. Although all these variables are visible to just one object, the first two kinds (**anObject** and **last**) are even less visible; they are usable only within the single method that defines them. By contrast, instance variables like **numerator** are usable by any of the object's methods.

Begin variables that are shareable among many objects with an uppercase letter. The most common kind of uppercased variable is a *global variable*. Global variables are universally visible; any object in Smalltalk can see and use them. You're already familiar with one variety of global variable—classes. More precisely, names like **Fraction** and **Whale** are global variables (that happen to point to the actual classes for fractions and whales). The other common variety of global variable consists of the ones you invent so that you can refer to an object at a later time. An example is the global variable **X** in the expression **X := Whale new**. **X** provides a handle by which you can refer to the whale instance. (Recommendation: Experienced object programmers limit their use of global variables, because globals are the antithesis of encapsulation. Your goal is to hide as much as possible, and global variables have the opposite effect. But you can't shun global variables entirely: for example, you can't do much in Smalltalk without classes.)

Another kind of shareable (uppercase) variable, a *class variable*, is not quite global. These are variables that may be shared among all the instances of one class and its subclasses. For example, a graphical icon might be a class variable, because every instance of a class does not need to have its own private copy of the icon. Or, if we want to copy and paste text among several text windows, it might be convenient for all text window instances to share a **TextBuffer**. Class variables, being visible to more than one but not all objects, occupy a middle ground between global variables and the variables that a single object enjoys.

Another kind of shareable (uppercase) variable is known as a *class instance variable*. Class instance variables are handy for implementing *solitaires* (page 230); I will save their explanation until then.

Summary: To conform to the preponderance of Smalltalk code in the industry, begin global, class, and class instance variables with an uppercase letter, and begin any variable that makes sense to only one object with a lowercase letter.

3.8   Pitfall: variables ≠ objects

It bears repeating that a variable is not an object (page 20). Rather, a variable refers to or "points to" an object. At one moment the variable **X** could refer to the integer **92**, at another moment, merely by reassigning it, **X** could refer to the string **'Call me Ishmael'**. Smalltalk permits **X** to refer to any type of object at all. That's why you will hear people say, "Smalltalk is an untyped language." (Remember that, until Chapter 17, it is safe to think of "type" as just another word for "class.")

Although the type of a variable can vary from moment to moment, the type of an object is never ambiguous. **92** is and always will be an instance of class **Integer** (actually **SmallInteger**, the subclass of **Integer** consisting of the 31-bit positive and negative integers) and **'To be or not to be'** is always an instance of class **String**. Thus one can say, "In Smalltalk, variables are untyped, but objects are strongly typed." The only exception is a powerful Smalltalk method, **become:**, which can actually alter the class of an object. (See the discussion on proxies and ghosts in Chapter 18.)

3.9   Classes are objects

In the spirit of "everything is an object," Smalltalk classes (factories) are themselves special kinds of objects. Like other objects, they can receive messages, **new** being the most frequent. This is no mean feat—classes are decidely not objects in most other object-oriented languages. That's why you hear the expression: "Smalltalk classes are first-class objects."

The methods that apply to classes are called *class methods* and those that apply to instances are called *instance methods*. Both kinds of messages occur in the expression:

    Whale new talk

The object that receives the **new** message is class **Whale**; thus **new** is a class method. The object that receives the **talk** message is the whale instance that comes out the factory door; thus **talk** is an instance method.

Smalltalk browsers present instance and class methods to us separately. This browser:

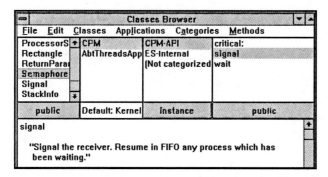

shows three instance methods at the upper right. We know they are instance methods because the pushbutton near the middle of the window says *instance*. Toggling this button gives us:

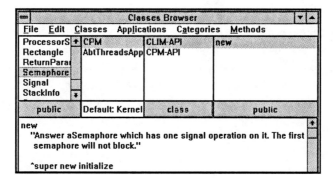

Class **Semaphore** defines only one class method, namely **new**. This reflects the general situation: Smalltalk has many more instance methods than class methods. That shouldn't be a surprise, for it's the instances themselves which you want to do most of your useful computing.

3.10   Control flow

One of the earliest facts you learn about programming is that programs need to be able to branch conditionally (if–then) and loop, as well as sequence statements one after the other. Yet Smalltalk has language statements for neither conditionals nor loops. Smalltalk accomplishes these in the only way it knows how to do anything, via messages. We need one additional language element first.

A *block* is a special kind of object, delimited by brackets [...]. A block acts like a chunk of code without a name. Here's a simple block:

```
[Whale new talk]
```

Since it's an object, you treat it like an object, assigning it, passing it as an argument, and sending messages to it. For example, I can assign it to a variable by *executing*:

```
MyBlock := [Whale new talk].
```

Smalltalk obliges, but nothing appears on the screen. That's because all I've done is assign the block to **MyBlock**. I haven't done anything to execute the block. To do so, I send the block a special message named **value**:

```
MyBlock value
```

And now Smalltalk finally responds with *'I spout and sing!'* Blocks, in effect, are a way to defer the execution of code until it is appropriate.

Now, conditionals and loops. Here's an example of a conditional branch:

```
MyValue < 17
    ifTrue: [Whale new talk].
```

Because binary messages (<) precede keyword messages (**ifTrue:**), Smalltalk first determines whether **MyValue** is less than **17**, resulting in either the **true** object or the **false** object. If the answer is the **true** object, the **ifTrue:** method evaluates the block. Control then passes to any subsequent statements. If the answer is the **false** object, the **ifTrue:** method does nothing; it doesn't bother to evaluate the block of code, and control still passes to any subsequent statements. The result then is as you would hope: depending on the outcome of **MyValue < 17**, either the block executes or not.

There are several methods for looping. Here is a simple message that invokes such a method:

```
6 timesRepeat: [K := K + 1]
```

This message causes 6 repetitions of the block of code. Notice that the receiving object is **6**, a lowly integer. In other words, class **Integer** has behavior so rich that all its instances can control loops; they all understand the keyword message **timesRepeat:**. This example illustrates how extreme the Smalltalk object model is. Nothing stands in the way of giving rich behavior to innocuous objects like integers.

3.11   Commentary: metaclasses

This section takes an entirely optional glimpse at an advanced topic that I treat fully in Chapter 20. One of the consequences of admitting classes as first-class objects is that classes themselves must then be instances of some other class. In effect, a factory must come from some sort of higher-level factory. Thus every class, like **Whale**, is itself an instance of some class, which happens to be called its metaclass. Moreover, class **Whale** happens to be the one and only instance of its metaclass. As a matter of fact, every class is the one and only instance of its own metaclass.

Now, if every class has an associated metaclass, and the class is the only instance of this metaclass, that doubles the number of class-like objects running around the system. You're probably fearing the worst—that this goes on forever, with meta-meta-classes and so on. Fortunately not. The next level is much simpler. All the metaclasses are instances of one and the same class, whose name is, naturally enough, **Metaclass**. The explosion of class-like objects stops cold with this one class. You can even count them all up. If your system has 2000 ordinary classes—mind you, that's really 1999 plus one called **Metaclass**—then it also has 2000 metaclasses. And all 2000 of these metaclasses are instances of **Metaclass**. That's just 4000 class-like objects in all.

Now, 4000 is 2000 more than a class browser really needs to make you aware of. The class browser is a practical tool and was designed to conceal those 2000 meta-classes. How? By giving you the convenient toggle you saw that lets you look at "class methods." The so-called class methods of **Whale** are actually the instance methods of **Whale's** metaclass! By this sleight-of-hand, the Smalltalk browser conceals **Whale's** metaclass, and portrays its methods to us as an artificial breed of method called "class methods."

You can program for a long time in Smalltalk without knowing as much as I've already said about metaclasses. The noteworthy theme is that metaclasses preserve the conceptual consistency of Smalltalk. ("Everything is an object, and everything is therefore also an instance of some class.") This consistency is unlike what you'll find in most other object-oriented languages. C++ classes are not objects; they aren't eligible to receive messages, for example. C++ classes are limited to the role of describing the system rather than participating in it.

Again, the details of the metaclass story appear in Chapter 20. Meanwhile, the next step is to begin programming in Smalltalk.

CHAPTER 4

Exercises—Foundations

Smalltalk is so compact that almost all its essentials can be practiced in one sitting. This chapter covers these essentials—the language elements in Chapter 3, plus tools for maneuvering through Smalltalk. It consists entirely of hands-on exercises. Only by experiencing Smalltalk firsthand will you understand what is unique about object-oriented programming in Smalltalk. Reading this or any other book without doing Smalltalk will get you nowhere. Do the exercises, look around, try experiments, be curious. Set aside at least half a day for this effort.

Warning

Do not get distracted by the myriad menus and options present in the Smalltalk environment, nor by the code version and management tools that are available. These exercises emphasize the nature of objects in Smalltalk, and only enough menu options and tools to survive. You will acquire the rest gradually, through experience and self-discovery. Confronting fundamental conceptual matters is more valuable now than becoming proficient in mechanical skills.

4.1 Precautions

I mentioned in Chapter 1 that each Smalltalk workstation has a crucial file known as the "image." The image contains executing objects, and it therefore grows and shrinks. The name of this file varies among Smalltalk dialects, but in IBM Smalltalk and Visual-Age, the default name is simply *image*. You should imagine it as consisting of objects and their methods, but not their source code. Although source code may be present in

44

the images of some dialects, this is an artifact of the dialect rather than an inherent characteristic of Smalltalk. Source code is needed to describe objects and their behavior, but it is not part of the objects themselves; hence it is not an essential ingredient of an image.

Of course, developers need access to a reliable copy of their source code. Smalltalk stores code that you write either in a text file or in a special library or repository. The standard versions of IBM Smalltalk or VisualAge use a text file called *changes.log*, local to each workstation:

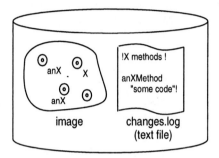

Standalone

(You may notice exclamation points peppering files like *changes.log* that contain Smalltalk source. They delineate methods and other chunks of code, and they are read and inserted automatically by the tools that handle source code.)

The team and professional versions of these products use a shared library with a qualifier of *dat*, such as *manager.dat* or *abtmgr30.dat*.

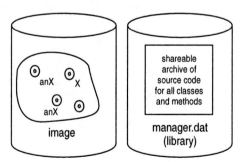

Team or Professional

Notice that the image contains instances of class **X** as well as class **X** itself. This is a reminder that in Smalltalk, classes are first-class objects. The class **X** wouldn't be a live object in C++, nor is the idea of an image relevant.

The point of this discussion is that you need two things—a sound backup image and a reliable repository of your source code—in the event that your image becomes corrupt, as it inevitably does sometime in every complex development project. Then you can always reconstruct an up-to-date image by merging your work into the backup image. The bottom line is that you should conscientiously back up *changes.log* or *manager.dat*, plus at least one trustworthy image.[1]

4.2   Finding things in Smalltalk

Finding things is a basic survival skill. Smalltalk developers most frequently need to find classes and methods.

Classes

❑ One workhorse tool is the browser on *all* the classes in the system. To open one, pick *Smalltalk tools > Browse Classes* from the menu bar of the system transcript window. Familiarize yourself with this browser by clicking, double-clicking, and scrolling around; don't try to read any code yet, though. Spend a few minutes (no more) trying to find class **Set**; if you fail, read on.

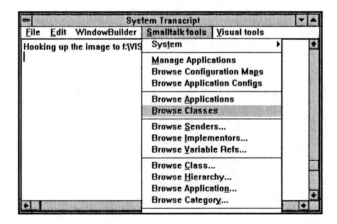

---

[1] In the standard environment, you might as well back up both *image* and *changes.log* at the same time. This precaution ensures that the live objects and the source code are in step with one another.

❑ This browser's alphabetical listing doesn't help much if you're looking for a class that's nested deeply in the hierarchy. For example, because **Set** isn't a direct descendant of **Object**, it doesn't appear in the browser's initial alphabetical listing. To find it, pick *Classes > Find Class* from the browser's menu bar. Type *Set* in the dialogue box, and click *OK.*

Methods

❑ Suppose you want to find all the implementations of the **at:put:** method. Pick the *Smalltalk tools* menu from the transcript again, but this time pick *Browse Implementors.* Type *at:put:* in the dialogue box and click *OK.* A list of the many implementations of **at:put:** that exist in Smalltalk appears. Select one for a glimpse at the source code; don't try too hard to understand the source code yet, though.

❑ Anything that happens in Smalltalk happens, ultimately, by way of a message. In particular, the effect of the *Smalltalk tools > Browse Implementors* menu sequence above is to *execute* this message:

```
System implementors
```

Instead of using the menu, type this message in the transcript, highlight it, and *execute* it, then produce a list of all the implementations of the **+** message.

By the way, the transcript is an obvious place to type and experiment with messages, but you can actually type them and try them in any textual window in Smalltalk. In general, if you can type somewhere you can also execute there. Regardless of which window you happen to have typed and executed messages in, you are making Smalltalk use live objects in the image.

❑ Similarly, you can find every method that sends a message by *executing:*

```
System senders
```

or by picking *Smalltalk tools > Browse Senders.* Use either technique to produce a list of all senders of the message **at:put:**. Use the other technique to produce a list of all senders of the (recursive) message **factorial**.

❑ To understand a method, say **remove:**, we often need to understand the methods it invokes in turn. Let's investigate class **Collection**'s **remove:**. Since there are **remove:** methods in many classes, Smalltalk developers use the notation **Collection>>remove:** to distinguish **Collection**'s method from the others. Select **Collection>>remove:** from the list, then pull down the *Methods* menu (or pop it up with a right mouse click), pick the *Browse Messages* menu item, then its *Implementors* sub-item. Smalltalk brings up a list of the messages that **remove:** sends. There are only two in this case. Selecting either one produces a list of all its implementors. We could repeat this procedure indefinitely. That is, we can drill as deeply as we wish into the implementation of any method by repeatedly picking *Browse Messages > Implementors*.

❑ Apply this technique to the method that tests whether a date occurs between two others. In other words, by alternately selecting *Browse Messages* and *Implementors*, trace the implementations of this chain of methods: **between:and:, <=, <,** and **year.**[2]

4.3 Elements of Smalltalk

Establishing global variables

❑ Add the global variable **T** to your image:

```
Smalltalk declareVariable: #T.
```

This message establishes an entry for **T** in the so-called system dictionary.

Global variables should generally be avoided. Professional developers use them sparingly because they conflict with the object-oriented spirit of limiting the visibility of information, and there is almost always a way around using them. But they can help illustrate ideas and facilitate experimentation, and in this opening chapter we use a few of them.

Global versus temporary variables

❑ In the transcript window, *display* this entire chunk of code (remember that periods separate statements, and the final period is optional):

```
T := 'dig' copy.
T at: 2 put: $o.
T.
```

❑ Repeat the experiment with this chunk:

```
|t|
t := 'dig' copy.
t at: 1 put: $p.
t.
```

---

[2] In older versions of IBM Smalltalk an additional > method occurs in this chain.

❑ Now *display* the global variable **T**. Then try *displaying* the temporary variable **t**. The latter is no longer defined; it was valid only when it was highlighted together with its declaration |t|.

The ^ (caret)

❑ Smalltalk methods always return some object. The ^ specifies the object. Use the classes browser to refamiliarize yourself with the hierarchy under class **Magnitude** that we examined on page 14. Locate the method whose selector is **max:** and read through its code. Notice that the ^ precedes the object that the method returns. The ^ also terminates execution of the method.

Many methods contain no ^ at all. Nevertheless, the method must return an object. In this default situation, that object is **self**, the receiver of the message. Notice that unless you look into a method's code, you cannot be sure of what it returns because you can't know if and where there are any ^'s. Sometimes, as you will see shortly, the returned object isn't what you expect.

Execute versus Display

Execute and *Display* both compile and execute the highlighted code. The only difference is their treatment of the returned object. *Execute* ignores it. *Display* prints it on the screen.

❑ Declare a new global variable **W**. Then *execute*:

```
W := 3.14 - 2 * 2.
```

Next *execute*:

```
W
```

Nothing should appear on the screen. But you can verify that the code has compiled and executed by *displaying*:

```
W
```

❑ Similarly, merely *executing*:

```
Array with: 'Tolstoy' with: W
```

produces nothing on the screen, but *displaying*:

```
Array with: 'Tolstoy' with: W
```

displays the resulting array instance on the screen. (The **with:with:** class method is an easy way to produce an array instance.)

❑ As a final example, *execute*:

```
Transcript show: 'War and Peace'
```

In this case, the effect of the execution is to echo back the string to the transcript window. But don't confuse this effect with the return. What is the returned object? Short of reading source code, you can find out by *displaying*:

```
Transcript show: 'War and Peace'
```

The same effect will occur, *and* Smalltalk will print the returned object—*an EtTranscript*—which is Smalltalk's description of an instance of class **EtTranscript**. As a matter of fact, that's what **Transcript** is—a global variable pointing to an instance of **EtTranscript**.[3]

The next exercise illustrates several returns, one of which astonishes nearly everybody.

Messages

❑ *Display* the returns from each of these messages:

```
4 factorial
8 max: 5
8 between: 5 and: 7
#(vanilla ice cream) at: 2
#(vanilla 'ice' cream) at: 2
'milk and ' , 'honey'
'salt' at: 1 put: $m "Remember that literals are immutable"
'salt' copy at: 1 put: $m
```

The return from the last message surprises most people. They expect **at:put:** to return the (modified) string that received the message; instead it returns the argument **$m**! This experience emphasizes that you cannot always guess the return. You must either read the method's code or experiment by sending a message.

❑ Finally, either *displaying* or *executing*:

```
#salt copy at: 1 put: $m
```

brings up a walkback window. The error occurs because symbols are unique, so that the **copy** message is ineffectual; it returns the original literal symbol, which is immutable.

---

[3] In other dialects of Smalltalk, **Transcript** points instead to an instance of class **TextWindow** or **TranscriptWindow** or **TextCollector**.

Parsing precedence

Remember that unless overridden by parentheses, unary messages precede binary messages, which precede keyword messages.

❑ Apply this rule to predict and confirm the returns for:

```
#(6 5 4 3 2 1) at: 2 * 3
```

and:

```
'oat bran' size * 4 between: 6 negated and: 3 factorial * 5
```

Classes and instances

❑ Examine the hierarchy of **Animal** classes you built on page 26. Predict and confirm the returns from these messages:

```
'oat bran' class
Penguin new class superclass
(2/7) class superclass superclass
String allInstances size
Penguin allInstances size
```

❑ Create a new global variable, P, then *execute* **P := Penguin new.** *Display* the returns from:

```
P isKindOf: Animal
P isMemberOf: Animal
```

❑ Finally, count the number of penguins in the system again by *displaying*:

```
Penguin allInstances size
```

Inspectors

❑ Examine the penguin object by *executing* **P inspect**. This window is called an *inspector*; by clicking on its entries, you'll see the values of the penguin's instance variables, including any it inherits from its superclasses. You can also inspect an object by highlighting it and using the *Inspect* menu option. Try this technique too.

❑ You can use inspectors to plunge through several layers of complex object structure. For example, inspect this object:

```
Array with: P with: 'ice cold' with: -273
```

and double-click on the array's three instance variables to examine the underlying objects.

Cascading messages

Smalltalk offers an economical syntax for repeatedly sending messages to the same object. Instead of writing:

```
SomeObject msg1.
SomeObject msg2.
SomeObject msg3.
```

you can *cascade* the messages by writing:

```
SomeObject msg1;
          msg2;
          msg3.
```

A cascaded message—one following a semicolon—is delivered to the same object that the previous message was delivered to. Here's another way to think about it: figure out the last message before the first semicolon; whatever object received that message also receives all the other cascaded messages.

❑ *Execute*:

```
Transcript cr;
          show: 'If I had a';
          cr;
          show: 'hammer'.
```

(The message **cr** just instructs the window to do a carriage return.)

❑ What is the return from:

```
5 + 2 * 3;
      + 7;
      + 9.
```

Verify your answer by *displaying* this code.

❑ The simple but handy message **yourself** returns whatever object it is sent to. Putting **yourself** together with a cascade gives us a convenient way to see the effect (instead of the return) of **at:put:**. Try *displaying*:

```
'salt' copy at: 1 put: $m;
          yourself
```

Writing methods

❑ Bring up an application browser on the animal application you prepared earlier. (Just as before, first *Manage Applications*, then select your application, then finally *Browse Application*.)

❑ Select class **Animal,** check that the *instance/class* button is toggled to *instance,* pull down the *Methods* menu and pick *New Method Template.* Write a **display:** method that looks like:

```
display: aString
        "Display aString in the transcript"
        Transcript cr;
                show: aString;
                cr.
```

Compile the method by picking the *Save* menu option.

❑ Now write a **talk** method in **Animal** so that animals say *'I have nothing to say'.* This method uses the method you just wrote, and is simply:

```
talk
        "Speak tersely"
        self display: 'I have nothing to say'.
```

❑ Test your work by *executing:*

```
P talk
```

Assuming that **P** is still your penguin, the response should be *'I have nothing to say'.*

❑ As in the Smalltalk/V animal hierarchy, we are going to make parrots behave a little differently. Parrots should have vocabularies. Define an instance variable **vocabulary** in class **Parrot.** Also write and compile a method **setVocabulary:** that assigns a string to this instance variable. Last, write a **talk** method for parrots with this code:

```
talk
        "Repeat my vocabulary"
        self display: vocabulary.
```

❑ Assign a new parrot to a new global variable **P2.** Ask this parrot to talk. Do you understand this response? Now give **P2** a vocabulary (**'I want a cracker'**) by sending it the **setVocabulary:** message. Ask **P2** to talk again.

❑ In class **Animal,** write and compile a **setName:** method that assigns a string to the **name** instance variable.

❑ Create a **Human** subclass of **Mammal.** Assign a new human to a global variable **H.** Does **H** have a name? (Inspect **H** to confirm your answer.) Give **H** a name (**'Claude Monet'**) by sending it the **setName:** message. Finally, write a **talk** method so that all humans will say *'My name is _____ '.* Verify that **H** says his name properly.

Special variables self and super

❑ Write a new instance method **blab** for humans. The method's body should simply be:

    `self talk`.

Predict and confirm the result of *executing* **H blab**. Replace the variable **self** with the variable **super** and recompile **blab**. What is the result of *executing* **H blab** now?

Here's the explanation. Changing **self** to **super** alters Smalltalk's rule for searching for methods. Instead of beginning the search in the class of the object—**Human** in this example—**super** causes Smalltalk to begin searching in the *superclass* of the method containing **super**. In this example, Smalltalk bypasses the **talk** method in class **Human** and begins its search in class **Mammal**. Thus, **super** is a way to access a superclass method that would ordinarily be eclipsed by an overriding subclass method. Notice that **super** and **self** both refer to the same object; they differ only in how they affect the starting point for method lookup.

❑ Make a small addition to your **talk** method in class **Human** so that humans say *both* '*I have nothing to say*' and '*My name is _____*'.

Now that you've developed some code of your own, you should save your work by saving the image. It's prudent to get into this habit, because a recently saved image simplifies recovery if and when the system crashes.[4]

Accessing variables

Consider a class hierarchy like this:

Suppose **Up** defines an instance variable named **u** and a class variable named **U** and **Down** defines an instance variable **d** and class variable **D**.

❑ Sketch an instance of **Up** and an instance of **Down**. Can instance methods of **Down** use **u**? Can instance methods of **Up** use **d**?

---

[4] In Professional IBM Smalltalk, VisualAge, or any Smalltalk dialect with the *Envy* library control system add-on, you can also create a *version* of your code. A version is a permanent snapshot of your code.

❑ Can instance methods of **Down** use **U**? Can instance methods of **Up** use **D**?

❑ Can class methods of **Down** use **u** or **U**? Can class methods of **Up** use **d** or **D**?

If you are uncertain about your answers, create a brand-new application and perform the experiments. (To create a new application, use your Application Manager. Pop up a menu and pick *Applications > Create*.)

Blocks [...]

Like everything else in Smalltalk, a *block* (sometimes also called a *context*) is an object. It is defined by placing code between brackets [...]. But it is stranger than most objects, because the code it represents might never execute. Meanwhile, you can assign it to a variable, pass it around as an argument of a message, and send it messages—in short, you can treat it like any other Smalltalk object. The code will execute only if the block receives an explicit request for it to do so. Here's an example.

❑ If you *execute*:

```
X := [ H talk ]
```

the assignment to the variable **X** occurs, but the code for talking does *not* execute. Only by sending the message:

```
X value
```

does the code actually execute.

❑ Blocks occur regularly in conditional messages. *Execute* this:

```
(H isKindOf: Mammal)
        ifTrue: X
```

and:

```
(H isKindOf: Mammal)
        ifTrue: [ P2 talk ]
        ifFalse: [ H talk ]
```

❑ They also occur in loops. *Execute*:

```
6 timesRepeat: [ P2 talk ]
```

❑ With a little syntactic twist, blocks can also have arguments. For example, to multiply all the elements in a set, *display* (don't forget to declare global variables):

```
MyProduct := 1.
S := Set with: 5 with: 3 with: 4.
S do: [ :number | MyProduct := MyProduct * number].
MyProduct
```

The **do:** method is one of the most common ways to loop. It iterates over all the elements of S, substituting them one at a time for the variable **number** in the block. The name of this variable is arbitrary; it could just as well have been called **:element** or **:n** as **:number**.[5]

Class Date

Date objects occur frequently in applications. Class **Date** is unusual because it has many more class methods for creating instances than other classes do. For example, knowing a day from 1 to 366 and a year, the **newDay:year:** class method can create a date instance for this date. Or, from a day and a month and year, the **newDay:month:year:** class method can create a date instance for that date.

❑ *Display* the object returned from sending the message **today** to **Date**.

❑ Use the **newDay:year:** method to create December 31, 1999; assign it to a global variable **X**.

❑ Use the **newDay:month:year:** class method to create your birthday; assign it to a global variable **Y**. Read the comment in the method first to determine the form that it expects for its arguments.

❑ Verify that **X > Y** returns a sensible object.

Rendering any Smalltalk object into text

The **printString** message attempts to return a string from any object at all, although the string may not be very informative. Some examples:

❑ To see how useful it is to be able to render an object as a string, contrast *displaying*:

```
'The bird is ' , P2
```

with *displaying*:

```
'The bird is ' , P2 printString
```

---

[5] IBM Smalltalk also supports an infrequently used feature known as *block temporary variables*. These are variables that are declared inside a block for use only within that block. For example, in the block [|x| ...] the variable **x** has been declared and may be used freely within the block. If the block also has an argument, the form is [:number | |x| ...].

❏ Similarly, contrast *displaying*:

```
Y , ' is my birthday'
```

with *displaying*:

```
Y printString , ' is my birthday'
```

Many Smalltalk implementations have a single **printString** method, located in class **Object**. IBM Smalltalk has a few, but not many, more implementations of **printString**. (How many?) How then is **printString** rich enough to render practically every kind of object into a meaningful text string? In fact, it is not at all rich enough. Instead, it invokes another method that is implemented individually in many classes; it is this method and not **printString** that does the brunt of the work of rendering objects into strings.

❏ Find this method. How many implementations of it are there? (Hundreds!)

4.4 Smalltalk's debugger

Debugging

❏ Create a new application (or use one of yours), then a subclass **AAA** of **Object**, with an instance variable **iv** and an instance method **m** whose body is:

```
iv := 4.
self badMessage.
Transcript show: 'Done'.
```

Execute:

```
AAA new m
```

The debugger window that appears is called a *walkback* because the list in the upper left windowpane lets you scroll, or "walk back," through the method invocations leading to the error. Each line represents a class and method. The order is that in which the methods called each other, with the caller beneath the callee. In all, they depict the frozen stack of method invocations at the time of the error.

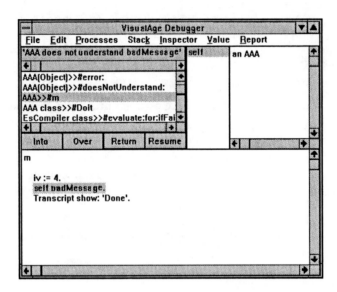

The line **AAA>>#m** indicates the method you wrote. Selecting this line displays your own code in the large windowpane, as you can see above. (The notation **AAA(XXX)>>#mmm**, means that although the object is an instance of **AAA**, the **mmm** method is inherited from the superclass **XXX**. Depending on the whim of the tool, the # may or may not be part of the notation.)

❑ Examine the present object (an instance of **AAA**) by double-clicking on **self** in the middle windowpane. An inspector opens on the object, from which you can determine the current value of the instance variable **iv**.

❑ You can fix the problem directly in the debugger, without having to use a browser: remove the erroneous message in the large windowpane, then *save* (recompile). Close the walkback window and verify that:

    AAA new m

runs correctly.

Controlling execution step by step

Once the debugger freezes the execution stack, you can often continue executing with the *into* button (which stops immediately after plunging down into the current, highlighted message), the *over* button (which stops after completely executing the highlighted message), the *return* button (which stops after completing the current method, just before returning to its calling method), or the *resume* button (which executes as far as possible).

❑ Replace **self badMessage** with **self halt** in the preceding exercise, and again *execute* **AAA new m**. This time, experiment with the buttons.

4.5 Provocations

Aliasing

❑ *Display* or *inspect*:

```
|r p|
r := Rectangle origin: 20@20 extent: 10@10.
p := r corner.
"p x: 50; y: 50."
r
```

Now remove the quotation marks, and *display* or *inspect* again. Did you expect **r** to change? **p** refers to **r**'s corner—**p** is an *alias* for the corner point. Thus, by changing **p**, **r** itself changes. In Smalltalk, aliasing occurs because variables are pointers, even though there is no syntactic cue that they are.

❑ Replace the third line with **p := r corner copy** and *display* or *inspect* again. This time, **r** is unaffected. That's because **p** is no longer an alias for the corner point itself, but a separate object that is a copy of the corner point.

Smalltalk shields programmers from the pointer bugs that afflict programs in languages with explicit pointers, but at the cost of making aliasing less apparent than in conventional languages.

Concise reuse

❑ Write a method **foobar** in class **AAA** with this body:

```
"... Lots of code ..."
Transcript show: 'To be or not to be'.
"... Lots more code ..."
```

❑ Create a subclass **BBB** of **AAA**. Make instances of **BBB** behave the same as instances of **AAA**, except that they respond to **foobar** messages with *'My kingdom for a horse'* instead of *'To be or not to be'*. The ground rules are not to copy code—

for example, copying "... **Lots of code** ..." to another method would not be a concise form of reuse. Instead, consider modifying the **foobar** method in **AAA** and defining brand-new methods in **AAA** and **BBB**.

Because no one can anticipate in general how code will be used, or reused—we did not know of the requirement for **BBB>> foobar** until after **AAA>> foobar** was working—no one can expect to produce reusable designs without considerable trial and error. "Not until you try to reuse do you discover what's wrong" [Sarkela 1989].

CHAPTER 5

Abstract classes

This chapter and the next introduce essential object-oriented concepts that build on and go beyond the elemental principles of objects, classes, and inheritance.

Abstract classes are a simple idea that profoundly influences software design. The definition sounds paradoxical: an *abstract class* is a class that never has any instances. Why bother to build a class that won't have any instances? We'll spend this chapter answering this question, going so far as to argue that such classes are indispensable in good object-oriented design. We begin with some examples.

Class **Magnitude** is abstract. (See the drawing on page 14.) No one has any use for something as abstruse as an instance of **Magnitude**. Nevertheless, class **Magnitude** has subclasses like **Date** and **Time**, whose instances are quite useful. An abstract class can act as a center for gathering behavior and expectations common to its subclasses. In this case, as we saw on page 15, the behavior common to **Magnitude**'s subclasses is comparability. For example, two instances of the subclass **Date** can be compared via messages like <=. Although **Magnitude** has no instances to enjoy this behavior, its subclasses evidently do.

Animal is another abstract class. We have little interest in an instance of class **Animal**—it's instances of **Whale** and **Dog** that we care about. This idea is not just a programming nicety; it's a cognitive distinction in the everyday world. The concrete objects we visualize are whales and dogs, not animals. What after all would something as abstract as an animal look like?

In Smalltalk, the most abstract of all abstract classes is class **Object**. An instance of class **Object** is too nebulous to be useful to a programmer. Yet class **Object** is an invaluable center for gathering expectations we have about all Smalltalk objects: all objects should be copyable, displayable, testable for equality with other objects, and so on. The idea sounds tidy, but there's a rub. Copying or displaying an object depends a lot on the particularities of the object. It would be naive to hope that we could write code in class **Object** for copying or displaying and have it work meaningfully for all subclasses. That's why an abstract class is a repository for *expectations*. We *expect* objects to be displayable and we *expect* animals to move, but how they do it depends on the kind of object or animal. The actual code to display and copy is likely to reside in concrete subclasses, not the abstract class.

5.1   Exercise in object-oriented design

Consider this fictitious hierarchy of class **Table** and its subclasses. An instance of **ArrayTable** is organized as an array; that is, its elements are stored at consecutive offsets in memory, the first at the first offset, the second at the second, and so on. An instance of **Link-Table** is organized by a chain of pointers; its elements are scattered through memory, the first pointing to the second, the second to the third.... We are going to examine the object-oriented implications of searching these tables.

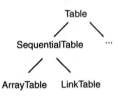

Here's some plausible pseudo-code for a search method:

```
search for an <item>

        start
        loop while (not end and next ≠ <item>)
                end loop
        if end then return not_found
                else return found
```

Underlines indicate methods. Thus the **search** method calls three other methods, namely **start**, **end**, and **next**.

❑ In which classes should each of these four methods be coded?

5.2   Solution and discussion

We begin with **next**. The way in which a table advances to its next element depends on the kind of table. An **ArrayTable** adds 1 to its current index (**index := index + 1**) while a **LinkTable** updates a pointer (**current := next**). Since the logic is different, the two subclasses will need their own separate versions of the **next** method.

The situation for the **start** method is similar. An **ArrayTable** starts by initializing the index to the first element (**index := 1**) while a **LinkTable** initializes the pointer to the head of the chain (**current := head**). Again, separate versions of **start** must occur in the two subclasses. There also must be two versions of the **end** method: an **Array-Table** must test for the upper limit of the array (**index > upper**) while a **LinkTable** tests for a null pointer (**current = nil**).

So far, then, we're forced to write separate versions of the **start**, **next**, and **end** methods in the two classes **ArrayTable** and **LinkTable**:

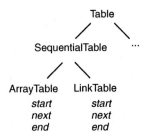

Do we also need two versions of the **search** method? That would be foolhardy, for the code in both versions would be identical; both would simply be based on the pseudo-code illustrated above. Instead, we will write it once, in class **SequentialTable**, and let the subclasses inherit it:

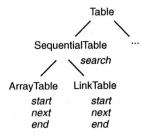

Now, why not move **search** still higher, into class **Table**? Because our **search** method has a strongly sequential flavor, and some kinds of tables behave in non-sequential ways. Consider a hash table, for example. A hash table searches directly instead of sequentially. Given a search item, the table uses the item itself to calculate ("hash") a position where the item may reside. This kind of table doesn't iterate through its items one by one. Hashing calculations don't resemble the sequential pseudo-code above at all. Therefore a hash table needs its own version of **search**, so we end up with our methods distributed through the hierarchy like so:

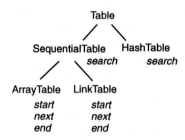

5.3   Pure virtual (subclassResponsibility) methods

So far, **Table** has no behavior at all. We dared not write **search** there, because its sub-classes required their own versions. On the other hand, one could argue that a class with a name like **Table** ought to be searchable; we *expect* any table to be searchable. Object designers settle this quandary by boldly writing a **search** method in **Table** anyway, but one that does nothing. This disembodied method is variously called a *pure virtual* function (C++), *implementedBySubclass* or *subclassResponsibility* method (Smalltalk), a *deferred* routine (Eiffel), or an *abstract* method (Java). I will use these terms interchangeably, even the C++ term *pure virtual*, because it is so evocative. (What could do less than something that is purely virtual?)

Why bother with a method like **Table>>search** that does nothing? There are two reasons: it announces to potential consumers of **Table's** subclasses that they ought to be able to find things in any table by using a method named **search**. And it announces to the programmers who will write any **Table** subclasses that they are obligated to sup-ply a **search** method. At the very least, then, a pure virtual method is effective docu-mentation. In Smalltalk, it's little more than this; the pure virtual **search** amounts to an informal contract between **Table** consumers and **Table** developers. Nothing enforces this contract. But in a language like C++ where the compiler can settle con-tract disputes, once the designer specifies a pure virtual function, the subclasses must provide a concrete ("do-something") implemetation of the function, or the code will fail to compile. That is, a pure virtual function in C++ enforces the contract between consumers and developers.

Notice one logical consequence of pure virtual methods: a class that has such a method is necessarily an abstract class. An instance of **Table** is nonsensical, since it has no working code for its **search** method.

5.4   Exercise: discovering pure virtuals

❑ Returning to our example, the hierarchy contains, in addition to **Table**, one other abstract class. Which class is this, and does it present another opportunity for pure virtual methods?

5.5   Solution and discussion

Do any other classes in the hierarchy have no instances? **SequentialTable** is such a class. Its subclasses can have instances because they support a full complement of behavior, namely **start, next, end**, plus an inherited **search**, but any instances of **SequentialTable** itself would be worthless. Hence **SequentialTable** is an abstract class.

Now an abstract class is rather hollow unless we have a sense of what can be expected of it. The mechanism for recording these expectations is to declare pure virtual methods. What should these methods be for **SequentialTable**? The suspects are, of course, **start, next**, and **end**. Not only are these natural qualities of sequential-ness, the **search** pseudo-code actually demands their presence. What better way to remind the **ArrayTable** and **LinkTable** developers to implement them than to declare them as pure virtual, subclassResponsibility methods? The final hierarchy, then, looks like this:

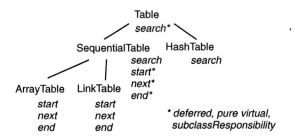

5.6   Ensuring no instances

We have determined that **Table** is an abstract class; an instance of it would be worthless because it would not have sufficient executable behavior. It would be nice if object-oriented languages could protect programmers from mistakenly creating such an instance. Smalltalk can't quite. The best it can do, if a wayward instance of **Table** has been created, is to alert the programmer at the time the instance receives a **search** message. If **Table>>search** is absent, the message triggers the familiar **doesNotUnderstand:** walkback that occurs whenever an object receives a message that it can't resolve.

The walkback duly alerts the programmer, but the preferred technique is not to omit **search**, but to write the method as follows:

```
search: anItem
        self subclassResponsibility
```

Then any attempt to send the **search** message to an instance of **Table** will invoke the **subclassResponsibility** method. This method too produces a walkback, but one that specifically describes its cause as the absence of a proper implementation of **search**. As we discussed earlier, writing **search** in this way also delivers the most important service of pure virtual methods—documentation of the. abstract class.

Compiled object-oriented languages like C++ can do even better. By specifying even one pure virtual function in a class, the compiler rejects any code that declares an object of that class. Thus, the mere presence of a pure virtual function guarantees that the class will have no instances and will really be abstract.[1]

In either case, Smalltalk or C++, the goal is the same: we don't want programmers to use instances of the abstract class because the abstract class lacks a full complement of behavior. It presents expectations but doesn't have the assets to back them up.

Technical aside: Sometimes a shrewd designer will write a benign method in an abstract class with no code at all, not even the message **self subclassResponsibility**. Here's an example:

```
customInitialize
        "This method does nothing, not even cause a walkback!
        It executes harmlessly, but if you wish to provide
        some subclass-specific initialization code, feel free to
        override it in your subclass."
```

Let's say that some method in the abstract class (perhaps its **initialize** method) executes some standard code, but along the way also executes **self customInitialize**. The programmer of a subclass can optionally override **customInitialize** to do something special, but if she does not, the inherited **customInitialize** method executes harmlessly. The designer has therefore opened an optional back door for custom code, analogous to what was called a *user exit* in the heyday of mainframe system software. Today these back doors are sometimes referred to as *hook methods*.

---

[1] The C++ jargon for an abstract class is an ABC, or *abstract base class*.

5.7 Concrete behavior in abstract classes

Lest you write off abstract classes as devoid of substance, you should know that it's possible and often beneficial to imbue them with *concrete* behavior too. In other words, not all methods in an abstract class need be pure virtual. The class may still have lots of code that is shareable among its subclasses. For example, Smalltalk's **Collection** class is an abstract class with plenty of behavior its concrete subclasses—**Array, Set, SortedCollection,** and many others—gratefully inherit.

A concrete method in an abstract class will sometimes appear to invoke one or more pure virtual methods. This is not as odd as it sounds. In the table example we just studied, the **search** method in class **SequentialTable** is a concrete method that appears to invoke **SequentialTable**'s pure virtual methods **next, start,** and **end.** These pure virtual versions actually never execute. Instead, because we use only instances of the subclasses of **SequentialTable,** the concrete, overriding versions execute. This is such a typical characteristic of sound object-oriented designs, and so often misunderstood by newcomers, that I want to belabor the point by examining another example.

Consider a method **max:** that returns the maximum of two magnitude objects. Nothing deters us from implementing **max:** concretely in the abstract class **Magnitude:**

```
max: anotherMag
        self < anotherMag
              ifTrue: [ ^anotherMag ]
              ifFalse: [ ^self ]
```

The odd aspect of this code is that although it is in class **Magnitude,** it uses a method, <, that cannot be implemented in class **Magnitude.** (That's because comparisons like < depend on the internal representation of an object, and these representations differ from subclass to subclass. For instance, the representation for objects of the **Time** subclass differs from that for the **Float** subclass. That's the "catch" we discussed on page 15.)

With this background—that **max:** uses a method that must be defined in subclasses—what kinds of objects in the **Magnitude** hierarchy can execute **max:**'s code? Clearly not instances of **Magnitude** itself, since **Magnitude** is abstract and should have no instances. Hence, only instances of subclasses qualify. Consider **13.7,** an instance of **Float,** and the message:

```
13.7 max: 17.3
```

The relevant portion of the class hierarchy is:

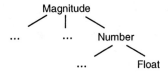

Now **13.7**'s class, **Float**, doesn't implement **max:**. Thus **13.7** searches up its inheritance tree until it finds a superclass that does implement **max:**—in this case **Magnitude**. The **max:** code above then executes. The first line sends the binary message < back to **self** (**13.7**). This time **13.7** recognizes < as a method that its own class **Float** implements, and hence executes it without recourse to inheritance. The result is **true** (because **anotherMag** is **17.3**), and so the code executes the branch that returns **17.3** (**anotherMag**) as the final result.

To recap, the code for **max:** was written in **Magnitude** with the full understanding that it depends on pure virtual methods that can't possibly be written correctly in **Magnitude**. No instances of **Magnitude**, only instances of its subclasses, can successfully execute **max:**. And finally, because the code in **max:** refers to **self**, execution can flow from the superclass method (**max:**) *down* to the subclass method (<).

This example is typical of sound object-oriented design. It maximizes reuse because there is just one **max:** method and as many versions of < as necessary, but no more than are necessary. More important, subclass implementors can direct their attention to subclass-specific methods like <; they enjoy the benefit of **max:** without thinking about it.

You should seek opportunities to write reusable methods like **max:** in your own applications. Unfortunately on larger projects, where different subclasses are written by different developers, opportunities for unifying common function aren't often recognized. In effect, each developer writes a slightly different version of **max:**. The price is redundant thinking, design, code, and especially maintenance. The redundancy can cost hours and days when the methods in question are more complex than **max:**

5.8 Summary: methods in abstract classes

The methods in an abstract class have three primary forms. Some are pure virtual (subclassResponsibility, deferred, abstract, implementedBySubclass); subclass developers must override them with concrete implementations. Some are concrete and self-contained; subclass developers inherit them without any obligations. And some are like **max:** (or **SequentialTable>>search**) above; subclass developers are obligated to provide some concrete behavior that the method needs, but they do not override the whole method.

There is no consensus on terminology for distinguishing the three forms, but [Wirfs-Brock et al. 1990] and [Johnson and Russo 1991] call them *abstract methods* (the *Java* term), *base methods*, and *template methods*, respectively. [Gamma et al. 1995] also call the last kind *template methods*. I think of them as *yo-yo methods* because execution bounces up and down with respect to a subclass, and framework designer Kirk Wolf refers to the phenomenon as an *apparent down-call*.

You will see in Chapter 19 that abstract classes and these three kinds of methods are at the heart of object-oriented frameworks.

CHAPTER 6

Containers and other indispensable ideas

In the everyday world, *containers*—things that contain other things—are everywhere. Pots, spoons, baskets, buses, countertops, books, CD-ROMs, and pea pods are all containers. Containers commonly even contain other containers. My kitchen contains a pantry, which in turn contains shelves, which in their turn contain boxes and cans, which contain cereals and soups. My kitchen also contains a refrigerator, which contains shelves and a door, both of which are also containers.

Containers are such indispensable everyday objects that we should expect them to also be indispensable software objects. The patterns that occur among software objects should reflect the ones that we observe among everyday objects.

For a programmer, important containers include queues, stacks, arrays, sets, and the like. Object-oriented programmers, and especially Smalltalk programmers, sometimes call containers *collections*. That's because the container classes in Smalltalk are all subclasses of an abstract class named **Collection**:

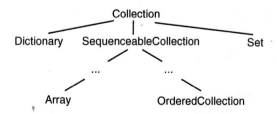

For our purposes, *collection* and *container* are interchangeable.

The hierarchy above shows just a few of IBM Smalltalk's container classes. Here are the most commonly used Smalltalk containers, and some of their distinguishing characteristics.

Class	Characteristics
Dictionary	Like a real dictionary, it organizes information by a lookup key.
Array	Its elements are arranged in consecutive slots. Also, its size is fixed.
OrderedCollection	Like an array, but its size may increase or decrease.
Set	Its elements are not arranged in any order. Also, an object can occur in it at most once.
String	It contains 0 or more characters.
ByteArray	Like an array, but its elements are bytes.
SortedCollection	Smarter than an ordered collection, it maintains its elements in an ordering determined by some sorting criterion.
IdentityDictionary	A special, efficient dictionary, suitable mainly if the keys are **Symbol** or **SmallInteger** objects.
Stream (not a collection, but similar)	Smarter than a collection, it remembers where it was last accessed.

A final word of introduction to the study of containers: practically every object-oriented design you do will require one or more containers, including your first sizable design exercise in the next chapter. Learning to recognize the need for containers in your designs is a major step toward becoming a good object-oriented designer.

6.1 Heterogeneity and homogeneity

In the everyday world, some containers, such as drawers, hold many kinds of things and others, such as three-ring binders, hold just one kind of thing, such as pages. Smalltalk's containers are like the drawers. That is, a typical Smalltalk container won't verify that its contents are all of the same type; it can hold integers, or whales, or even a mixture of integers and whales. This drawer-like property, the ability to hold *heterogeneous* elements, is attractive but potentially dangerous. Its attraction is evident: you can pick up and use a container without worrying about whether it will work for the kinds of objects you want to hold—it'll hold any Smalltalk object. On the other hand, if your container is one that maintains elements in sorted order (see the exercise in the next section), what good would it be to hold a mixture of integers and whales, or for that matter, whales alone? Or, suppose you have a set that presently holds integers, but you've accidentally deposited a whale into it. If you double all the elements, the whale will protest, via a walkback, that it doesn't understand multiplication by two.

6.2   Exercise: heterogeneity and homogeneity

❑ Ordered collections are like arrays, except that their size is not fixed. Define a class **Whale**, then explore heterogeneity by *displaying* the following. (Don't forget to declare global variables like **OC**.)

```
OC := OrderedCollection new.
OC add: 'a';
    add: 'c'.
"OC add: Whale new."
OC.
```

Remove the quotation marks and try again. This exercise demonstrates that the ordered collection is able to accommodate any kind of object. However, if you want to do something meaningful to **OC**, its heterogeneous contents are a problem. Why does *executing* the following code produce a walkback?

```
Pet := 't'.
OC do: [:elem | Pet := elem , Pet].
Pet
```

But if you now re-comment the whale line by replacing the quotation marks, and *display* the whole sequence of statements, from beginning to end, the errors vanish and Smalltalk displays *'cat'*.

❑ Another subclass of class **Collection** is **SortedCollection**. An instance of class **Sorted-Collection** is a collection whose objects are always in sorted order. *Display*:

```
X := SortedCollection new.
X add: 3; add: 2; add: 5.
X
```

What defines the order? The answer is that every **SortedCollection** object has a sort block that defines the ordering operation. The default operation is **<=**. Reverse the order by *displaying*:

```
X sortBlock: [:a :b | a >= b].
X
```

❑ How heterogeneous is a sorted collection? Unlike a set, which accepts any object you add to it, a sorted collection starts sending comparison messages as soon as you add more than one object. If an object you add isn't comparable, the sorted collection will protest with a walkback. For example, *execute*:

```
X add: Whale new.
```

Thus the first object you add to a sorted collection can be of any class, but all subsequent ones had better be comparable to the first.

6.3 Exercise: dictionaries

❑ Looking things up—in dictionaries, phonebooks, software help files, relational database tables, and so on—is an elemental activity for both humans and computers. Smalltalk's container class for this activity is **Dictionary**. Dictionaries are among the most widespread containers in a typical Smalltalk application. (Arrays, however, are even more prevalent.) To see the relative occurrence of these objects in your current image, *display* these lines, one by one:

```
Set allInstances size.
Dictionary allInstances size.
Array allInstances size.
String allInstances size.
```

❑ A Smalltalk dictionary consists of entries that Smalltalk calls *associations*. Each association has a key and a value. *Executing*:

```
X := Dictionary new.
X at: 'Kilauea' put: 'Most active volcano';
      at: 'Denali' put: 'Formerly Mt. McKinley'.
```

constructs a new dictionary with two associations whose keys are geographic names and whose values are descriptions of the associated places. You can look up an association by *displaying*:

```
X at: 'Denali'
```

or you can examine the entire dictionary by *executing*:

```
X inspect.
```

6.4 Preparatory exercise: identity versus equality

Like any object system, Smalltalk maintains a critical distinction between *identity* and *equality*. You will need to grasp this distinction to understand identity dictionaries in the next section.

To say that "two" objects are identical is to say that they are actually the same object. The message selector that tests for this condition is ==. As an example, X == X results in the **true** object, no matter what object the variable **X** may refer to.

❑ The == message can be used to resolve some fundamental questions in Smalltalk. For one, do different occurrences of an integer refer to different objects or the same object? To answer this question, *execute* the first two lines below, *one at a time,* then *display* the last line:

```
X := 3.
Y := 3.
X == Y.
```

Since the result is the **true** object, we conclude that there is only one **3** object in all of Smalltalk. (The same is true for any "small" integer, which means technically any instance of the class **SmallInteger**. Each dialect of Smalltalk has a range, beyond which an integer is no longer an instance of **SmallInteger** but **LargeInteger**. For IBM Smalltalk, this range is from -2^{30} to $+2^{30}-1$, or -1073741824 to $+1073741823$.)

❑ Symbols are like integers: there can be at most one symbol with a given spelling, as you can verify by *executing* these lines, *one at a time*, and *displaying* the last one:

```
X := #Hobbes.
Y := #Hobbes.
X == Y.
```

On the other hand, repeat the experiment, again line by line,[1] with:

```
X := 'Hobbes'.
Y := 'Hobbes'.
X == Y.
```

---

[1] In some Smalltalk dialects, including IBM's, the behavior of examples like these depends on whether the code is compiled all at once, or piece by piece. When compiled all at once, the compiler can perform optimizations that camouflage the striking results we want to see.

The result, **false**, forces us to conclude that the two instances of the string **'Hobbes'** are distinct from each other. In other words, strings are not identical, even if they consist of exactly the same characters! Picture it in this way:

The other test, *equality*, uses the message selector =. This is a weaker test than identity. In rough terms, equality merely measures whether two objects are "indistinguishable." The precise meaning of "indistinguishability" depends on how the programmer defines it for a given class; that is, on how the programmer overrides the = method.

❑ *Execute* the first two lines, one at a time, and *display* the last:

```
X := 'Hobbes'.
Y := 'Hobbes'.
X = Y.
```

The result, **true**, tells us that the two strings are *equal* to each other, even though we have just seen that they are not the same, *identical* string object. Thus, objects may be equal—indistinguishable—without being identically the same object. On the other hand, identical objects are necessarily equal.

Identity is such a fundamental Smalltalk notion that if you override the == method Smalltalk ignores your override.[2] By contrast, you can override the = method at will. Therefore, in your own classes, the definition of equality—"indistinguishability"—is entirely up to you. As a case in point, Smalltalk's designers decided on their own definition of equality for strings, namely that two strings are equal if they contain the same characters in the same order. But before you override equality in your classes, read the upcoming section "Overriding equality."

6.5 Identity dictionaries

Class **Dictionary** has a famous subclass named **IdentityDictionary**. These two kinds of dictionaries use different tests to determine whether two keys are the "same." Ordinary dictionaries use the equality test, and identity dictionaries use the identity test.

---

[2] Actually, there is an uncommon way to force your own == method to execute. See the technical aside on page 197.

What's more, in many Smalltalk products, the implementations of **at:put:** and **at:** in class **IdentityDictionary** execute faster than in class **Dictionary**. And identity dictionaries occupy less storage than ordinary dictionaries. When performance matters, identity dictionaries may be preferable. But you can use them only if equal keys are also identical. For example, using strings as keys in identity dictionaries is inadvisable. That's because most programmers who write code like:

```
someDictionary at: 'Hobbes' put: '17th century philosopher'.
someDictionary at: 'Hobbes' put: 'stuffed tiger'.
```

expect the second **at:put:** to replace the value **'17th century philosopher'** by **'stuffed tiger'** at the (sole) dictionary entry for **'Hobbes'**. Ordinary dictionaries indeed behave this way. If, however, the dictionary is an *identity* dictionary, we know that the two strings are distinct objects, so that, contrary to expectation, a separate second entry will be created.

To summarize, almost all identity dictionaries in practical use have keys that are either small integers or symbols. These make suitable keys for identity dictionaries because for these kinds of objects, equality implies identity. For most applications, ordinary dictionaries suffice, and they have the advantage of operating reliably for any kind of key at all.

6.6   Exercise: identity dictionaries

❑ Explain why this code, executed line by line, produces a walkback:

```
X := IdentityDictionary new.
X at: 'Heidegger' put: 'Difficult existentialist'.
X at: 'Heidegger'.
```

6.7   Overriding equality

We've seen that developers have the prerogative of overriding the = method as they please in their own classes (page 74). Those who do, however, risk introducing a subtle bug into their programs. They will find, for instance, that objects they add to a set may appear not to be there later on. I call this the "anomaly of the disappearing element," and you will experiment with it in the exercise in the next section.

Here's how the anomaly occurs: sets use hashing to determine where to insert an added object, and the default hashing algorithm produces different hash values for two distinct (non-identical) objects. The set therefore tends to place non-identical objects in different positions, which is ordinarily desirable and harmless. But if the developer overrides the = method so that the two distinct objects are equal, adds the first one to the set, then searches the set to see if the second, equal one is present, *expecting that it is,* he will find that it isn't. That's because the set will begin its search at a different position, determined by the different hash value of the second object. The developer's error was to expect the second object to behave as though it were identical to the first, when in fact it is only equal to the first.

This scenario may seem unlikely, but it arises in client/server systems, which commonly use a proxy for an object to stand in for the object itself. To determine which proxy stands for which object, the system uses an overridden equality test that compares a problem-specific datum (like a social security number or other unique identifier) in the proxy and the object. Although the proxy and its object aren't identical, they are equal because they have the same identifying datum. The system then treats the proxy and its object as though they are the same, which was the purpose for overriding equality. But it also exposes the system to the "anomaly of the disappearing element." The different hash results of the proxy and the proxied object specify different positions for the two objects:

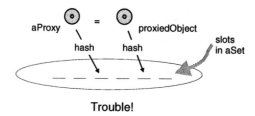

Trouble!

To prevent this anomaly, whenever you override the = method for a class, also override the **hash** method. Whatever the = method compares, write the **hash** method so that it hashes the same thing. In the client/server example above, if the = method compares a social security number, write the **hash** method so that it too hashes the social security number. This ensures that when a set hashes to determine the position of an object, it will compute the same position for both the proxy and its object.

6.8 Exercise: anomaly of the disappearing element

❑ Write a subclass **Book** of **Object** with an instance variable **isbn** and methods **setIsbn:** and **getIsbn** that simply set and answer the instance variable. Override the = method so that it compares ISBN numbers:

```
= anotherBook
        ^self getIsbn = anotherBook getIsbn
```

The following code will construct a library with an initial capacity of 100 holdings, add a holding, then test the library for the holding. *Execute* the first two lines, one at a time, then *display* the last line:

```
Library := Set new: 100.
Library add: (Book new setIsbn: '0-671-20158-1').
Library includes: (Book new setIsbn: '0-671-20158-1').
```

The result, **false**, demonstrates the anomaly of the disappearing element. (The set is large enough that it is statistically unlikely for the result to be **true**, but if it is, adjust the size of the set.) Now amend class **Book** so that the anomaly does not occur.

❑ Once you've solved the preceding exercise, here is an additional wrinkle. An object's identity may occasionally change. Perhaps the book has been re-assigned a different ISBN number. This change affects future searches through the library: the book will again not be found. Why not?

6.9 Exercise: excursion into Streams

Stream classes are not officially under Smalltalk's **Collection** hierarchy, but streams are so closely allied with collections that this chapter is a sensible place in which to introduce them. Streams do something that collections cannot: a **Stream** *remembers where it was.* You can work somewhere in the middle of one, go away for a while, and then continue working on it at the same place you were before. For example, a stream over a string can remember where you last accessed one of its characters, so that at any time you can ask the stream for its *next* character. Collections cannot remember where something last happened to them.

❑ Predict the result of *displaying* this code:

```
|stream|
stream := ReadStream on: 'Van Gogh'.
stream next; next; next; next; next; next.
```

Notice that the stream remembers its position between **next** messages.

❑ One of the most common everyday programming problems is having to construct a string from various sources of information, then passing it off as an argument to some distant object. Complete this code sequence:

```
|string|
string := "You write a few lines".
Transcript show: string.
```

in such a way that *executing* the sequence will produce this text in the transcript:

Sunflowers

Irises

Starry Night

Hint: When you want your string to advance to the next line, you have little choice but to physically advance using the <enter> key on the keyboard. Unfortunately, the resulting code is awkward to read and maintain.

It is more elegant to create a stream and incrementally add chunks to it until it is complete. For incremental processing, streams excel and strings founder. It is contrary to a string's nature to grow, since a string has a fixed length.

❑ To illustrate this approach, reproduce the result above by completing this code sequence:

```
|stream|
stream := ReadWriteStream on: ''.
stream     cr;
           nextPutAll: 'Sunflowers';
           "You write a few messages".
Transcript show: stream contents.
stream close.
```

To summarize, if you need to access or add consecutive elements of a collection, you will have to write code that keeps track of the positional information. Better to use a stream, which relieves you of this obligation by absorbing the responsibility into its own behavior.

6.10 Containers versus aggregations

Aggregations and containers share a main characteristic: a bigger thing holding smaller things. They differ in that an aggregation is, by convention, a rigid relationship between an object and its parts. The makeup of a container, by contrast, is expected to evolve, with elements taking up residence and departing over time. A telephone, comprising a handset, a dial, and so on, is an aggregation. So too is a compiler, comprising a lexical analyzer, a parser, and a code generator. On the other hand, a set or a queue is a container, one of whose principal responsibilities is the comings and goings of objects within it. Containers should therefore respond to add and remove requests.

You can verify this property by browsing through Smalltalk's **Collection** hierarchy and noticing all the **add:** and **remove:** methods.[3] An object like a telephone for which pickup and dial, rather than add and remove, are the more apparent behaviors, should not be designed as a container.

The trouble is that this apparent distinction is sometimes not so crisp. Whether an object has the rigidity of an aggregation or the plasticity of a container is a distinction in degree only. Consider the leaves on a branch. They are rigidly located at fixed locations on the branch, yet they come and go from year to year. One could argue that a branch is an aggregation or a container.

In many situations an object is predominantly an aggregation but also has containment properties. A human body is an aggregation of limbs and organs, yet it also contains blood cells that are continually replenished. That doesn't make the body a container—you wouldn't define it as a subclass of **Collection**. It is an aggregation, but one of the components of the aggregation happens itself to be a container, namely, the **circulatorySystem**, which is a container of blood cells. The component of the body, rather than the body itself, is the container.

Similarly, a class browser, though principally an aggregation of user interface widgets, also contains the collection of methods for the class it browses. Again, the browser itself is not a container, but one of its constituents—its **methods** instance variable—is an instance of **SortedCollection** that contains methods.

Designs that resemble these decompositions are plentiful. A body and its circulatory system, a browser and its methods, or a refrigerator and its vegetable drawer are all objects with many sub-objects, one or more of which is a container object. You will see several of these designs in this book; they represent a design pattern, the *smart container*, in Chapter 18.

6.11   Shallow and deep copying

Copying an object sounds straightforward. In fact, it's one of the subtlest and most trouble-prone areas in object-oriented programming. The essential question arises when an object refers to other objects. Consider a container. If we copy the container, what should happen to the elements in it? For an even simpler example, suppose one object has an instance variable **v** that points to a second object and we copy the first. What should happen to the second?

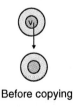

Before copying

---

[3] In some dialects, **add:** and **remove:** are pure virtual (subclassResponsibility) methods in **Collection**, reminding us that the subclasses are obligated to support adding and removing.

The question has two possible answers. If the element or referenced object is also copied, the copy is *deep*; if it isn't copied but instead shared, the copy is *shallow*.

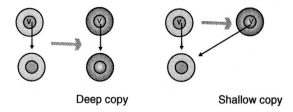

Deep copy   Shallow copy

As the drawing illustrates, shallow copying is appropriate when you intend to share the referenced objects. Container objects are usually shallow copied because we intend to share their contents. In fact, shallow copying is the prevalent (and default) copy in Smalltalk. A realtor, for example, would prefer a shallow copy of the county's collection of real estate listings because he can then be sure that he and everyone else is modifying the same, shared entries. (He'd be even happier to have access to the master collection itself rather than any kind of copy at all, for then he could also keep up with deletions and new listings.)

Deep copying is appropriate in some situations. A Xerox copy is a deep copy because the copy and the original don't share anything. The copy is a complete clone of the original. Deep copying is also often appropriate for aggregations—a house and its garage, for example, or a bicycle and all its parts and, recursively, all their subparts. Two houses shouldn't share one garage, nor should two bicycles share one seat. Aggregations generally retain rigid associations with their components.

There is, however, a gray area between deep and shallow copying. Suppose the house has an instance variable for its builder and we intend for copies of the house to share the same builder. Then copies of the house should have both shallow and deep characteristics. They must be shallow, to share the builder, and deep, to replicate the garage, as well as the kitchen and other rooms. This example illustrates that the developer of any class whose objects are likely to be copied must design its copy method in accordance with the sharing requirements of the object's instance variables.

6.12   Commentary: value and reference semantics

Smalltalk is based on *reference* semantics. Its programming model relies on pointers that refer one object (or variable) to another. In Smalltalk, though you may think of a bicycle object having a seat object embedded in it, the bicycle object merely has a pointer to the seat object. Thus, when a message passes argument objects, it is really passing pointers to those objects. (At a machine level, little objects like characters and small integers are passed around bodily and indeed embedded in bigger objects rather than pointed to by those bigger objects. But a Smalltalk programmer's conceptual view is pointer-based; that is, reference semantics.)

By contrast, C++ supports *value* semantics as well as reference semantics. A C++ programmer may optionally embed a seat solidly into a bicycle. Also, messages frequently pass an object around by passing a copy of the object instead of a pointer to the object. Because of this tendency for C++ code to copy objects, C++ programmers discipline themselves to think rigorously about whether their copies should be deep or shallow. Copying demands so much attention in C++ that each class has a special feature (a *copy constructor*) with which the programmer defines just how copying of its instances should work. Smalltalk programmers tend to be less disciplined in thinking about copy behavior, and get away with it because copying occurs so much less frequently in Smalltalk.

6.13   Commentary: containers in C++

C++ containers are like three-ring binders: they generally hold objects from a single class (or subclasses of that class). These containers are less flexible than Smalltalk's, but safer, for any code that attempts to add an object of the wrong class to a C++ container fails to compile. This safety comes at a price, though, because you need to develop a class of container specialized for each kind of object you intend to hold—a **SetOf-Whale** as well as a **SetOfInteger**. A C++ language feature (*templates*) simplifies the definition of such container classes, but container libraries in C++ still tend to be unwieldy, complex, and difficult to write. The need for fast, robust containers has spawned a cottage industry for container libraries. Sometimes these libraries are called *foundation* libraries, to acknowledge their essential place in object programming. Sadly, foundation libraries are sometimes not interchangeable,[4] because they are often integrated into larger libraries or frameworks that provide other services like windowing or communications or persistence. By contrast, every Smalltalk dialect includes an integrated foundation library—the subclasses of **Collection**. This library cannot be decoupled from Smalltalk because so much of Smalltalk itself is built using collection classes.

---

[4] Standardization will help. The ANSI C++ standard now specifies a *Standard Template Library*.

CHAPTER 7

CRC cards

We now shift from the essential concepts of containers and object identity to a concrete design problem, and some techniques to help solve it. After working through the design here you will, in Chapter 8, write the Smalltalk code to implement it.

Probably no object-oriented subject fuels as much debate as object-oriented design methods.[1] The question of what contributes to a good design method is large and interesting, but not our focus in this book. Rather, I present a simple technique that helps with one inescapable step in designing an application—discovering classes. This technique is a simplification of *CRC cards,* an idea published in 1989 by Kent Beck and Ward Cunningham. Since then CRC cards, or *Class-Responsibility-Collaboration* cards, have been widely used and imitated. (See the commentary at the end of this chapter.)

Start with a pile of index cards, 3 × 5 inches or 4 × 6 inches, as you wish. (Their paper stipulated 4 × 6 inches, but Kent and Ward themselves don't agree.) If you don't have index cards, tearing up several full sheets of paper into quarters is almost as good. On each card, sketch an instance of an object:

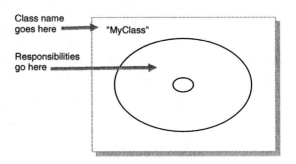

---

[1] Also known as *methodologies. Methods* is the trendier, more precise term, but suffers from already meaning something else to object-oriented programmers. I'll use the terms interchangeably, except where there is risk of confusion.

Record as responsibilities whatever you think instances of the class ought to be able to do, the "know-how" that instances should have. Record them at a level of detail you find helpful. For example, you may first want to describe the responsibilities of a traffic-light object broadly: "Mediate orderly flow of vehicles through an intersection." Later, if you're almost to the point of writing code, you might describe responsibilities more concretely: "advanceColor," "initializeGreenDuration:," and so on. Whatever you do, don't use the cards dogmatically. They are an *informal* tool, and they should stimulate your creativity rather than limit it.

If you feel unhappy about something you've written, throw away the card and start again. Cards are inexpensive, and disposability is one of their happiest virtues. In this early phase, the price one pays for stupidity ought to be low; the more dumb ideas you can discard early, the better your final design will be. This is an eternal human truth, even for the most successful thinkers. Francis Crick, who shared a Nobel prize for discovering the double-helix structure of DNA, said, "If we deserve any credit at all, it is for...the willingness to discard ideas when they become untenable" [Crick 1988]. The software designer who doesn't explore some dead ends won't learn much.

Another virtue of CRC cards is tangibility. Designers wave them around for emphasis, move them as arguments of a message, or arrange them on the table to illustrate relationships. This tangibility explains why attempts to represent CRC cards in computerized tools have been disappointing. Entombing them in a computer, no matter how advanced the user interface may be, constrains your thinking at a time when you need to excite your imagination and brainstorm as much as possible. The time for methodical thought comes later.

7.1 Design exercise

❑ Use CRC cards to design a simple personal-computer application that could keep track of a checking account. Transactions should be retained in a log or register, and ordered by date.

Remember to explore competing alternatives and throw away cards that are least promising. In the next chapter you will write the code for this exercise, so keep the design simple—don't get bogged down in all the detailed kinds of data that a full-blown application needs, and don't go overboard into extensions like on-line checking. Aim for a range of two to five cards. Finally, remember the lesson in Chapter 6: containers are essential participants in almost every object-oriented design.

7.2   Solution and discussion

If you have trouble getting started, try looking for nouns and verbs in the problem description. Nouns are candidates for objects, and verbs are candidates for responsibilities or methods. This is a suggestion, not a general rule. (For example, in Chapter 15, verbs will *also* be excellent candidates for objects. Design always depends on the problem at hand.)

From the problem statement, these nouns are promising: account, log, transaction, and date. We know from our earliest glimpses of Smalltalk that class **Date** is already available in Smalltalk. Let's concentrate then on the other three classes, beginning with some plausible responsibilities for them:

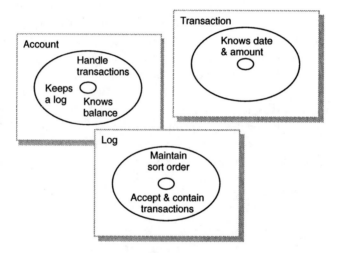

Although account balances and transaction amounts are not explicit in the problem statement, they seem like unavoidable elements. On the other hand, I've chosen to omit a host of ancillary elements—account number and description, check number, payee, memo—on the grounds that they would contribute little to understanding the essential object interactions that we are after. Adding such information would be straightforward and accurate but distracting. Note that I've overlain the edge of the **Log** card on the **Account** card to emphasize the close collaboration implied by the responsibility, "The account keeps a log."

So far, the transaction objects are bland. This is about to change. The log's chief responsibility—sorting—recalls a class we worked with in Chapter 6 with exactly this responsibility. That class was **SortedCollection** (page 71). Thus, rather than defining a new **Log** class, we will reuse the **SortedCollection** class. Remember that a sorted collection object sorts the objects added to it, provided that its **sortBlock** makes sense for the objects. The default **sortBlock** assumes that the objects understand the **<=** method. That's why integers and their kin are all automatically sortable. To ensure that transactions are sortable via the default **sortBlock**, they too must be comparable via **<=**. Therefore an additional responsibility for the transaction card above is, "Comparable to one another."

With an eye toward eventual implementation, we can summarize our observations with a more detailed, Smalltalk-biased version of the cards:[2]

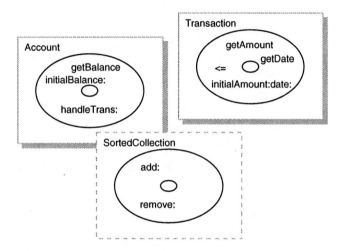

The dashed lines around **SortedCollection** indicate that it doesn't warrant a new card or class because, like **Date**, it is already present in Smalltalk. That leaves just two classes to write, **Account** and **Transaction**. The kinds of objects the methods expect as arguments, omitted from the drawing to reduce visual clutter, are:

- **handleTransaction:** *aTransaction*
- **initialBalance:** *anInteger*
- **initialAmount:** *anInteger* **date:** *aDate*
- **<=** *anotherTransaction*
- **add:** *aTransaction*
- **remove:** *aTransaction*

where *anInteger* represents a monetary amount, such as dollars.

---

[2] Spelling out actual method selectors departs from the responsibility-based spirit of pure CRC cards. We are slanting the design toward Smalltalk, and also blurring the distinction between "what" a class does and "how" it does it. But a little help with method names now will help you write the code in the next chapter.

Now we turn to relationships like inheritance and aggregation. Inheritance is irrelevant for the classes in this design, but aggregation matters. The usual way to implement "knowing" and "keeping" responsibilities of a CRC design is to define instance variables. Thus, for the responsibility, "An account knows its balance," define an instance variable in **Account** named **balance** to hold the account's current balance. And for an account to "keep a log," define an instance variable **log**, which will refer to a sorted collection. Similarly, because transactions "know" their amounts and dates, they ought to have instance variables **amount** and **date**.

What about the log's responsibility for "containing transactions"? Since we intend to reuse class **SortedCollection**, which Smalltalk has already implemented for us, we don't really have to worry about the details for discharging this responsibility. (Here, nevertheless, is an aside about the internals of containers like sorted collections. A container cannot practically describe each object in it by an instance variable with a name. A Smalltalk container therefore has an unspecified number of *unnamed* instance variables, and the number of such variables appears to increase or decrease as one adds or removes objects to or from the container.)

If we enlarge the insides of our objects to emphasize instance variables (and the "knowing," "keeping," and "containing" relationships they imply), our cards suggest this arrangement of objects:

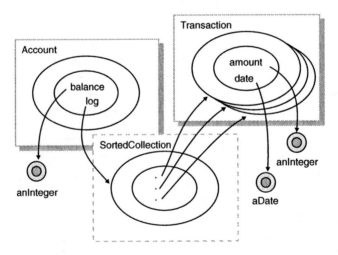

Although I have said little about the "collaboration" part of CRC cards, you can see that instance variables impart collaborative relationships to a design.

The progression in this section is more orderly than you should expect from real, large-scale problems. Experienced designers working together on large problems will, at times, shuffle dozens of cards as fast as they can scribble notes on them; between the frantic scribblings will be lulls consisting of hard thinking and discussion. The crude product of all this effort eventually needs to be rewritten with more thoughtful and lucid wordings, to communicate the ideas to developers who weren't present for the session.

7.3 Common questions and answers

There is little chance that everyone who tries the problem above will arrive at exactly the same conclusion along exactly the same path. Some of the common deviations are:

1   Why not use plural names for classes, like **Accounts** and **Transactions**? The short, irrefutable answer is that it is a convention among object-oriented designers to use singular names for classes. But another answer, subtle but important, is that using a plural name suggests a collection, and we wouldn't want to mislead anyone into thinking of a class as a collection. The preferred way to think of a class is as a factory (Chapter 2).

2   Why not subclass **Account** (**Checking, Savings,...**) and **Transaction** (**Check, Deposit,...**)? These extensions would make the design more realistic. It is nevertheless almost always better to master the simplest form of a design first, and save the embellishments for later. One danger in enriching a design too early is in making it so rich that developers never implement it. This is a frequent cause of failed projects. Better to have accomplished something simple than nothing at all. (Our solution is so simple that our mechanism for distinguishing deposits from checks is to use a positive transaction amount to denote a deposit and a negative one to denote a check or debit. It is simple enough that you will be able write the code for it in one sitting.)

3   Why not make transactions responsible for "processing themselves"? This is an acceptable alternate design, consistent with the term "transaction," which computer professionals define as a "unit of work." On the other hand, home users of this kind of application feel that a typical transaction like a check is relatively inert, and that accounts are the center of activity. I've deferred to the user's viewpoint rather than the professional's.

4   Where should you record class responsibilities or methods on a CRC card? Good question. Methods like **new** don't belong in the picture of an instance because an instance doesn't understand them. Only the class understands them. If they are worth capturing, I generally scribble them in the upper-right corner of the card.

In addition, you can prefix them with a special symbol, like a $ as in some notations [Rumbaugh et al. 1991].

5   Can we shift the responsibility for comparison from the transactions to the **log**? Yes, this is an attractive alternative. In the present design, the **log** does not know it contains transaction objects; it assumes only that the objects it contains respond to <= messages. Removing the <= from **Transaction** implies that the **log** (a sorted collection) must assume more knowledge of its contents. The **log**'s **sortBlock** must now retrieve and compare the dates from the transactions. To specify such a **sortBlock**, send the message:

```
log sortBlock: [:t1 :t2| t1 getDate <= t2 getDate].
```

This **log** doesn't entrust comparison to the transactions; instead it compares their dates itself. The same idea can be used to sort the transactions by other criteria, like amounts. Just update the **sortBlock** by sending the message:

```
log sortBlock: [:t1 :t2| t1 getAmount <= t2 getAmount].
```

7.4   Commentary: analysis, design, and implementation

Methodologists often partition software development into three phases: *analysis* (fully expressing the application's requirements in a vocabulary comprehensible to users), *design* (determining software structures to solve the problem), and *implementation* (rendering the design in a specific operating environment and computer language(s)). Each phase is, in effect, the "how" of the preceding phase's "what."

Unfortunately, one person's "what" is another's "how," and so the phase boundaries blur unavoidably. Is deciding how to make "an account have a log" the act of designing or the act of implementing? (You could define a **log** instance variable in class **Account**, as we've done, or you could add a single entry to a dictionary whose keys are account objects and whose values are logs. The dictionary is overkill for the small personal system we studied, but it may be more attractive in a distributed computing environment where account information—like name, number, PIN—and transaction histories may reside on different computers. As you weigh these two alternatives, are you designing or implementing?)

Even the level of abstraction—design or analysis—you ascribe to the relationship, "an account has a log," is inconclusive. Nothing precludes a relationship from appearing at two levels of abstraction. Indeed, in object-oriented methodologies, objects and their relationships generally endure from one phase to the next. Despite the inherent ambiguities, it is still customary to try to distinguish among analysis, design, and implementation phases. Thus one usually ascribes the responsibility cards in the diagram on page 84 to the design phase, and the prescription of Smalltalk-style method names in the diagram on page 85 to the implementation phase.

Rigid progressions from analysis to design to implementation, historically known as "waterfall" models of development, are out of vogue. Problems can rarely be fully understood until after users have examined a prototype. Nothing will expose more misunderstandings or fuzzy analysis or elicit more feedback than a working mock-up or prototype. For this reason, current design or analysis methods almost always emphasize "spiral" or "iterative" development, which explicitly acknowledge that what you learn from downstream phases induces rework of upstream phases.

The greatest shortcoming of CRC cards is also their greatest strength, namely, their disconnection from the biases and constraints of actual computer systems. They provoke discussions, but they leave little trace of these discussions. The cards fall out of date and are eventually lost, along with the ideas and associations they once engendered. Of course, a project is obligated to preserve as much of value as possible from those early CRC discussions. The prevailing schools of thought for solving this documentation problem are to: (1) produce computerized diagrams that illustrate the analysis or design, supplemented by text, (2) write thoughtful comments embedded in the code, or (3) combine these. There has never been a completely satisfactory solution, even before objects or CRC cards, and each project must set and enforce a suitable policy.

Any policy must rely heavily on the names and comments of methods. That's because these are practically the only development artifacts (along with class names) that are relevant and meaningful to everyone on the project—analysts, developers, testers. Everyone can understand them, and if anyone changes them, everyone else can understand the changes. Class and method names therefore constitute a common language for sharing the conceptual model (page 144) of the problem. A conceptual model that people do not have to translate for one another is a side-effect of a successful object-oriented project.

Good analyses and designs also treat the dynamic behavior of a system—that is, sequences of messages among several interacting objects. CRC cards promote rudimentary forms of dynamic design because the cards can be waved about and at one another while enacting scenarios, but one must again turn elsewhere to document the knowledge so acquired. More on this subject in Chapter 10.

The original CRC cards [Beck and Cunningham 1989] had two columns of text, the first listing responsibilities and the second collaborators; that is, classes on which the current class depends to fulfill its responsibilities. Variants abound, however. The simplification in this chapter, underplaying the collaborators, is among the least orthodox. Whether as part of using CRC cards or another method or at a later stage in design, the developer must think through collaborating classes. Rebecca Wirfs-Brock's "responsibility-driven design" methodology follows the original card format, but also documents superclass and subclasses on the card, and suggests that collaborators be grouped with the responsibility they support. Her use of cards does not emphasize their physical manipulation, however. Her book [Wirfs-Brock et al. 1990] is a good source of larger CRC examples than this chapter's, and is also one of the standard textbooks on object-oriented design and analysis. Others include those by [Rumbaugh et al. 1991; Booch 1994; Jacobson et al. 1992; and Coad and Yourdon 1991].

Last but not least, failure as a necessary element of good design is the theme of [Petroski 1985]. He examines engineering failures, but the underlying principle is universal.

Exercises—Implementing a design

You now have the basic skills to begin developing Smalltalk applications. Your first application will be a prototype of the application we designed in the preceeding chapter. Rather than spell out every detail of the implementation, I'll just guide you through the mileposts and encourage you to think through the details. As you know by now, Smalltalk programmers explore a lot as they develop applications, so you should *expect* to explore and experiment as you proceed. Allow about three hours for this chapter.

8.1   Create the classes

❑ First create a new application for the work you are about to do.

❑ Then create both classes **Account** and **Transaction**.

❑ Define the instance variables for these classes. To review the appropriate instance variables, look at the figure on page 86, and to review how to create classes and instance variables, review your work in Chapter 4.

8.2   A test case

A good way to stay honest is to write a method you can use as a test case.

❑ Create a *class* method named **example** for the class **Account**. It won't make sense to execute it yet, since none of the methods it invokes exist.

```
example
        "Test by executing:

        Account example inspect

    "
    |account transaction|
    account := Account newBalance: 2500.
    transaction := Transaction newAmount: -300 date: Date today.
    account handleTransaction: transaction.
    ^account
```

This test uses class (factory) methods to create an account and a transaction, processes the transaction, and returns the account. The reason for so much white space in the comment is to make **Account example inspect** an easy target for highlighting with the mouse and *executing*. You can execute the method while you are browsing it, instead of having to move over to the **Transcript** every time you want to run a test. Not essential, but a convenient trick. Also notice that unlike most other **new** methods you've seen, the methods for creating new instances of **Account** and **Transaction** above expect arguments.

8.3   Write "new" methods

❑ Because you will be creating new instances of both classes in the application, write a "**new**" method for **Account** and **Transaction**. Remember that these are class methods, not instance methods. Here's an example of the method for class **Account**:

```
newBalance: anInteger
        "Answer a new instance of the receiver with balance anInteger"
        ^self new initialBalance: anInteger
```

Notice that you will also need an instance method named **initialBalance:**.

By the way, you don't have to use names with "**new**" in them, like **newBalance:**, although it is common to do so for class methods that create new instances of the class.

8.4   Write instance methods

❑ Prepare instance methods for the classes **Account** and **Transaction**, according to our design. Refer to the CRC cards on page 85.

The <= method often puzzles beginners. Remember that the design assumes that transactions are smart enough to compare themselves with other transactions, for which they need the binary method <= in class **Transaction**, like so:

```
<= anotherTransaction
        "Answer true if my date is before anotherTransaction's date,
    false otherwise"

        ...
```

But how? The code must explicitly compare my (the receiving transaction's) date with the date of the *other* transaction. How do *I* access the inside of *another* object? That's the basic prohibition of encapsulation: I can't. I can obtain the information only if the other object has a method that obliges. Thus transactions must also support a method of the form:

```
getDate
        ^date
```

8.5   Test your solution

Now run the test case by *executing* **Account example inspect** (or equivalently, *inspecting* **Account example**). An inspector window should open on an account, but if something goes wrong, like getting a walkback, use it as an opportunity to practice your debugging skills. (Review the exercise on page 57 if necessary.) Once you have an inspector window on an account, verify that it holds your transaction. You can do so by *double-clicking* on the entries in the inspector; this action opens another inspector on whatever you double-clicked. By repeatedly double-clicking, you can drill down and examine the account's log, any transactions inside the log, and dates and amounts inside the transactions.

This first test was too simple to thoroughly test your code—one transaction doesn't make for an interesting sort. Write another test case, **example2**, similar to the first, but that handles at least two additional transactions with different dates. You can produce different dates in several ways: look through the class methods of **Date** or review your work with dates on page 56. Run **example2**, and double-click through inspector levels to verify that the log contains all your transactions, and that they occur in chronological order.

8.6 Engineering discipline

The Smalltalk environment, dynamic as it is, encourages programmers to try changes quickly, sometimes at the expense of sound engineering practices. For example, unless cautioned otherwise, many students modify **example** directly instead of writing an *additional* **example2** and keeping the original **example** for regression testing. Make it a practice to think twice before discarding any test case. Old test cases are one of the best ways to ensure that you haven't introduced unwanted changes to your code. Lest you fear having to retype or copy-and-paste test methods, notice that by merely overtyping the first line of a method and saving (compiling), you create a new method— different name, same code. Using this technique, you can effortlessly create a clone of the original and then proceed to modify the clone as much as you wish. Thus, you can retain the original until you consciously want to purge it.

8.7 A minor variation

Some people prefer a solution in which the account object itself builds new transactions and processes them, so that a test method contains expressions like:

```
account transactionAmount: -300 date: Date today.
```

❑ Prepare a test method in this spirit, then implement the variation by writing the instance method **transactionAmount:date:** for class **Account**. This method will contain just one Smalltalk expression, and you need not write or modify any other methods.

8.8 "Private" methods

In Smalltalk's early days, a method was deemed *private* if it was to be invoked only by other methods in its same class (or subclasses); a method was *public* if it could be invoked by methods from other classes. Private methods were for use only by the programmer who was developing the class in question. Programmers working on other classes were not to invoke them. With this understanding, the owner of a class could rewrite it, revamping the class's private methods at will, as long as the public methods retained their names and functions.

In the last few years, many Smalltalk programmers have relaxed the interpretation of a private method. They now sanction invocations of a private method not only from the same class but also from closely cooperating classes. Privacy has evolved into an understanding within a subsystem or framework of classes rather than within an individual class.

In some Smalltalks you indicate that a method is private simply by adding the word "private" to the method's comment. Other Smalltalks have enhanced browsers that let you earmark a method as private, either by placing it in a special category or by means of a button that toggles between a list of all private selectors or all public selectors.

In all cases, though, designating a method private is only informational. Unlike a C++ compiler, the Smalltalk compiler has no way to determine whether a method your code invokes even exists, let alone whether it happens to be private. Therefore your code can freely invoke any method you like, private or not, even though the author of the method may have intended otherwise. In short, Smalltalk privacy is a recommendation only; it is not enforced.

❑ Browse through some Smalltalk classes and find some private methods.

❑ Which methods in your checking account solution ought to be marked private? Make them private by pulling down or popping up the *Methods* menu and selecting *Change public/private.*

8.9   Commentary: getters and setters

Simple methods like **getDate**, which merely return an instance variable, are called "getter" methods. Smalltalk stylists usually write getters more economically like this:

```
date
    ^date
```

This style is not ambiguous, in spite of how it may appear: the first **date** is the method selector and the second is the instance variable in the transaction object.

The opposite of a getter is a "setter," with a selector like **setDate:** or simply **date:**. The method would be written:

```
date: aDate
    date := aDate
```

Getters and setters (together called *accessor* methods) are common, pedestrian methods in object-oriented programming, but take care not to overuse them. Writing a public getter and setter for every instance variable violates the spirit of encapsulation, because it announces that any other object may access the instance variables.

On the other hand, one stylistic school of thought recommends that you write private getters and setters for *every* instance variable. The object itself should access its own instance variables *only* by invoking the getter and setter methods, never directly. This convention makes the design less brittle. For example, imagine that you decide later to move information that is now in an instance variable to an entirely different object. Without a getter and setter, every method that touches the instance variable breaks. With a getter and setter, only the getter and setter methods must be rewritten.

For a discussion of this and other Smalltalk coding conventions and their rationales, see [Skublics et al. 1996].

8.10 Summary

In the exercises of this chapter you produced a complete working application, however small or artificial. By this I mean that all the application logic is there, and it executes correctly. But you have probably noticed that the windows and buttons and scrollbars that people have come to expect of Smalltalk applications are absent. Your application has no user interface to speak of.

This absence is no accident. As you will see in Chapters 11–13, serious object-oriented developers work hard to separate their user interface code from their application logic. When we designed the checking account application in Chapter 7, we concentrated solely on the application objects, not a user interface. Windows come later.

CHAPTER 9

When (not) to inherit

Now that you have worked through serious Smalltalk code, we return to conceptual challenges. In Chapter 2 I suggested that aggregation and inheritance are independent, separable ideas. In fact, they are not so independent, and for some problems it is difficult to decide which of the two to apply. This chapter exposes the tension between them. (Further discussion appears in Chapter 14, on polymorphism, and in the commentary on page 255.)

9.1   Historical background

In recent years, inheritance has received much more attention than aggregation, mostly as a matter of fashion. Aggregation is the older facet of programming life. Programmers have used it for decades, so unwittingly that they never bothered to give it a glamorous name. In Pascal, an aggregation looks like this:

```
type Flight = record
                    gate: integer;
                    terminal: char;
                    onTime: boolean
                END;
```

and in C, like this:

```
struct Flight {
            int gate;
            char terminal;
            int onTime;
        };
```

Both samples express the idea of composing an airline flight from three constituents. Of course, nowadays the flight and its constituents are all likely to be objects, but the underlying idea is still aggregation. In Smalltalk, one would have:

```
Object subclass: #Flight
        instanceVariableNames: 'gate terminal onTime'
        ...
```

Notice the disappearance of type information in the Smalltalk code fragment. This absence is not a characteristic of object-oriented programming in general, but of Smalltalk in particular. The C++ version looks much like the C version, including the type information, with the principal difference being the word **class** instead of the word **struct**.

9.2   Inverting hierarchies

With inheritance as well as aggregation in our vocabulary, the potential complexity of a design doubles. When a language gains power, it also presents opportunities for confusion. Consider this innocuous aggregation:

Face
|
Mouth
|
Tongue

I suggest that by inverting this aggregation, I can produce a legitimate inheritance hierarchy:

Tongue
|
Mouth
|
Face

Here's my argument. According to the discussion of inheritance in Chapter 2, we agreed to the rule of thumb that instances of a subclass have *more* properties than instances of their superclass. **Mouth**, then, should be a subclass or special kind of **Tongue**, because a mouth is a tongue embellished with teeth, gums, and lips. Even more striking, **Face** should be a subclass or special kind of **Mouth** because a face is a mouth plus lots of additional properties like eyes, nose, ears, and cheeks. A face even does everything a mouth does (it eats), and also sees and smells and hears. This analysis, preposterous as it sounds, is completely consistent with the definition of inheritance. Nothing in Smalltalk or C++ prevents you from designing and implementing a class hierarchy in this way.

Hence the dilemma: should these classes be designed using aggregation or inheritance? In this case, trust your intuition. Although it's entirely possible to use inheritance, thinking of **Face** as a special kind of **Mouth** just isn't intuitive. And what isn't intuitive to the designer is unlikely to be intuitive to other programmers who will use the design. The essence of programming objects is the cognitive economy they promise; a good design reduces mental translations. This observation alone justifies designing a tongue as part of a mouth and a mouth as part of a face.

But we are not ready to dismiss the example yet. The decision may not be so clear in other languages. Smalltalk supports *single inheritance*—each class has exactly one immediate superclass. Other languages, like C++, support *multiple inheritance*, where a class can inherit from several immediate superclasses. Designers using these languages sometimes employ a technique called *mix-ins*. Mix-ins are simple classes like **Mouth** and **Nose** that are used as superclasses for creating more complicated subclasses like **Face**. The subclass gets its properties and behavior by inheriting from as many mix-in superclasses as it needs. Thus, **Face** could inherit from *both* **Mouth** and **Nose**. Notice that although mix-ins clearly rely on the inheritance *mechanism*, the designer is *thinking* of composition or aggregation—building an aggregate object like a face from components like a mouth and nose.

9.3   Buy or inherit?

The problem in the previous section illustrates one of the most characteristic object-oriented design quandaries, that of *buying* versus *inheriting*. To *buy* an object is simply to acquire one for use, often by aggregation. *Buy* is a simple, evocative word, to my knowledge first used in the context of programming objects by Bertrand Meyer [Meyer 1988]. (You can also use the stuffier synonym, *compose*.)

In the preferred design above, class **Face** buys class **Mouth**. We implement this design in Smalltalk by defining an instance variable in the **Face** class that will refer to a **Mouth** object:

```
Object subclass: #Face
        instanceVariableNames: 'mouth ...'
        ...
```

The method that initializes **Face** will include a statement like:

```
mouth := Mouth new.
```

If, instead of buying a mouth we wish to inherit it, as in the less desirable design, we would have:

```
Mouth subclass: #Face
        ...
```

These two designs represent the full range of options open to the designer. *There are two techniques an object-oriented designer can use to access a class's behavior or properties: buy or inherit.* If you like what you see in class **Y** and want to incorporate it into class **X** you must either buy from **Y** or inherit from **Y**; these are the only ways to give **X** direct access to **Y**. (Indirect relationships are another matter: see the discussions on many-to-many relationships on page 217 and lawyer objects on page 233.)

This is a bold claim, but it is entirely consistent with your experience. Every direct relationship you've designed or seen so far either buys or inherits. For example, in the checking account exercise in Chapters 7 and 8, the **Account** class *bought* a **SortedCollection** to use as its log.

9.4   Exercise

Remember that in Smalltalk, class **Collection** is an abstract class that is a superclass of many subclasses with container-like properties. One of these subclasses is **OrderedCollection**. An instance of **OrderedCollection** maintains its elements in relative positions: it has a first, second, ... and last element. It has methods that remove or add to either end of it. Thus, it resembles an array whose size may grow or shrink. For this exercise, we care most about the methods that stretch or contract from the far end, namely **addLast:** and **removeLast**.

❑ Design a **Stack** class. Because class **OrderedCollection** already offers stack-like properties, you will want to exploit **OrderedCollection** directly. Sketch a solution that buys, then a solution that inherits from **OrderedCollection**.

9.5   Solution and discussion

Here's a design for buying an ordered collection:

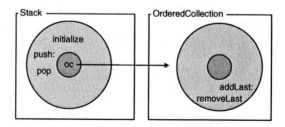

The instance variable **oc** enables the stack to access the ordered collection it is buying. The essential methods for a stack are **push:** and **pop**. Their code buys an appropriate method from the ordered collection, simply by forwarding the request across the instance variable. Thus for pushing:

```
push: anObject
    oc addLast: anObject
```

And for popping:

```
pop
    oc isEmpty
            ifTrue: [ ^nil ].
    oc removeLast
```

(The first statement prevents a walkback in case someone tries to pop from an empty stack.) Initialization sets up the instance variable to point to a valid ordered collection:

```
initialize
    oc := OrderedCollection new
```

Contrast this with a design for inheriting instead of buying from class **Ordered-Collection**:

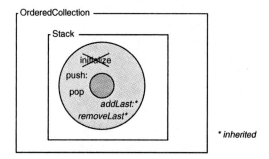

Because we're not buying, there's no instance variable to forward requests across. And because we are inheriting, the stack inherits the **addLast:** and **removeLast** methods from its superclass. The stack *is* an ordered collection; that's what inheritance means. That's why the drawing shows only one object. The code for **push:** is therefore:

```
push: anObject
    self addLast: anObject
```

The only difference from buying is that **self** receives the message instead of **oc**. In fact, **self** is the one and only object available for receiving messages.

The code for **pop** changes in the same small way. And the **initialize** method disappears, because there is no instance variable to set up.

9.6 Conclusions

Either technique, buying or inheriting, works. Inheritance generally yields a smaller solution. In the example, inheritance lets us dispense with the **initialize** method, as well as the **oc** instance variable. The net saving in this small example is only about two lines of code, but it still illustrates the general rule that inheritance saves code.

Another consequence of inheritance is *tight coupling*: inheritance couples the subclass to its superclass so tightly that absolutely everything that applies to the superclass also applies to the subclass. Whether this coupling is desirable or not depends on the situation.

In our example, tight coupling would be undesirable. It would imply that any of the dozens of messages that make sense for an ordered collection would also make sense for a stack. That's much more than we bargained for; it is treacherous for a stack to respond to **OrderedCollection** messages like **at:put:** or **removeFirst**. A trustworthy stack ought to respond only to messages **push:** and **pop**. Thus, to prevent subversive messages in Smalltalk, the designer must buy instead of inherit. That is what the first solution showed: buying safeguarded the stack from responding to **OrderedCollection** messages.

Inheriting, thereby tightly coupling two classes, is a long-term commitment, because as the software ages and undergoes maintenance and enhancements, any changes to the superclass will automatically reflect into the subclass. Again, whether this commitment is desirable or not depends on the situation. The designer must consider not only the economies of coupling the classes, but whether users of the classes expect them to evolve in tandem. Do they expect public methods added later in the superclass to be relevant for the subclass too?

In our example, it is unlikely that enhancements to the public protocol of **OrderedCollection** will ever matter for stacks. Stacks should *not* do much besides push and pop. Thus, subclassing **Stack** from **OrderedCollection** confers no maintenance benefit and may even deceive users of stacks into expecting more similarities with ordered collections than they should.

For this exercise on stacks, then, software engineering considerations militate in favor of buying. The modest code savings from inheriting **Stack** from **OrderedCollection** aren't worth the reliability and maintenance implications.

The buy versus inherit decision is a fundamental activity in object-oriented design. Initial intuition is often valid, but you should weigh the trade-offs—(1) code reduction, (2) subversive superclass messages, and (3) maintenance—summarized in this table:

	Buying (Selectively access methods of another class)	**Inheriting** (Access all methods and instance variables of another class)
Code bulk	More	Less (good!)
Subversive superclass messages	Preventable (good!)	Possible
Maintenance	Evolve independently (loose coupling)	Evolve together (tight coupling)
Familiarity with the superclass's internals	Less	More

The last row in the table indicates the degree to which the developer will have to study a class before buying or inheriting from it. Buying requires less familiarity with the internals than inheriting does. For this reason, buying is sometimes known as *black-box reuse* and inhteriting is sometimes known as *white-box reuse.*

The table is not the last word on the buy versus inherit dilemma. We will discuss a powerful reason to inherit—*polymorphism*—in Chapter 14. Also, the commentary on page 255 summarizes buy or inherit decisions in the context of object-oriented frameworks.

The situation in other object-oriented languages is not as clear as the table suggests. C++ designers use inheritance more than Smalltalk designers do, partly because it is their only means of expressing polymorphism, but also because the C++ language has facilities that can limit the wholesale inheritance of superclass features. Because Smalltalk has no such facilities, Smalltalk designers must heed the cautions above.

If in doubt, consider buying. Novice designers tend to overuse inheritance; experienced ones make an effort to buy. As a rule of thumb, buying is less brittle than inheriting.

9.7   Commentary: multiple inheritance

Multiple inheritance (page 99) is a powerful facility of some object-oriented languages. What do you do if your language (Smalltalk) doesn't support it? According to the principle spelled out in this chapter, only one choice remains: buy. If X and Y are two classes from which you would like a class C to multiply inherit, and Smalltalk limits you to singly inheriting from just one of them, then you will have to buy from the other.

The difficulty is that you may really want to inherit from both **X** and **Y**. That is, you may really want **C** to behave as though it were both an **X** and a **Y**, which means that **C** should respond automatically to all the same messages that **X** and **Y** do. Inheritance has this automatic property. But buying doesn't. In this situation buying is therefore a poor substitute. Smalltalk is not adept at simulating multiple inheritance to the degree that would satisfy a C++ programmer.[1]

The argument over multiple inheritance isn't completely one-sided. Its detractors argue that it leads to problems that require complicated linguistic rules to resolve, and these unfortunate problems occur so commonly as to counterbalance its benefit. Here is a simple illustration of a problem known as *repeated inheritance*, so called because a class will inherit more than once from another class.

Certain television programs mix dramatizations of historical matter with archival documentary footage to produce *docudramas*. A multiple inheritance hierarchy for this situation is shown on the right.

```
        TVShow
        /    \
     Drama  Documentary
        \    /
       DocuDrama
```

Consider an instance variable defined in class **TVShow** for the show's **director**. Classes **Drama** and **Documentary** evidently inherit this instance variable. Class **DocuDrama** thus stands to inherit two directors, one from each of its superclasses, which would be an artistic nightmare. We would prefer that **DocuDrama** inherit just one **director** instance variable.

On the other hand, consider another **TVShow** instance variable, **duration**. Classes **Drama** and **Documentary** again inherit this instance variable, but now we may prefer that **DocuDrama** inherit two copies of the instance variable, so that it can separately capture the minutes of dramatic material and the minutes of documentary material.

To attempt to accommodate either possibility—sharing some multiply inherited instance variables and replicating others—languages that support multiple inheritance introduce additional, complicating facilities. For the details, see C++'s *virtual base classes* [Stroustrup 1991] and Eiffel's *renaming* [Meyer 1992]. In short, multiple inheritance adds power to a programming language, but at a cost of complexity.

Here is a closing historical curiosity: multiple inheritance appeared briefly in Smalltalk-80, but was withdrawn because the benefits were deemed insufficient to compensate for the ensuing complications.

---

[1] Buying may not substitute for inheritance, but what about the converse: can inheritance substitute for buying? Rarely in Smalltalk, because of the reasons discussed in Section 9.6. It turns out though that C++ supports a form of inheritance called *private inheritance* that resembles buying much more than Smalltalk's inheritance does.

CHAPTER 10

Use cases and dynamic relationships

Until now, we've concentrated on the static relationships in an object-oriented application—aggregation, inheritance, the methods and instance variables of an object, and the like. The dynamic relationships—the order in which methods execute, the births and deaths of objects and their interactions during their lives—are just as crucial for understanding a design. These are the relationships that weave the objects together to actually do something. Without them, an object model (or object analysis or object design) is as empty as a ghost town.

Long before the dawn of objects, software engineers knew that dynamic relationships were important. They used diagrams they called "flowcharts" to represent the idea. Two decades of object-oriented programming passed before anyone thought to introduce the same idea into an object-oriented design method. (See the historical commentary on page 114.) Nowadays, finally, dynamic relationships are a standard feature of all the major object-oriented design methods.

10.1 Interaction diagrams

A *use case*, as coined by Ivar Jacobson, is a scenario involving a user and an application. In his words, it's "a behaviorally related sequence of transactions in a dialogue with the system" [Jacobson et al. 1992]. Now, this definition may make sense to a computer scientist, but it's a little esoteric for non-technical people. And non-technical end users are usually the people who are supposed to help us understand new problems by describing their use cases. Therefore I like to use a more accessible definition, like "an activity or task that the computer can help the user perform." This wording is simple enough that it won't stand in the way of a meaningful dialogue between computer professionals and computer users.

An example of a use case is, "Ask an Automated Teller Machine for the balance in an account." A detailed rendition of this use case might be, "The customer inserts his card, the machine prompts him for a PIN…." Textual descriptions like these can be cumbersome or vague, so the designer may choose to sketch an *interaction diagram* like this:

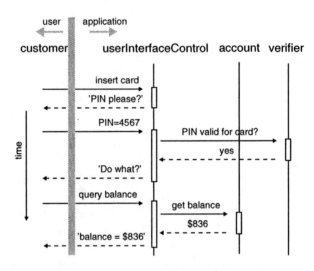

Each vertical line represents an object (labeled at the top of the line). Horizontal solid arrows represent messages and dashed arrows depict the object that a method returns. The vertical boxes illustrate the duration of each method. Notice the *time* dimension. That is what differentiates these interaction diagrams from pictures of class hierarchies and aggregation relationships.

Interaction diagrams illuminate dynamic behavior better than any static picture can hope to do, just as flowcharts and dataflow diagrams did for earlier, pre–object-oriented methodologies. As a rule, whenever a design seems fuzzy in your mind, pause (don't write code) and examine its dynamic structure with use cases and interaction diagrams.

Concurrency warning: Nothing is concurrent about these interaction diagrams, nor is object-orientation inherently concurrent. In particular, nothing in the Smalltalk and C++ languages has anything to do with concurrency. This news comes as a surprise to many newcomers, because the terminology of objects emphasizes *messages*, a word that conjures up numerous senders and receivers communicating simultaneously. Concurrency is possible in Smalltalk and C++ as well as most other languages, but not because the languages support it directly. Instead, you have to go outside the language by call-ing operating system services. For example, you can use UNIX forks and semaphores or create OS/2 threads from either C++ or Smalltalk.[1]

In interaction diagrams like the one above, what may appear to be concurrently executing threads or processes (like the vertical bars for *query balance* and *get balance*) only indicate ordinary call-return semantics. The sending operation (*query balance*) blocks (does not proceed) until the message it sends (*get balance*) returns, just as a call-ing procedure in a conventional programming language blocks until a subprocedure it calls returns.

Sometimes an activity of the system under study is at such a low level and so far from the user that you would be hard pressed to describe the activity as a use case. But inter-action diagrams can still be illuminating. The following example emphasizes low-level Smalltalk message flows; the user's role is only a mouse click. The diagram tracks what happens from the time Smalltalk starts looking for an event, through converting this raw operating system information into an actual Smalltalk message, and finally scheduling this message for subsequent execution by placing it in the **CurrentEvents** container.

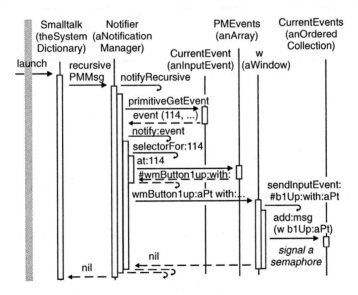

---

[1] Although Smalltalk has classes for processes and semaphores, their instances *simulate* concurrency and are not necessarily related to concurrent behavior in the underlying operating system. Future releases from Smalltalk vendors may associate Smalltalk's concurrent objects with actual operating system threads. Java and Ada95 are commercial object-oriented languages that have built-in concur-rency features.

Messages to **self** are depicted by solid arrows that hook back to the object they come from. Dashed, hooked arrows depict the objects returned from such methods. When successive return values are the same, the returned object isn't repeated each time: for example, the last four return values are all the **nil** object, even though the two hooked arrows aren't labeled. Sometimes a return value—frequently the default return value of **self**—is unused and uninteresting; then the dashed arrow is omitted entirely, as you can see for the **add:** method that finally schedules the Smalltalk message **w b1Up: aPt**. There's no standard notation for these diagrams; I often use the conventions above, but use whatever works for you.

This scenario applies to a specific Smalltalk (Smalltalk/V) and a specific operating system (OS/2) and window manager (Presentation Manager, or PM). Several of us who were concerned with event handling in that environment used this diagram off and on for years as a reference.[2] The diagram is most likely not relevant for your problems, so you should not study its details. But other use cases and interaction diagrams of complex scenarios specific to your own problem domain will be valuable to your development team. Even a rough hand-drawn sketch is worth the effort. (See the examples in the analysis and design discussion that begins on page 110.) Try to retain some form of your sketches, no matter how rudimentary. Not only will other developers appreciate them, but you will discover that testers find use cases and interaction diagrams more useful than inheritance and aggregation diagrams. Testers test what software *does*, not the static relationships between classes and objects.

10.2   Exercise

In Chapters 7 and 8, you added transactions to a log (an instance of class **Sorted-Collection**), and with no more support than a **<=** method for class **Transaction**, the log sorted the transactions chronologically. For many students, this is a mysterious happening.

❑   Work through a simple scenario until you are comfortable with the object interactions. You can sketch an interaction diagram for the scenario, but you may find that anthropomorphizing the objects—representing them as people or pencils or coins— is just as effective. If you sketch an interaction diagram, keep in mind that the value of the exercise is in thinking it through, more than in producing a pretty picture.

---

[2] The event happens to be number 114, which the operating system has defined as an up-click of the left mouse button, and the resulting Smalltalk message (**w b1Up: aPoint**) is a message to the window telling it that the click occurred at a specific point in the window. Another scenario, not illustrated here, iterates through the **CurrentEvents** container and executes each of the messages therein.

10.3   Solution and discussion

Before you examine the interaction diagram below, it's important to develop a sound intuition for the objects and their static relationships. That's because interaction diagrams, sadly, contain nothing to help you reconstruct that static information. Let's review this static information. Refer to the drawings on pages 85 and 86 for this review.

The log, being an instance of **SortedCollection**, by default uses the comparison **<=** to sort. When we add a new transaction to it, it will ask the transaction to compare itself (using **<=**) to the transactions already present, one at a time, until it finds the right position in which to insert the new transaction. What does this new transaction use to compare itself with the other transactions? It uses its own date, comparing it with the other transaction's date. This is a key piece of static information—that the dates are encapsulated within the transactions. Keep in mind that the log contains transactions, that each transaction encapsulates its own date, and that transactions have a **getDate** getter (often named simply **date**) to access this encapsulated date. All this information is static. The interaction diagram that weaves this information together is:

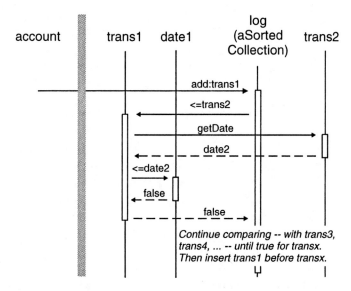

Note that two instances of **Transaction** appear in the diagram. We need at least that many to illustrate a comparison. Also note that although **trans2**'s date **date2** participates critically in the interaction, at this level of detail we cannot see it receive or initiate any messages.

10.4   Use cases and interaction diagrams in analysis and design

Use cases are valuable in the early stages of analyzing a new problem. Here are two examples.

1   To build a subsystem for a new pharmacy application, we asked users of the old application to think about the tasks they wanted the computer to help them with. They first listed about four tasks, such as "enter a drug order" and "dispense drugs." These are both use cases. Because they had already used CRC cards to identify a number of objects, we began next to work through interaction diagrams. Not unexpectedly, they observed that there were some important variations to the initial use cases. We identified those as additional use cases. When we had completed this preliminary inquiry, they had found about eight use cases for the subsystem in question, and we all had a good idea of the main objects and their interactions. Together with the CRC cards, we had the information we needed to develop a crude mockup of the subsystem.

2   In the requirements analysis for a banking application, although we had iteratively developed important CRC cards and use cases, not until we worked through an interaction diagram for a use case did the software developers and bankers reach a real understanding. The bankers recognized for the first time how objects they conceptualized could really do work for them by sending messages to one another, and the developers saw both what the bankers were really thinking and how we had to design the software to solve their problem. For both parties, this was a cathartic moment.

These experiences illustrate one technique for object-oriented analysis. The first two steps (their order is not critical) are to elicit CRC cards and use cases from the users. Then, by working through message flows, the developers and users together can refine both the CRC cards and the use cases to produce an initial round of object-oriented requirements. The entire discussion can occur without introducing any technical complications—no one has to use words such as class, inheritance, or polymorphism. Everyone can communicate using cards (objects), activities (use cases), and telegrams or messages (interaction diagrams).

A general aside about analysis: Good analysts are flexible, spontaneous people. They need to be able to switch gears when they sense that users are getting frustrated. The larger the group of users, the worse the problem. Different people think in different modes, and get frustrated for different reasons. Adapting to this variability in human cognition is at the heart of successful analysis. A technique that inspires one person stifles another. And a technique that works on one aspect of a problem won't on another. In the banking application above, after many successful sessions with objects and scenarios, one murky area remained. The banker charged with helping us developers understand it was as frustrated as we were. So we stopped talking about objects entirely, and started to sketch window layouts and how they might relate to one another. This shift produced such responses as, "No, not that way.... Yes, yes, good!" that got the whole effort moving again. Of course, developers imagine objects under windows, and we were therefore subconsciously gathering object-oriented requirements, but the conversation had been unshackled from any object baggage, much to everyone's benefit.

I don't mean to suggest that drawing windows is a universal remedy for analysis gridlock. It happened to work for those people on that aspect of that problem. That is the point. Different approaches will work for different people and problems. The successful analyst needs the creativity and optimism to keep trying approaches until one works for the situation at hand. Methodologies won't help.

It is worth repeating that it is possible to spend too much time documenting message flows with interaction diagrams. Not every message flow deserves the time it takes to make it pretty on a computer:

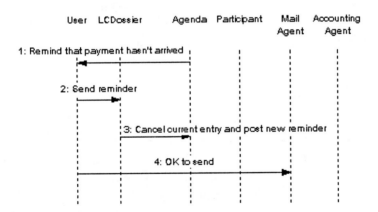

Real analysis sessions are so harried that we must capture message flows by hand—computers are too slow for the dynamics of creative human interaction. Sometimes we do not even have the luxury of thinking through the *objects* that send and receive messages. We may be pleased to walk out of a session with precious scribblings from a whiteboard that resemble:

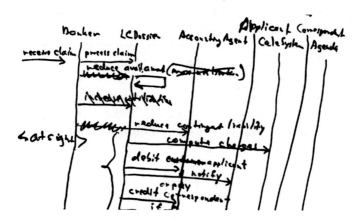

Hastily hand-drawn flows like this are not very readable or shareable. On the other hand, transcribing diagrams to a computer can take more time than your schedules allow. Moreover, for many diagrams the chief benefit comes through the human exchange in which they were created, rather than from the appearance of the final artwork. You will have to decide, after considering the usual factors—shareability, project standards, available staffing, management expectations—just how many sketches are worth the considerable expense of transcribing into attractive computerized form.

10.5   Limitations

Interaction diagrams have limitations which may frustrate or disappoint you if you expect too much from them.

- Interaction diagrams cannot represent loops and conditionals. You must either limit your diagram to a scenario having a single path or annotate the diagram informally with text. The single-path assumption is often acceptable because it is mainline processing that you're often trying to illuminate. Another way to produce non-branching diagrams is to decompose a highly branching diagram into many small non-branching ones; these small diagrams turn out to be reusable units for reassembling other complicated diagrams.

- Not everything is a message. For a Smalltalk designer, assignment is the main culprit. Interaction diagrams represent messages between objects nicely, but that's all. An assignment isn't a message to an object, and thus doesn't lend itself to interaction diagramming. (Try diagramming **balance := 2500**.) For a C++ designer, the situation is even worse: ordinary function calls, which lack a preferred receiver object, aren't messages either. You can't express them in interaction diagrams, which require well-defined sending and receiving objects.

• Interaction diagrams are graphical, but they aren't memorable. Because they constrain the objects to appear in just one dimension across the top edge, they lose the spatial benefit of placing objects above, below, or near or far from each other, with connecting lines indicating, say, aggregation relationships. In other words, interaction diagrams express time wonderfully, but are virtually devoid of static information.

The first two limitations are troublesome mostly in lower-level interaction diagrams. If you stay at a high enough level, like the first example in this chapter, the account balance query, you can often avoid these limitations.

10.6 Summary

I think of the design of a complex application as a misshapen multidimensional blob. There is no simple formula for describing or understanding the blob; all one can do is slice it in different ways and examine the cross-sections to get an idea of its structure. The most familiar slices are static; they are usually class diagrams that show responsibilities, plus inheritance and aggregation and other relationships.

But a static slice tells you nothing about what the application is supposed to do for its users. For that you need dynamic slices. The simplest dynamic slice is a one-sentence use case, then comes an expansion of the use case into a sequence of statements, and finally we have interaction diagrams with their objects and messages. These slices describe the functionality of the application.

Early in analysis and design, the dynamic slices clarify the static slices. That's because as you work through dynamic slices you realize that your CRC cards or class diagrams are missing various objects and responsibilities. Later, when the blob has settled down a bit, the dynamic slices become test cases for system testers: if a use case or interaction diagram doesn't work as documented, the tester knows something has gone wrong. (Static diagrams are almost useless for system or integration testers, again because they say nothing about what the application ought to be tested for.)

When you think about something from a different perspective you usually learn something worthwhile. Thinking through the dynamic dimension usually illuminates murky areas of the blob. If a design problem stumps you, try outlining a use case or an interaction diagram; at the very least this tactic will give you a fresh outlook on the problem. Often, it will propel you into a clarification of a murky area.

Unfortunately, for a lot of blobs not a scrap of documentation exists, yet they have somehow gotten themselves realized into Smalltalk. Sooner or later you will need to understand one of these blobs. The only surviving artifact is code, so you have no choice but to slice through it. You can slice statically, by drilling down through method invocations with browsers (using *Browse Messages > Implementors*, again and again). Eventually, you will also have to slice dynamically, setting up experimental conditions and stepping through execution paths with the debugger. This procedure is like skillfully examining specimens with a microscope: instead of selecting tissue slices and preparing them with appropriate dyes, you scaffold appropriate objects together and set up conditions for a good debugger session. In effect you are reconstructing what interaction diagrams would have told you had there been any.

10.7   Commentary: historical note

The value of understanding the dynamic aspect of a problem was appreciated long before objects became popular. Software engineers used flowcharts and hardware engineers used timing diagrams. What is surprising, or embarrassing, is how long it took for an object-based variation to appear. Jacobson first alluded to use cases in [Jacobson 1987]. By now, every mainstream object-oriented design method advocates some technique for representing an application's dynamics. These techniques go by assorted names: *interaction diagrams, message flow diagrams, event traces* [Rumbaugh et al. 1991], *timing diagrams* [Booch 1994], *scenarios* [Reenskaug 1996], or *scripts* [Gibson 1990; Rubin and Goldberg 1992].

For a different, higher-level look at application dynamics, see *timethreads* in [Buhr and Casselman 1992].

CHAPTER 11

The venerable model-view-controller

An application's or system's *user interface* (UI) consists of everything the user interacts with—the screens and sounds, menus, keyboard and mouse, and so on. This chapter begins the discussion of user interfaces; the discussion concludes with Chapter 13, which addresses the substantial challenges in actually *designing* a satisfactory user interface.

We are going to set a goal: to separate UI from non-UI software elements as practically as we can. The idea of this separation, known as the *model-view-controller* (MVC), dates back to the late 1970s and is the most important milestone in the history of object-oriented user interface design.

11.1 Model-view-controller example

Imagine that someone needs a computerized counting tool. Here are two applications that would do the trick:

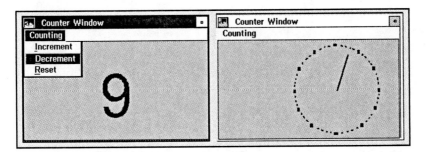

These two applications evidently display their values differently, one digitally and the other like an analog clock. The two kinds of displays are known as two kinds of *views*. Strictly speaking, a *view* is just a way of displaying information. At this moment, the digital view displays *9* and the analog one displays *3*.

There are no connections between the two applications, even though they appear side by side on the screen. You can increment either independently of the other, by means of their respective menus. The applications therefore each rely on their own underlying counter object—an object with an increment and decrement method and an instance variable representing the current value:

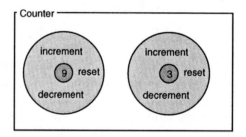

These two instances of **counter**, known as *model* objects, operate independently of each other, just as the views above operate independently. A model is responsible for changing and maintaining the state of the underlying application—in this case, the underlying counter. Models are ignorant of how their information is displayed; that is, they are ignorant of their views. Models aren't visible on the computer's display.

We'll discuss the mechanism that connects views to their models shortly, but first consider another possible configuration: both views could share one model object. The two views would then operate in lockstep: if you increment either, the other also increments because it is merely another view of one and the same model object. Here are the two views:

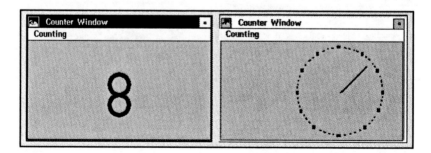

And here is the model object both share:

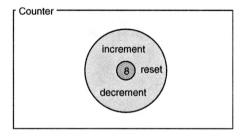

So far, all the counters we've considered still operate in the same way, by means of menu selections. The next step is to introduce an entirely different input mechanism, like the buttons here:

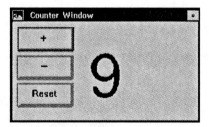

This application has the same kind of digital view we've already seen, and also the same kind of model as before, but a different kind of *controller*—the technical term for the input mechanism. This kind of controller also could have been associated with the analog view, producing this counter application:

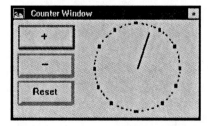

In theory then, we can decompose the design of an application into independent elements—models, views, and controllers. In practice, such a decomposition may be more or less feasible depending on the framework of classes in which you are compelled to work. For example, we shall see later that a full three-way decomposition is more likely to occur in VisualWorks than in other Smalltalk environments.

You can think of a controller as an object that handles input events and a view as an object that handles output events. More precisely, a controller handles events that the user generates, like pressing a mouse button, and a view handles events that the model generates, like increasing the value of a counter. A view provides a *look* and a controller provides a *feel*. The model underlies the views and controllers, and as we will see in the next section, the ideal model is independent of views or controllers. The model neither knows nor cares about any of them.

11.2   Exercise

The screen below displays several counter applications. The top two counters are simple ones that operate by mouse clicks: a left click increments the count and a right click decrements it.

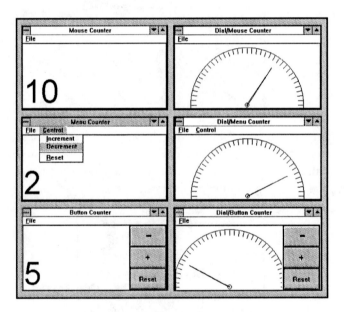

❑ How many *kinds* of models are there?

❑ How many *kinds* of views?

❑ How many *kinds* of controllers?

❑ How many *instances* of models?

11.3   How MVC works

Here is how the user interacts with an application based on an MVC decomposition:

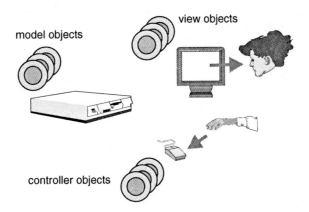

The view objects render information to the user and the controller objects accept the user's input. The user has no direct contact with model objects; she imagines their presence and characteristics only from her interactions with the views and controllers. (How and what she imagines are the subjects of Chapter 13.)

In classical MVC, the relations among these three kinds of objects are indicated here:

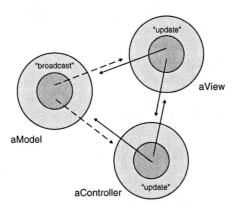

You can see that views and controllers have instance variables that refer to their model as well as each other. They know their model. But the converse is false. The model does not have explicit instance variables pointing to its views or controllers. This is a crucial omission. The underlying application should function without knowledge of how the user interface happens to display information or interpret input. The application should not know or care what kind of view or controller happens to be attached to it, nor even whether several views and controllers may be attached, or different ones as time passes. The essence of MVC is this radical decoupling of the model from the user interface components.

If the model has no instance variables referring to its views and controllers, how does it inform them of changes in its state? In other words, how can the model proclaim ignorance of views and controllers, yet still inform them of changes? The answer is that it informs them indirectly, via a concealed relationship known as *dependency*: the model's dependents are indicated above by dashed arrows. Whenever the model sustains a change that it wants to convey to its dependents, it sends a message to itself—**self broadcast**[1]—which eventually causes a message to be sent to each of its dependents—**dependent update**. The dependents decide what they want to do, if anything, to update themselves; that is the function of the **update** methods above. In the counter example, the view's **update** method would send a message to its model to fetch the current value of the counter, with which the view could refresh its display.

Roughly speaking, there are two mechanisms for implementing dependency relationships. One uses a global dictionary, where the keys are models, and the value associated with each key (model) is a collection of the model's dependents. The **broadcast** method searches the dictionary for the model in question, then sends the **update** message to each of the objects associated with the model. The upcoming exercise illustrates this mechanism.

The second mechanism gives each model object its own **dependents** instance variable that refers to an ordered collection of its dependent objects. The **broadcast** method then sends the **update** message to each object in this collection. You don't want to write code for dependency and broadcasting every time you construct a new class of models, so if you adopt this second mechanism you should write the code you need once in an abstract class called **Model**, and subclass all your model classes from it. This technique conceals the relationship just as we wanted; application programmers who build model objects don't have to know that the **dependents** instance variable is present.

A refinement of the second mechanism offers a sharper form of broadcast, in which a cluster of messages is broadcast in response to a given event. This form is now available in all the major Smalltalk dialects (see the table on page 125). For example, in VisualAge the class **AbtObservableObject** does entirely away with the simple **dependents** instance variable; instead it has an instance variable called **eventDependents** that is a dictionary-like object whose keys are events and whose values are clusters of messages. Therefore, instead of a fixed broadcast resulting in the same **update** message

---

[1] This message is **self changed** instead of **self broadcast** in some dialects.

being sent to every object, an **AbtObservableObject** can selectively broadcast the cluster of messages associated with any one of its events. And these messages may have any names or receivers at all. In effect, broadcasting can be surgically precise.

This sharper form of broadcast is sometimes called *event notification*. Event notification is increasingly popular and may eventually displace the older, more basic forms of broadcast.

11.4 Exercise: the original dependency mechanism

❑ All major Smalltalk dialects support a general dependency mechanism that lets any object depend on any other. In most Smalltalks, this mechanism uses a class variable of **Object** named **Dependents**. Inspect **Dependents**[2]. What kind of object is it, and what does it currently contain?

❑ *Execute*:
```
X := Penguin new. "Any object will do!"
X addDependent: 17.
X addDependent: 12.
Dependents inspect.
```

What does **Dependents** contain now?

❑ Next *execute*:
```
X broadcast: #update.
```

Smalltalk broadcasts an update, but you should see nothing. That's because integers don't respond to **update**. Now write an **update** in **Integer** whose body is:
```
Transcript cr;
        show: 'I am ', self printString.
```

(The Professional version of IBM Smalltalk may require you to put the method into a new application edition. Any edition, including a "scratch" edition, suffices.) Again try:
```
X broadcast: #update.
```

This general dependency mechanism is serviceable, but by object-oriented standards it is not well encapsulated. After all, any object can access the class variable **Dependents** in class **Object**. If you want to use a dependency mechanism, consider building or reusing one in which an object encapsulates its own dependents. The major Smalltalk dialects all come with such a mechanism. (See the table on page 125.)

---

[2] In some dialects, you must first inspect the class **Object** and then inspect its **classPool**.

11.5   MVC: benefits and difficulties

A clean MVC decomposition keeps the designer honest. It forces him to separate concerns, which is a basic goal of software engineering. He can focus on the coherence of
the underlying model (more on this subject in Chapter 13) without worrying about
presenting it on the screen. Conversely, he can invent new ways of presenting the
model without having to reprogram the model objects. In short, development of the
user interface and the model can proceed separately. The objects will then be smaller
and less complicated and the prospects for reusing them will be better.

MVC also provides a pathway for porting an application from one platform to
another: model objects should port with little or no trouble—good models are not
cluttered with platform-specific code. The porting problem therefore reduces to
rewriting only the UI code. The benefit depends on the relative proportions of UI and
model code in the application. For the counter example above, with its simple model,
the benefit is almost negligible. But for an application like a network simulation with
rich algorithmic content, the benefit is considerable. In any case, ideally, the programmer responsible for the port will not need to know or learn anything about the underlying application or problem.

Desirable though it may be, a pure MVC separation is a lofty goal. Here are some
difficulties.

- *Simple rendering.* In MVC, we strive to keep model objects ignorant of anything having to do with their presentation. Strictly speaking, it would be unfaithul to MVC to
taint a circle object with a method that paints a circular arrangement of pixels on a
graphical window, or even a method that spells out the characters '*Circle*'. Similarly,
a purist may challenge a method (such as we will see in the next chapter) for a checking account transaction object that returns a string detailing its date and amount.
Such methods have to do with views, not models, the argument goes. If you insist on
not tainting model objects with these rendering methods, however, you will have to
pay the price for another layer of objects that are responsible for rendering. That can
be an overblown response to relatively minor MVC infractions.

- *Validity and constraint checking.* In a screen in which the user enters, say, a telephone
number, the UI has an opportunity to validate that the number's structure—country
code, area or city code, number, and extension—is acceptable. The UI could even
refresh another field, perhaps the name of the country. The more business-specific
knowledge the UI brings to bear on such checking—which countries are acceptable,
whether to allow letters as well as numbers for the phone number, and the like—the
less pure the MVC decomposition becomes. The penalty for making the UI more
powerful in these ways is that as the business evolves, UI logic as well as model code
must be rewritten.

- *Partial refresh.* In classic MVC, the UI informs the model of specific changes, and the model then broadcasts a generic update back to the UI. For a drawing application, the UI would update by fetching *all* picture elements from the model, blanking the canvas, then refreshing the whole canvas. But if the specific changes affect only a small portion of the canvas, blanking and refreshing the whole canvas would be both slow and distracting. Classic MVC is not flexible enough to refresh just the small, affected portion; this localized refresh requires closer cooperation between view and model. The view still informs the model of the changes, but it must selectively fetch just those elements it needs from the model, and refresh just the altered portion of the canvas. This optimization does not relieve the model from having to broadcast—there may be other views, after all—but the current, active view should ignore the broadcast, lest it respond by blanking and completely refreshing itself, which is what we've been trying to avoid.

- *Drag and drop.* When the user drags an icon across the screen, the icon may change its appearance as it moves over different targets. For example, when a drop would be illegal many UIs change the icon to a "Do not enter" symbol. The legality of a drop commonly depends on a simple consideration, like whether the graphical element being dragged lies over a particular window. But the legality could conceivably depend on more complex considerations, such as the states of the underlying objects. A prescription icon may not be dropped on a patient icon if the patient is allergic to that drug; a letter may not be dropped on a mailbox if the letter has no addressee; an insurance policy may not be dropped on a client if the client is an assigned risk; and so on. In these situations the underlying model objects must participate in the negotiation, because only they know the relevant state information. Icon objects, which are merely visual artifacts, aren't smart enough to help; they do not even know what questions they ought to ask the model objects. MVC, with its broadcast metaphor, has no bearing on this fine-grained, real-time problem. A solution to this problem is to use *lawyer* objects (page 233). A lawyer knows both an icon and an underlying model object, and it negotiates with other lawyers that represent other icon and model object pairs. The UI maintains a collection of lawyers, one for each icon, and the lawyers decide whether one icon may be dropped on another, by negotiating between the model objects they represent.

The last three difficulties underscore the lesson that broadcasting is sometimes too slow and heavyweight. Users of today's computing systems expect immediate feedback; they cannot wait for the model to issue a generalized broadcast to the view objects. Instead, the view objects must become more intimately involved with model objects than they would be in an ideal MVC partitioning. MVC is not sufficient for every situation.

11.6   What's become of MVC?

The MVC idea originated in 1978–1979 during Trygve Reenskaug's visit to the Xerox PARC Smalltalk team, which formalized it in the Smalltalk-80 product, later to become VisualWorks.[3] Digitalk carried essentially the same ideas into its early DOS Smalltalk/V products, where it was renamed to MPD (model-pane-dispatcher).

Nowadays, controller objects are commonly absorbed into view objects, so that the classical MVC threesome reduces to a twosome. To see the rationale, think about the pushbutton controllers in the counter applications above. These controllers have view-like characteristics: the buttons are visible and they appear to bounce down and up when the mouse is clicked over them. A button controller is, in effect, already bound to a view-like object, and messages flow back and forth between the controller half and the view half to coordinate their behavior. Because controllers often have both view and controller characteristics, object-oriented UI classes usually coalesce views and controllers into one kind of object, which relieves the programmer of the burden of managing communication between two different objects.

Another reason for coalescing views and controllers is that unified view-controllers are a natural match for the built-in user interface "objects" (scrollbars, buttons, menus, and so on) found in native windowing environments such as X-Windows, OS/2 Presentation Manager, Windows, and Macintosh. It is simpler for a layer of programming objects above the windowing environment to mirror the underlying architecture than to dismantle it into separate view and controller constituents that aren't there to begin with.

These modern view-controller objects still go by the name *view*, or occasionally *interactor*. Instead of a classic three-way MVC decomposition, we decompose applications into this simpler MV form:

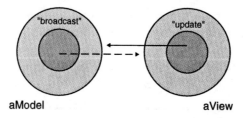

aModel   aView

---

[3] Trygve's account of the early history appears in [Reenskaug 1996].

In short, coalescing views and controllers simplifies the programmer's task, at the cost of some loss of flexibility in mixing and matching looks and feels. Today, almost all UI frameworks, whether based on Smalltalk or C++, coalesce controllers and views. Examples include MacApp, Smalltalk/V, Interviews, and the X/Motif widgets used in IBM Smalltalk. VisualWorks is the most notable product that sustains full MVC separation.

From now on we will focus on MV separations instead of MVC separations. Thus the primary software engineering obligation of UI developers is to separate models and views. You should strive to avoid excess seepage of model behavior into views. Powerful GUI (graphical user interface) builders increase the temptation, because developers sometimes become so enamored of GUI building that they overlook the design of a coherent layer of model objects.

As I implied on page 120, several broadcast or dependency mechanisms are suitable for achieving MV or MVC separations. This table illustrates the variety available in the major Smalltalk dialects:

	VisualAge (IBM Smalltalk)	Visual Smalltalk (Smalltalk/V)	VisualWorks (Smalltalk-80)
Abstract **View** and **Controller** classes (supports full MVC)	No	No	Yes
Dependency supported by a class variable in **Object**	**Dependents**	**EventHandlers** (**Dependents** in older versions)	**Dependents**
Dependency supported by an instance variable in an abstract class	**AbtObservableObject** broadcasts message clusters[a] (aka event notification)	**EventManager** broadcasts message clusters (aka event notification)	**Model** broadcasts message(s) like **update** to all dependents[b]

[a] As of version 3.0, instances of subclasses other than **AbtObservableObject** can also broadcast message clusters. The protocol is the same as the one in **AbtObservableObject**, but the methods are reimplemented in **Object**, using the auxiliary class **AbtCLDTAdditions**.

[b] ParcPlace-Digitalk intends to make **EventManager** the foundation for its instance-based broadcast protocol in its combined VisualSmalltalk/VisualWorks offering.

The class variable in **Object** is convenient for quick and dirty broadcasts but should generally be avoided, because it is accessible from any object. It is therefore tantamount to a global variable, which we know to be generally undesirable. This mechanism also involves more message sends, which could degrade performance in designs with many (probably too many) broadcasts. Thus you should try to use the built-in instance-based support (from the last row of the table), or build an abstract class of your own once, and subclass from it.

Because of the many workable approaches to broadcasting, it is unlikely that the ANSI standardization committee will specify a broadcast or dependency protocol as part of the forthcoming Smalltalk standard.

CHAPTER 12

Building windows

This chapter deals with building windows in the IBM Smalltalk environment. You are going to build windows from scratch—almost—with only a little help from a simple abstract class. This will be an excursion into the heart of user interface programming. The specific classes and methods in this chapter apply only to IBM Smalltalk, not other dialects. Windowing frameworks differ so widely between Smalltalk dialects that you will have little hope of reinterpreting this material for other dialects.

Using the techniques in this chapter to handcraft complicated windows would be inefficient. For constructing lots of intricate windows, programmers nowadays mostly use a GUI (graphical user interface) builder such as VisualAge or WindowBuilder Pro (for IBM Smalltalk) or VisualWorks (for Smalltalk-80). These have the advantage of simplifying the tedious aspects of window construction, although some also obscure the layer of window components where the programmer may want to fine-tune the behavior of the user interface. This layer is the subject of this chapter and, GUI builder or not, it is desirable to know a little about it.

Before you can build a first, simple window in IBM Smalltalk, you must learn a little about *Motif.* Motif is a standard programming interface for building GUIs. It was developed by the Open Software Foundation (OSF), a consortium of large computing companies. Motif is not an object-oriented programming system; it consists instead of many conventional functions.

IBM Smalltalk's user interface components include a layer of classes and methods whose names and arguments mimic Motif reasonably well. These classes therefore have a strong affinity with systems that support Motif, which happen to include many UNIX systems. But OS/2 and Windows don't support Motif; instead they have their own window managers. Nevertheless, by incorporating a common Motif-like layer on these platforms as well as UNIX, IBM Smalltalk ensures that applications built on this layer will be highly portable among the three platforms—UNIX, Windows, and OS/2. Moreover, because this Motif layer ultimately translates to the underlying platform's windowing system, the look and feel of user interfaces conform to the platform's native look and feel.

12.1   What you need to know about Motif

Conventional Motif is itself built atop another standard, *X-Windows*. The X-Windows interface consists of a collection of function calls called *Xlib*, or the *X/Library*. Motif is an example of an X *toolkit*; X toolkits are built on an interface called the *Xt Intrinsics* (*X toolkit Intrinsics*), which in turn is built from the Xlib. Thus, the conventional Motif layering looks like this:

| Motif ("an X toolkit") |
| Xt Intrinsics |
| Xlib |
| Unix (X server, X client) |

IBM Smalltalk presents a layer of Smalltalk classes and methods that look like Motif[1] services, but are built atop the operating system's GUI services. In other words, the IBM Smalltalk Motif layer is built on whatever the underlying platform offers, be it raw OS/2 or Windows GUI services, or a real Motif toolkit and Motif window manager (*mwm*) like the picture above. The picture for IBM Smalltalk is:

| application's windows |
| Motif-like layer in IBM Smalltalk |
| Windows or OS/2 or Motif window manager |

Two other abbreviations—*Cw* and *Cg*—occur commonly in IBM Smalltalk's UI classes. "Cw" stands for *common widgets*. *Widget*[2] is the term that X programmers use for any UI component—be it a button, a scrollbar, a textual field, a label.… The counterparts in IBM Smalltalk of Motif's widgets are known as common widgets, and their class names are prefixed by "Cw." Similarly, functions in the Xlib for graphics—drawing, bitmaps, fonts, color palettes—have been structured into Smalltalk classes that are prefixed by "Cg," for *common graphics*.

The first window you build will contain a textual widget that displays *'Hello San Francisco'*. Although this window, labeled **myWindow** below, is about as simple as they come, it relies on several Motif widgets, intertwined by instance variable relationships:

---

[1] By the way, Motif is sometimes abbreviated to *xm*, which stands for *X/Motif.*

[2] Non-UNIX programmers often use the word *control* instead of *widget*. For our purposes UI widgets and UI controls are synonymous.

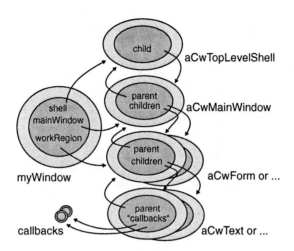

You can see where a textual widget would be, at the bottom of the sketch. Note that it is a child of a **CwForm**. Forms are container widgets; a form typically will contain several other widgets, although in your first application it will contain only one text widget, a **CwText**, for presenting the string *'Hello San Francisco'*. The highest level in the sketch is a **CwTopLevelShell**. As its name implies, it is the Motif widget that forms a "shell" over all the other widgets. A *main window* (**CwMainWindow**) is also a container; in addition to its forms it can contain a menu bar, should an application require one.

Notice also the *callback* objects at the lower left. Callbacks or, more precisely, callback handlers, are methods that are triggered by events like resizing or exposing a window. Widgets can respond to events like these by executing an appropriate callback handler. I will say more about callbacks later on.

The sketch above is schematic. The actual instance variable names are somewhat less readable. They have names like **cwChild**, **cwParent**, and **xmNChildren**.

Each of the Motif-like common widgets in the sketch above encapsulates a similar but more primitive object, which in turn encapsulates a really primitive operating system object known as a *window handle:*

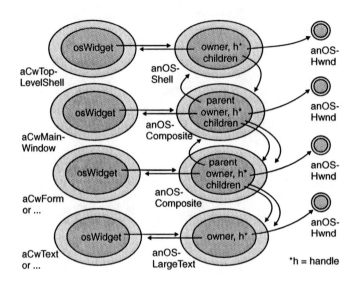

These primitive objects tie the common widgets to the real operating system. Fortunately, though, you can write all the code you need at the common widget level, and trust that the rest has been correctly encapsulated to do your bidding.

12.2   Widget resources

Widgets must be customized for each application. Customization covers everything from where the widget should be positioned to how it responds to events like button presses. To customize a widget, you send it appropriate customization messages. Customization is also known as setting the widget's *resources*. Here are some examples of setting resources for a widget **w**:

w topAttachment: XmATTACHFORM	Attach the top of **w** to the top of its form
w bottomAttachment: XmATTACHPOSITION; **bottomPosition: 10 "percent"**	Attach the bottom of **w** 1/10 of the way down from the top of its form
w topAttachment: XmATTACHWIDGET; **topWidget: anotherWidget**	Attach the top of **w** to the (bottom) of another widget referred to as **anotherWidget**

w editMode: XmMULTILINEEDIT	Assuming **w** is an instance of **CwText**, let it handle multiple lines of text, instead of just one line
w value: self myMethod	Assuming **w** is an instance of **CwText**, set the text it contains to a string that **myMethod** returns
w items: self yourMethod	Assuming **w** is an instance of **CwList**, set the items in the list to a collection of strings that **yourMethod** returns

w addEventHandler: ButtonPressMask
    receiver: self
    selector: #pushMe:clientData:callData:
    clientData: nil;
	Assuming **w** is an instance of **CwPushButton**, let its response to a button press be defined by a method named **pushMe:clientData:callData:**

The peculiar-looking constants **XmATTACHFORM**, **ButtonPressMask**, and so on are defined in pool dictionaries, which I'll explain in the next section.

12.3   Excursion: pool dictionaries

Any software that talks to an external system must use the same low-level indicators (typically flags or masks that are bits or integers) that the external system uses. For example, on OS/2 the color dark blue is indicated by 9, and red by 2; any software running on OS/2 must use these same numbers for the same colors. We would like to think about the numbers as little as possible, of course, and instead refer to them by names like **ClrDarkblue** and **ClrRed**. Similarly, Motif resource values like **XmAT-TACHWIDGET** are easier to remember than arbitrary integers. (**XmATTACH-WIDGET** happens to be 3 in Motif.)

Smalltalk pool dictionaries are handy objects for bundling constants like these. Pool dictionaries are dictionaries that have strings such as **'ClrDarkblue'** for keys and values such as **9**. (In IBM Smalltalk, pool dictionaries are instances of the special class **EsPoolDictionary**, which accepts only strings as keys.) For example, the global variable **PlatformConstants** refers to a pool dictionary that contains color constants as well as many other constants. And the global variable **CwConstants** refers to a pool dictionary that contains the resource values for Motif widgets.

So far in this discussion, we haven't used pool dictionaries in any unusual way. If you were to access one of its entries, you would have to write something like:

```
widget topAttachment: (CwConstants at: 'XmATTACHWIDGET')
```

just as you would refer to an entry in any other dictionary. The effect would be to pass **3** as an argument, but of course we don't want to write a **3** in our code.

The attraction of a pool dictionary appears when you specify one as part of the definition of a class:

```
Object subclass: #MyClass
    instanceVariableNames: ''
    classVariableNames: ''
    poolDictionaries: 'CwConstants '
```

Now if you want to access an entry in a method, you can simply write:

```
widget topAttachment: XmATTACHWIDGET
```

No need to specify the dictionary or use the **at:** message! The Smalltalk compiler searches through the class's pool dictionaries for a key that matches the string **'Xm-ATTACHWIDGET'**. When it finds the key in **CwConstants** it compiles the association into the compiled method.

In short, pool dictionaries make code more succinct by saving you the trouble of typing the name of a dictionary every time you want to refer to an entry.

Here are some characteristics of pool dictionaries:

- The keys are strings.

- The values are often integers. (But not always. Try *inspecting* the pool dictionary **PlatformFunctions**, then double-clicking on one of its entries.)

- A global variable refers to it. (Otherwise there is no name by which to specify it when defining a class.)

- The dictionary should be fully populated beforehand. (If a key is absent, a method that uses it cannot compile.)

To solidify your understanding of pool dictionaries, try these simple exercises:

❑ What is the underlying value of **ButtonPressMask? ClrYellow?**

❑ Construct a pool dictionary as follows:

```
Smalltalk declarePoolDictionary: #MyPool.
MyPool at: 'ABC' put: 55.
```

Now build a subclass of **Object** called **MyClass**, being careful to specify **MyPool** as a pool dictionary. Write this instance method:

```
test
    " Test by displaying:
            MyClass new test
    "
    ^ABC
```

Predict the result and run the experiment to confirm your prediction. What happens if you write another test method that returns **XYZ** instead of **ABC**?

Technical curiosity: A pool dictionary can begin life as an ordinary dictionary, that is, as an instance of **Dictionary**. As soon as you use it as a pool dictionary though, IBM Smalltalk automatically converts it to an instance of **EsPoolDictionary**.

12.4 Exercise: a first window

The goal for your first window is something like:

❑ Create a new application, or add to one of your old ones. Change the *prerequisite* applications to include **EtBaseTools** so that you can access class **EtWindow**. Add a subclass **HelloWindow** to **EtWindow**.

❑ Write an **example** class method for testing:

```
example
        "
                HelloWindow example
        "


        ^HelloWindow new open
```

❑ Write an instance method that answers any string you like:

```
myHello
        ^' Hello San Francisco'
```

❑ Remember that abstract classes come with expectations that their subclasses fulfill certain obligations. For the abstract class **EtWindow**, its subclasses must implement the method **createWorkRegion**. Write this method in your **HelloWindow** class.

```
createWorkRegion
        | textWidget|
        textWidget := workRegion
                createText: 'My text widget'
```

```
                    argBlock:
                        [:w |   w
                                        editMode: XmMULTILINEEDIT;
                                        value: self myHello;
                                        leftAttachment: XmATTACHFORM;
                                        rightAttachment: XmATTACHFORM;
                                        topAttachment: XmATTACHFORM;
                                        bottomAttachment: XmATTACHFORM].

        textWidget manageChild
```

This method looks more formidable than it is. The important messages are the resource-setting messages inside the block. You should recognize their purposes from the last section.

❑ Finally, test your **HelloWindow** class by *executing* your **example** method.

12.5   Exercise: a window for the account balance

You are about to add a simple user interface to the bank account you developed in Chapter 8. You want to end up with a window representing the account, with separate widgets to contain the transaction log and the current balance. We'll proceed in three steps: first a window that displays only the balance, then one that displays only the transaction log, and finally one window that displays both the balance and the log, using two widgets.

❑ Begin by choosing a suitable application, like the one in which you wrote your earlier account exercise, and change the prerequisites so that they include **EtBaseTools**. Add a subclass, **BalanceWindow**, to **EtWindow**. The fundamental difference between this exercise and the preceding "Hello" exercise is the need for the window to know about an account object. Create an instance variable named **account** in **BalanceWindow** for this purpose.

❑ Prepare a test case by writing this class method in **BalanceWindow**:

```
example
        "
        BalanceWindow example
        "
        ^BalanceWindow new openOn: Account example.
```

This test case reuses **Account**'s class method **example**, which you developed on page 91.

❑ Note that you will need an **openOn:** instance method that takes an account as an argument. Write this method. It should do just two things: set the instance variable and open the window (by saying **self open**).

❑ Instead of **myHello**, write an appropriate method to return the account's balance. Don't forget that the returned object should be a string. In other words, don't forget to convert the integer balance to a string.

❑ Finally, write a **createWorkRegion** method and test by executing your **example** method.

12.6   Exercise: a window for the transaction log

In this exercise, you will need to transform one collection into a different, brand-new one. One way would be to write a loop. However, object-oriented developers rarely write loops to process collections. Mature class libraries have powerful methods (or even objects, called *iterators*) that process a collection's contents. In Smalltalk, the method **Collection>>collect:** processes each element in a collection and puts the resulting objects into a new collection.

❑ *Display* each of these lines:
```
(OrderedCollection with: 3 with: 2 with: 1) collect: [:x | x squared].
(SortedCollection with: 3 with: 2 with: 1) collect: [:x | x squared].
```

❑ Mimic the steps in the previous exercise: start with a class called **LogWindow**, write an **example** class method, and an **openOn:** instance method.

❑ Your **createWorkRegion** method should be similar to the one for displaying the account's balance. That one built a text widget, however, and this one should build a list widget. Thus, part of it should look like:
```
listWidget := workRegion
              createList: 'My log widget'
              argBlock:
                  [:w |
                      w
                          items: self myLog;
                          leftAttachment: XmATTACHFORM;
                          ...
                  ].
```
Write the **createWorkRegion** method.

❑ To complete the code, you must write the **myLog** instance method specified in your **createWorkRegion** method. **myLog** should use **collect:** to transform the transaction log into an **OrderedCollection** of strings.

❑ Execute your **example** method to test that your window displays the transactions in chronological order.

12.7 Exercise: a window containing both widgets

❑ Build a class called **AccountWindow**. This window should combine ideas from the preceding exercises so that it displays both the balance and the transactions.

12.8 Assessment: building windows

You've now seen what it takes to build simple windows using Motif. In general, one subclasses from a suitable abstract window class. **EtWindow** is one example, because it is the abstract window class for all the everyday browsers and tools you use in IBM Smalltalk. Theoretically **EtWindow** is not the best choice of superclass for a product that will be delivered to a customer. That's because it was designed as the basis for the development-time windows, and a product's code shouldn't depend on development-time code. In fact, Et stands for "Envy Tools," where Envy is a suite of team programming facilities that is also available in other Smalltalk environments.

Another starting point could have been the abstract class **WidgetWindow**, best found by loading the application **CwExamples** and its prerequisites. To use **WidgetWindow** as a superclass, you would write a **createWindow** method instead of the **createWorkRegion** you wrote in the exercise.

Another prospective starting point is the class named **WbApplication** (part of the public-domain application **WbApplicationFramework**), which is the abstract window class of the third-party product WindowBuilder Pro; you override the method **addWidgets** instead of **createWorkRegion**. **WbApplication** can thus serve as the superclass of handcrafted windows as well as of windows generated by the WindowBuilder Pro GUI builder.

Or, you could start by writing your own simple abstract class, including code to create the top-level shell, a main window, and any other standard fixtures you want your windows to enjoy.

These are all legitimate approaches to handcrafting windows. They are valid even for building elaborate windows consisting of numerous, carefully positioned widgets. But as I said earlier, you are most likely to use a GUI building tool to lay out such windows. For IBM Smalltalk, that is likely to be VisualAge or WindowBuilder Pro. VisualAge offers the attraction of *visual programming*, which means that you can connect user interface and model components together to produce working logic, without even writing Smalltalk code. WindowBuilder Pro uses fewer layers of objects and so offers efficiency plus the virtue of making Motif widgets accessible should you need to work with them.

Good sources of additional details about Motif programming in IBM Smalltalk are the product manuals [IBM 1995] and [Objectshare 1995].

12.9   Callbacks and events

Your windows so far don't respond to any inputs and therefore aren't too practical. Practical windows respond to mouse actions and other *events* (or *X events*) from the operating system. These include typing on the keyboard, moving the mouse, resizing or exposing a window, giving a window the focus, and so on. You can think of events as stimuli that the operating system detects from physical devices and passes on to your widgets. (In X-Windows, the component of the system responsible for this service is known as the *X server.*)

A widget won't respond to an event unless it has been sensitized to the event. To sensitize a widget to an event, you must establish an *event handler*. You will write event handlers in the upcoming exercise.

Sometimes it may be convenient to think of higher-level, or "artificial" events. For example, it would be reasonable to want to sensitize a button widget to a "click," which consists of two events, namely a button press followed by a button release, both of which must occur over the widget. A click lifts the programmer's level of abstraction above the raw hardware concerns of a mouse press and release occurring in just the right sequence and place. In Motif and other windowing systems, these artificial events are known as *callbacks*. (The callback for clicking on a **CwPushButton** widget is known as an **activateCallback** or **XmNactivateCallback**.)

The programmer writes event handlers for events, and *callback handlers* for callbacks. Both event handlers and callback handlers are special methods that execute whenever the expected stimuli occur. The reason for the name "callback" is that when the stimulus occurs, the operating system "calls your widget back" and gives it the opportunity to execute its handler. A callback is similar to arranging for someone to call you back later on the telephone: you expect the callback to occur and you will be ready for it, but you're not sure when it will happen.

Events and callbacks are similar. The programmer sensitizes the widget to either one by establishing handlers, and the operating system calls back when the stimulus occurs. The distinction between them—events being low level and callbacks being higher level—is a Motif convention. In other object-oriented environments, the word "callback" applies to all stimuli, whether they are low or high level. In fact, Smalltalk programmers frequently use the term "callback" for any call of a Smalltalk method that originates from outside of Smalltalk.

How does a callback (or event) differ from a conventional call? The distinction is partly one of degree. For one thing, most callbacks represent primitive stimuli and therefore carry less information (fewer and simpler arguments) than conventional calls can. But the principal conceptual distinction has to do with concurrency. After a view establishes a callback handler it continues to execute other code; it does not block and await the callback. Instead, the callback occurs asynchronously, at some unforeseeable future time, when the view could be doing anything at all. From the view's perspective, the callback has an event-driven flavor rather than a procedural one.

12.10   Preparation

A **CgDrawable** (and its subclass **CgWindow**) can display graphics that are "drawn" on it by a *graphics context*, an instance of **CgGC**. You can think of a graphics context as a drawing tool like a pen or brush. Here are examples of **CgDrawable** drawing methods:

```
CgDrawable>>drawPoint:x:y:
CgDrawable>>drawLine:x1:y1:x2:y2:
CgDrawable>>drawRectangle:x:y:width:height:
```

❑   What kind of object do you expect the first keyword argument in each of these methods to be? If you are uncertain, verify your answer by browsing class **CgDrawable**.

12.11   Exercise: mouse event handling

The result of this exercise will be a window in which you can "doodle" with the mouse.

❑   Load the **CgExamples** application into your image, if it is not already present. (To install it in the standard environment, start from your System Transcript and pick menu options *Smalltalk tools > Load Features...* then select *Smalltalk Programming Examples*. To load it in the Professional environment, start from an Application Manager window and pick menu options *Applications > Available > Application*.) You can now access the abstract class **CgSingleDrawingAreaApplication**. This abstract class has both a drawable widget (**CgWindow**) and a graphics context built into it; therefore its concrete subclasses can "draw."

❏ Which instance variable in the abstract class refers to the graphics context? Which refers to the drawable widget?

❏ From your Application Manager, create a new application in which to write your code. Change the application's prerequisites to include **CgExamples**.

❏ Add a subclass **DoodleWindow** to **CgSingleDrawingAreaApplication**. Add two instance variables, **oldX** and **oldY**. You will use these instance variables to retain the previous position of the mouse as the mouse moves.

❏ Write a class method to test your application:

```
example
    "
    DoodleWindow example
    "
    ^DoodleWindow new open
```

❏ Look at the inherited **buttonMotion:** and **buttonPress:** event handlers. Note that the argument they expect is an event, actually an instance of **CwMotionEvent** or **CwButtonEvent**. What methods can you use to get the *x* and *y* coordinates of the point at which the event occurred?

❏ Finally, override the event handlers **buttonMotion:** and **buttonPress:**, and test your window.

12.12 Challenging exercise: dynamic updates

❏ The account window displays both a balance and a list of transactions, but it is still relatively inert because it provides no way to add new transactions. Extend the window so that the user can create and handle new transactions. You can consider either of two UI designs:

- Add a button to the window. When the user clicks the button, another window or dialogue box should open and let the user fill in a date and amount for the new transaction. When the user completes this dialogue, the original window should refresh with an updated balance and transaction log.

- Add a date field, an amount field, and a button to the window. When the user completes the date and amount, then clicks the button, the balance and transaction log should refresh.

This is not an easy exercise. Without a GUI builder, it requires a healthy dose of exploration and experimentation. It is a good idea to have an experienced Smalltalk programmer around in case you get stuck.

12.13   Summary

Object-oriented user interface programming has an event-driven flavor. The programmer establishes handlers for system events or callbacks, and the specified handlers execute when the events occur. Typically, these events occur at a time and place determined by overt user actions, like clicking a mouse at a point on the screen. Thus the event-driven programming model tends to liberate users, letting them perform whatever actions they want whenever they want to. User interfaces that fulfill this promise, so that the user is rarely forced to deal with a fixed situation before proceeding, are called *non-modal* user interfaces. (Not every user interface programmed with objects is non-modal. For example, a user interface in which button clicks or menu picks present dialogue boxes that the user *must* complete before proceeding may look as if it has been programmed with objects, but it won't *feel* that way.)

Now consider a procedural or function-oriented programming model, in which the application decomposes into a tree of sub-functions. In the classic user interface for this model, interaction occurs mostly through a formidable hierarchy of menus. This kind of user interface puts the application squarely in control of the user, who feels psychologically straitjacketed by it. Such user interfaces, in which users must act in rigidly prescribed ways to proceed or extricate themselves from a situation, are an extreme form of modal user interface.

Events and callbacks originated in Smalltalk-80, where widgets were known as *views*. By supporting different handlers for an event, a view could be customized for different problems. They were therefore called *pluggable views*: if you needed a view with specialized behavior, it was enough to plug one of these views into the overall application window and establish specialized handlers for it. Without pluggable views, you would have had to add a whole new view class to get the behavior you wanted. In other words, you could either "buy" a pluggable view and customize it, or "inherit" from another view and customize that. Nowadays, the variety of widgets and their pluggability is rich enough that you don't need to create new widget classes for most ordinary applications.

So far, I have discussed only events or callbacks that pass through the operating system—that is, stimuli that arise from outside Smalltalk. A similar logical flow can occur strictly within the confines of Smalltalk. For instance, an MVC or MV broadcast is like a callback. The view establishes a handler, namely its **update** method, written according to the problem or model at hand, and this handler executes whenever the model calls the view back with a broadcast. Some broadcast mechanisms allow you to call back clusters of messages with arguments, instead of just **update**. The VisualAge and VisualSmalltalk products support such mechanisms. (Cf. the table on page 125.) Programmers and frameworks sometimes also use these mechanisms for model-to-model broadcasting. (But approach such usage warily, because excessive broadcasting can measurably degrade performance.)

Finally, today's GUI builders relieve you of having to *build* the UI, but you still have to *design* it. Good UI design is much more than assembling widgets into a window, and is the subject of the next chapter. Users of powerful GUI builders sometimes backslide from good model-view separations. Carried away by power and speed, they connect user interface widgets directly to low-level components like database elements, without thinking about appropriate model objects.

We can suffer the same lapse even without a GUI builder. In our rush to build **HelloWindow**, we didn't stop to think about a model class. We adopted a style of user interface programming in which we subclassed from an abstract superclass that provided standard view capabilities. *We thought of the application as a kind of window.* No model class encapsulated the application's logic. Such a fall from grace is pardonable for a simple example like **HelloWindow**, which has no interesting application logic. It is a benign step in the wrong direction; it is perilous only if we begin to build applications where a monolithic window class is suffused with application logic. We avoided this misstep with the account windows by using a separate model class (**Account**) that encapsulated the application's behavior.

CHAPTER 13

Designing the UI: a brief tour

The preceding two chapters covered the principle of separating models from views and the actual programming that goes into constructing windows. You should now have a solid grasp on the mechanics of a user interface. We next approach the hardest, most ineffable aspect of user interfaces—designing them.

13.1   User interfaces

The *user interface* (*UI*) is the sole point of contact between a user and the computer. As far as the user knows, the user interface *is* the computer. But even though the user interacts with nothing else, a lot happens in her mind. The appearance of the UI evokes images, just as a novel evokes mental images in the reader's mind. And the more the user interacts with the UI, the further she refines these images, imbuing them with their own imagined behavior, as a child imbues a talking doll with imagined behavior. Unfortunately, the UI's evocations are rarely as effective as the novel's or the doll's. The quality of that evocation is precisely what distinguishes bad user interfaces from good ones, hence bad computer software from good.

The premise in this chapter is that it is worth investing in the design of your application's user interface. An application's acceptability in the marketplace can pivot on the difference between a good user interface and a mediocre one. Although this chapter is not a complete treatise on designing user interfaces, I present some simple, generally overlooked principles that are at the heart of designing respectable UIs. Along the way, we will again meet the principles of object-orientation.

13.2 Elementary examples

Consider two user interfaces for a chess program, one in which the user interacts by typing commands of the form "Nd5," the other in which she uses a mouse to drag an icon depicting a pawn to a square on an image of a board. The game is the same, but the user interfaces create very different impressions on the user.

Or imagine an interactive video game, rendered not with images of protagonists in fast-breaking life-and-death situations and real-time feedback between a control stick and the images on the screen, but sentences on the screen describing the action and a keyboard for typing moves. Again, same game, different user interfaces. One works; the other elicits, at best, indifference. The quality of the user interface foretells a product's acceptability.

Designing a user interface for a game is not a hard problem. (Implementing it may be another matter.) The reason goes to the heart of this chapter: a computer user interface for a game should be a metaphor for the real game. No other user interface makes sense. If the game involves chess pieces, the user interface should represent chess pieces; if the game involves militant people or rocket ships, the user interface should represent militant people or rocket ships. The elements of these games are tangible, recognizable objects, and end users won't settle for less than faithful representations of these objects on their computers.

Contrast this situation with other applications: it is much harder to design a good user interface for a typical software application than it is for a game. A word processor deals with intangible, uncommon entities—styles, paragraphs, fonts, tables, frames, layouts, footnotes. It is altogether more complex than a game; devoid of blatant metaphors. What's more, a game has well-defined rules and actions, so the actions that its user interface should accommodate must be equally well defined. Not so for a word processor. Contemporary WYSIWYG[1] word processors confront users with a daunting array of icons and menus, offering much richer and less constrained capabilities than any sensible game does. No wonder it takes so long to become proficient at powerful software applications; users just cannot get much metaphorical guidance from their user interfaces.

The essence of the difficulty is the absence of a simple, underlying model. When such a model exists, as for a game, the UI can be designed to portray the model. Without a simple model, user interface designers facing an inherently complex problem like word processing have little to guide them.

---

[1] "What You See Is What You Get"

13.3   Coherent conceptual models

The models discussed in the last paragraph are *conceptual models*. By a conceptual model I mean words, metaphors, pictures, rules, or anything that you use to explain how you think something fits together. A superior conceptual model sharpens your understanding of the subject. Here are some examples from my own experience:

- Many people automatically call a tree with needles a pine. Some do so uneasily, because they know that other trees such as firs and spruces have needles too. But they still call them all pines. Their conceptual model for a pine is "a tree with needles." A better (and correct) conceptual model for a pine is "a tree with needles bundled in a sheath at their base":

With this conceptual model, it is hard to mistake a spruce for a pine.

- My conceptual model for a printer driver used to be "a piece of software that comes with a printer and allows the computer to send output to the printer." But every FAX program I've seen comes with a printer driver too. Why do I need a FAX printer driver? (I didn't know.) If I needed to print a FAX, wouldn't I simply have used my printer's driver? (Yes.) I eventually realized that a FAX printer driver was the means by which I could send FAXes through the modem in my computer, *instead* of printing them. To make sense of this revelation, I had to adjust my conceptual model of a printer driver to "a piece of software that handles an application's print commands." This improved conceptual model neatly implies that anything that is printable is also FAX-able.

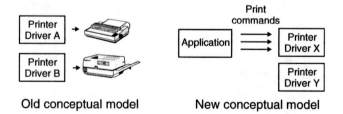

- A teacher of new computer users told me that when she asked them to "move the mouse to the top of the display," some of them lifted their mice into the air and placed them on top of their monitors. They were unfamiliar with the direct manipulation conceptual model, in which the mouse *is*, in effect, something on the screen.

Users are not to blame; if computing is to be attractive and helpful, the computer industry had better clearly convey conceptual models to its users.

If conceptual models are the means by which we understand a subject, it follows that they had better be *coherent*—their parts must fit together in a natural, easily understood manner. Only then will users find them memorable and meaningful. On the right is an attempt to portray a conceptual model for a face. A face designer would be satisfied that it contains all the right elements—eyes, nose, mouth, and so on.

Now consider an upside-down version of the same face. Study it carefully, without turning the page upside down. This lets you analyze it without being influenced by your usual intuitions about faces.

Aside from the irrelevant fact that it is upside down, is this model equally coherent? Can you discern any incoherent elements? It should take a few moments before you notice them: the mouth and eyes are oriented right side up. Thus, a face designer would eventually concede that the elements are not assembled coherently, even though all the right elements are present.

Users, on the other hand, do not have the designers' patience for analyzing a model's coherence. To appreciate

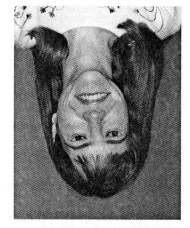

their perspective, turn the page upside down now. This conceptual model of a face is immediately and unmistakably incoherent. Users arrive at the same conclusion as the designer eventually ought to, but more quickly, and by a different cognitive process.[2]

The analogy here for user interface design is that to achieve a successful user interface the designer must describe not only a conceptual model, but one that is coherent. If the designer has no conceptual model at all, the user will never make sense of the user interface. A little better than having none at all is having one that is incoherent. This is the most common situation, where the designer settles for a conceptual model that nevertheless baffles the user. Best and rarest, and the only hope for comfortable, intuitive user interfaces, are coherent conceptual models.

In practice, conceptual models function at more than one level. In the word-processing example, one elemental conceptual model is that a word processor behaves something like a typewriter. Another is that the result can be stored indefinitely and recalled and changed at will. Another is spell-checking. Another is paragraph styles. The overall conceptual model of a word processor consists of how these hundreds of lesser models fit together. (Note that assembling them coherently is a herculean task.)

At another level, many word processors employ scrollbars, a toolbar with iconic buttons, menus, and dialogue boxes. For each of these widgets, users have developed expectations for their behavior: "dragging a scrollbar moves a window over the document," "clicking a menu title drops down a list of menu selections," and so on. These expectations are conceptual models for each kind of widget. Failure to recognize any one of these conceptual models at either level will be a major obstacle in using the word processor.

Because conceptual models are the means by which we understand the world, it behooves us to find effective ways to describe them. There is no one answer, but the next section brings one of humankind's most powerful cognitive tools to bear on the problem.

13.4   Metaphor

Metaphor is the use of one idea in place of another to suggest some likeness. If I tell you that my office is a pigsty, I am using a metaphor. I don't mean that pigs actually

---

[2] The brain has wiring for face (or landscape) recognition. Turning the image upside down disables this wiring. That's why we are unaware of how seriously amiss things are in the upside-down image. Some people lose this wiring completely, even for right-side-up images. They develop *visual agnosia*, a right-brain disorder in which they can no longer recognize faces, or assemble visual wholes from parts. See [Sacks 1985].

inhabit the place; rather I mean to suggest the disarray of a pigsty. A good metaphor is a powerful cognitive tool because it is a form of reuse. The mind applies its knowledge of something it already knows to something it doesn't.

Most people claim that it is difficult for them to think metaphorically. But in fact they use metaphors all the time without realizing it. "That sofa weighs a ton." "He reminds me of a politician." "She is dancing on air." When taken far enough, practically everything we say has a metaphorical root. Consider:

> [The dog] flashed and darted hither and thither as if fairly demented, screaming and shouting, swirling round and round in giddy loops and circles like a leaf in a whirlwind. [Muir ca. 1880]

How many metaphors do you count? Two are conspicuous: likening the dog to a lunatic and also to a leaf caught in a whirlwind.

But probe a little deeper. Where do words come from? Someone had to invent them. The word *flash* came about by onomatopoeia—it sounds like the idea it represents. Just hearing the word evokes the image of something that swiftly comes and goes. Someone made it up for this reason. *Darts* were originally pointed weapons thrown by hand (surviving today in the form of a game); here they are a metaphor for the dog's abrupt movements. Whoever first used the word *circle* was connecting it to the Greek word for ring, *kirkos*. For that individual, a ring was a metaphor for a circle, and we now accept the invention without reflecting on its metaphorical origin. The word *shout* goes back to an Old Norse word for a taunt, *skúta*. *Demented* derives from the Latin *de*, meaning out of, and *mens*, meaning mind. And so on.

In short, every word comes about because somebody connected it to an idea, and so a metaphor lies somewhere behind every word we use. Instead of insisting that it is hard for us to think metaphorically, we should concede that it is hard for us to think in any other way. Everything's meaning is based on the meaning of something else. Metaphorical thinking is part of our cognitive core, whether we consciously acknowledge it or not.

What metaphors could describe the conceptual models for the word-processing example? It is like a *typewriter*, but it can do more. It can *remember* documents. Text can be rearranged like *building blocks*. It works with a *dictionary* to check spelling. To someone who has never experienced word processing, or even a computer, metaphors like these may convey conceptual models more concisely and vividly than a literal description of the software's capabilities.

Just as conceptual models apply at different levels, so do metaphors. Here are some application-level metaphors that have profoundly influenced the computer industry:

Application	Metaphor
VisiCalc (first spreadsheet, precursor of Lotus 1-2-3)	Bookkeeper's ledger sheet
Pong (first video game)	Ping pong
Xerox Star (first office GUI, precursor of Apple Lisa and Macintosh)	Desktop
SQL	Predicate logic
Word processor	Typewriter + dictionary + style guide + ⋯

And here are some metaphors at the level of user interface components:

User Interface Function or Widget	Metaphor
Menu	Restaurant menu
Scrollbar	Sliding window
Dragging hand	Sliding paper
Drag and drop	Moving
Folder icon	Container
Radio button group	Radio presets

In Chapter 1, I emphasized the value of metaphors in thinking about programming objects. In this chapter we've extended their reach from programming objects to conceptual models. As before, I'm not interested in the fine distinctions among metaphor, simile, analogy, and imagery. Their important common characteristic is that they use one idea to suggest something about another idea.

13.5   Magic

The remaining consideration for designing good user interfaces is *magic*. If a computer application does neither more nor less than the metaphor it is based on, there's no point to it. A word processor that exactly duplicates a typewriter's function is no better than a typewriter. *Magic* is the term that user interface designers use to describe the ways in which a computer application goes beyond what the original metaphor suggests.

A spreadsheet program goes beyond a bookkeeper's ledger sheet in two stunning ways. First, it permits the user to enter formulas where the bookkeeper would have had to calculate a cell's value by hand, and second, it can automatically recalculate these formulas when the cells on which the formulas depend change. We take for granted these capabilities that VisiCalc first introduced in 1978. But VisiCalc, graced with this magic, became the first major commercial personal computer application and was an early driving force in the personal computer revolution.

Many people form minor addictions to the simple solitaire card game in Microsoft Windows. Its conceptual model (and metaphor) is the real card game, Klondike solitaire. The software provides exactly the same functions as the player with a card deck does. Its magic consists of the ways in which it is faster and less troublesome to play than the real version. Starting a new game requires only a menu pick, not a physical and time-consuming shuffle and deal; this magic overcomes the chief obstacle to playing "just one more game." Moving a run of cards by dragging and dropping is lazier and tidier than moving real cards. Turning over cards by pointing and clicking takes less energy than grasping and flipping a real card. Overall, the software version affords the same intellectual challenge as the real version, but requires markedly less physical effort to play, on account of its magic.[3]

Magic fosters good software, but magic gone awry is treacherous. Getting the right balance of magic is part of the challenge in user interface design. Consider the Macintosh trash can. To delete an item, the user drags and drops it into the trash can. The metaphor is so faithful to a real trash can that you can recover items by opening up the can and examining its contents. To permanently delete its contents, you must explicitly "empty the trash."

But the trash can has another magical property: if you want to eject a diskette from the diskette drive, you drag and drop the diskette icon into the trash, too. Every new Macintosh user I've observed, including me, has been puzzled by this behavior, and at least momentarily concerned that they might be erasing all the files from their diskette. They adjust soon enough, but not before the initial scare.

Another example: The OS/2 shredder is based on the metaphor of a paper shredder. This metaphor works nicely for documents: drag a document's icon and drop it on the shredder and the shredder disposes of the document. Sometimes, though, icons represent programs instead of documents. And often, two icons representing the same program are tucked away in different places on a desktop. As a new user, I worried whenever I wanted to delete an extra icon. In my conceptual model, the icon *is* its underlying object (the program). Hence, if I shred the icon, the program must go with it, which is different from my intent.

---

[3] Some critics believe this convenience is a bad thing. They argue that software games are detrimental because they distance their users from tangible reality. Essentially the same objections apply to television, breadmaking machines, digital images of art, even books.

Fortunately in this situation, the shredder deletes only the icon and not the underlying program. This behavior isn't consistent with my innocent conceptual model, but at least it provides a way to do what I want to do. But the story doesn't end there. After I adjusted to this behavior, I stumbled on situations where shredding the icon also deletes the program! On these occasions, the innocent conceptual model is correct: the icon identifies with the underlying program file. (Icons found by starting with the "drives" icon behave in this way.) Unhappily, this kind of icon and the kind of icon that doesn't identify with the underlying program are visually indistinguishable. Same icons, different behaviors. The magic of shredding was designed to present an irreconcilable obstacle to consistent use of the user interface.[4] (By the way, Windows and Windows95 suffer from the same ambiguity. In my experience, only the Macintosh is unambiguous about icon identity.)

A final illustration: in everyday life we often wish we could undo something that turned out badly. Examples range from staining the side of the house the wrong color, to disassembling a camera lens, to sewing an extra flap of fabric into a seam, to saying the wrong thing to someone. This wish occurs as often when working with computers as it does in real life. But in computer applications, it is theoretically possible to fulfill the wish. Some applications—the Microsoft Word and DeScribe word processors, the WindowBuilder Pro and VisualAge GUI builders come to mind—let their users undo an unlimited number of past actions. Users develop complete confidence that they can retrace their steps, and therefore are not reluctant to try bold new directions. Such undo magic is as good as it can get.

Unfortunately, most undo facilities are more limited. Some let you undo perhaps four actions, or warn you that specified actions are not undoable. This undo magic has gone awry. Users are burdened with remembering an arbitrary detail, like whether the state to which they wish to return is within the four-action limit. They stop using undo because they regard it as untrustworthy. The effect can be debilitating: they hesitate to risk actions whose results they are not sure of. One sees this hesitation in the use of photo-editing software, where they are inhibited from trying special effects because of the fear that they will not easily be able to return to an acceptable image.

Limited undo functions remind me of a timeless piece of wisdom, known as the "zero, one, infinity" rule: if you are going to design undo, make it support zero, one,

---

[4] Computer scientists call these kinds of problems *aliasing* problems. This is an example of aliasing on the user interface. But aliasing problems pervade software, and object-oriented programming is no exception. In C++, every pointer is an opportunity for an aliasing bug. Smalltalk is a little better, because it has no explicit pointers. But implicit pointers are everywhere, so you can still encounter aliasing surprises. Refer to the aliasing exercise on page 59.

or infinitely many undos. These are the only numbers that people can remember. We will revisit undo in Chapter 15, where we will discover an object-oriented design for infinite undo.

Magic is hard to get right. All of these examples—the Macintosh trash can, the OS/2 shredder, and undo facilities—are based on reasonable metaphors, but present disruptive magic. The resulting conceptual models aren't coherent.

Let's summarize the characteristics of good user interfaces: they are based on coherent conceptual models that are understood through carefully chosen metaphors. And they improve on these metaphors by just the right kind of magic—magic that adds power to users without disrupting their understanding of the user interface.

13.6 Exercise: design a user interface

Design the user interface for an application for managing addresses and phone numbers of friends, family, and associates. This is the "contact-management" component of products called *PIMs*, or *Personal Information Managers*. Be as imaginative and unconstrained as you like, but consider all these:

❑ Brainstorm until you have at least two metaphors for the user interface. ("It's like a _____.")

❑ Develop some high-level use cases. Brief descriptions of some of the user's tasks will suffice.

❑ Choose one of your metaphors and outline your ideas for a user interface based on it. Use your use cases to evaluate (a) ease of learning, (b) ease of use, and (c) magic.

❑ As a responsible user interface designer, try to articulate one or more underlying conceptual models to a prospective end user. A good test for coherence of your conceptual model(s) is to limit how much you say. (Twenty seconds? Three sentences? One picture?) Imagine just one brief opportunity to convey the spirit of the application. The conceptual model(s) can be the same as your user interface metaphor, but it need not be.

This exercise produces the most interesting results if you can do it in a group of up to four people.

13.7   Discussion of your results

People who do this exercise invent all kinds of ingenious interaction techniques. Most are variations on the fine details in their chosen user interface metaphor. As for the metaphors themselves, the list of candidates seems short—three that I can distinguish. And no matter what the metaphor, the same conceptual model always emerges. Let's begin with the metaphors.

The two most popular user interface metaphors for contact management are the address book and the Rolodex. A real address book has some obvious limitations: you can't add pages if you need more space, and you can't order the entries. For instance, all names beginning with "S" are together, but not in any logical order. These limitations present obvious opportunities for magic—unlimited names and automatic alphabetic sorting. The result is a more gratifying address book than a real one. Notice that although unlimited pages and sorting are magical extensions for the address-book metaphor, they are already part of the Rolodex metaphor.

One interesting feature of real address books is the index tab. Imagine the use case of searching for a name, say, "Segovia." I pick the tab for the letter "S" first, then scan that page for "Segovia." Not bad. Those tabs on manual address books and Rolodexes were an inspired way to cope with large numbers of names. Far better than, say, a telephone book. But that was before computers. A computerized contact manager that makes me select an index tab to get to the vicinity of the name I want feels, well, inefficient. Computerized Rolodexes and address books both give users this feeling.

To overcome this problem, contact managers often provide a fast-path facility in which the user can type letters like "S-E-G" and immediately reach the first name that begins with "Seg." This technique is an appealing form of magic, but it doesn't quite fit with address books and Rolodexes. The user looking at an address book sees an alphabetic tab for the letter "S" that entices him to pick that tab to find "Segovia." The user may not guess that typing two or three characters will lead progressively to a matching entry. The technique is ingenious, but it differs sufficiently from the base metaphor that it runs the risk of appearing to be inconsistent.

Perhaps a computerized contact manager should do away with index tabs. Does such a design depart too radically from the world of real contact managers? Or is there a real-world contact manager that has no index tabs, on which we could model the computerized version?

Absolutely. The simplest real-world metaphor is one that people carry on a sheet or two of paper—a *list* of names and contact information. If a list of names on a sheet of paper is too dreadfully mundane a metaphor, you may consider a fancier version of the metaphor—your local telephone book. Either way, the designer can spruce up the user interface with a little magic: the user can scroll a window over the list (continuously, and without artificial markers like the twenty-six letters of the alphabet); the user can search by typing "S-E-G" and the window will scroll farther as the user enters each letter; and selecting one name from the list can open a view of that individual's detailed contact information:

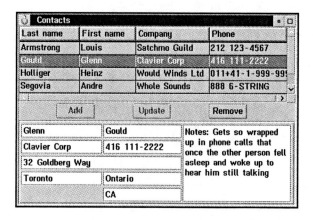

This user interface is unencumbered by superfluous index tabs that set expectations more appropriate for physical contact managers than computerized ones.

We have concentrated so far on the use case of searching for a name. Other essential use cases are adding a new entry, deleting an obsolete one, or altering an existing one. You may also have considered use cases like dialing a phone number, sending e-mail, or printing an envelope, or variations of the essential use cases such as copying or sharing contact information from another contact. Sooner or later, in a real design effort, you would have to walk through detailed versions of each of these use cases. You would find the challenge to be in balancing faithfulness to the metaphor you've chosen with the magic you need to make the computerized version more usable than its real counterpart.

Finally, can you as a UI designer articulate a coherent conceptual model to the prospective end user? This is a serious challenge. For example, the designer who wants to say that the conceptual model is a Rolodex or address book, and then adds multiletter, progressive searching, will have a tough time arguing for coherence. First, you must succeed in articulating a coherent conceptual model to yourself. Thinking back to model-view architectures (Chapter 11), a good place to begin is to imagine the model objects you would need.

Regardless of the UI metaphor you started with, it doesn't take long to concede that a **Person** or **Contact** class, and a suitable container to hold them, like a **Sorted-Collection**, are unavoidable. Rolodex and address-book UI designers also need a

Rolodex or **AddressBook** class, respectively. List or telephone-book UI designers quickly recognize that they will need a class that supplies the magical behavior for their views too. They might name this class **PaperList** or **TelephoneBook**. The striking result of all three approaches is that, regardless of the user interface metaphor, the model objects end up configured something like this:

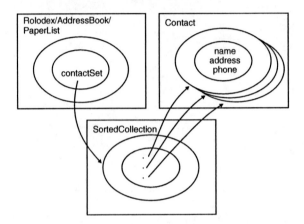

These model objects can service any of the three user interfaces—the three views. Any behavior beyond what a container like a **SortedCollection** can manage resides mainly in the **Rolodex/AddressBook/PaperList** class.

You have actually used this configuration of objects before, in the checking account exercise in Chapter 7. Compare the sketch here with the CRC cards illustrated on page 86. The resemblance is not coincidental; this configuration of objects solves many design problems. Recurring configurations like this are known as design patterns (Chapter 18).

Notice that this common conceptual model resembles address books and Rolodexes least. In fact, it's not very different from the paper-list metaphor. For one thing, the index tabs that are an artifact of the other metaphors and so strongly predispose users to search for and add names by tabbing to a specific letter, are absent. Because tabs don't intrude on a paper list, both it and the conceptual model are free of the biases with which magic multiletter progressive searching might clash. That the paper-list metaphor aligns so well with the conceptual model (they are *isomorphic*—see the next section) suggests that computerized lists may be desirable user interfaces for contact-management applications. The irony is that so many contact-manager user interfaces today look like address books and Rolodexes, in spite of the dissonance with the underlying conceptual model.

The sketch above is a satisfactory way for the user interface designer who knows about object-oriented programming to picture how the application fits together. It constitutes a coherent conceptual model. The same sketch can conjure up a coherent conceptual model for the user: the user can imagine a sophisticated main object that has a container of contacts. A conceptual model shared between user and designer—even one as simple as this sketch—is the essence of successful user interface design.

13.8   Isomorphism

The sharing of a conceptual model by user and designer is an example of isomorphism (from the Greek, *iso* = same, *morphism* = form). In a successful user interface, the user's and designer's conceputal models have the same form. If a user can learn the user interface quickly, this shared conceptual model is probably coherent too. This isomorphism is illustrated in the following picture, with the designer's thoughts at the left and the user's on the right:

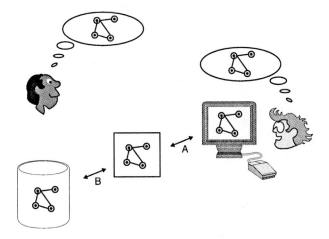

Once the product is out the door, the only way for the designer to convey the conceptual model to a user is through the user interface itself, represented by the monitor and mouse in the figure. (Manuals may be available, too, but they are getting smaller and becoming less of a factor.) Hence, the user interface had better also be isomorphic to the conceptual models of the designer and user.

Just as an isomorphism between user interface designer and user reduces mental translations, all other isomorphisms reduce mental translations. Thus, programmers benefit from an isomorphism (A in the picture) between the user interface and the programming language, and database designers benefit from an isomorphism (B in the picture) between the programming language and the database. Isomorphism A comes from an object-oriented language into which the programmer can translate the objects from the conceptual model. Isomorphism B comes from an object database system, into which the programming objects may be directly stored.

At least that is the theoretical ideal. Nowadays, all these isomorphisms are feasible—and desirable—except for the database isomorphism. The database solution for a problem is sometimes an object database, but the decision depends on a host of practical considerations: scalability, performance, distribution, transaction size and frequency, and the presence of legacy data. For example, in large-scale business problems, the database solution often necessarily involves an existing relational database management system.

Isomorphism brings us full circle, back to objects. Isomorphism means that the conceptual models of the user and designer have the same form; the user interface evokes this shared model; and the programming model and wistfully, the database model, are faithful to it. Metaphors help us impart our conceptual models to each other, but we cannot program in metaphors. So we use the universal language of objects to express our metaphors in a form that object-oriented programming can handle.

13.9 Summary

Designing a first-class user interface is orders of magnitude more difficult than most people think. If we had a prescription for success, many more of us would be great user interface designers, and many more great user interfaces would be on the market. Unfortunately, great user interfaces are rare. In particular, we have seen that they can appear only in conjunction with great overall designs. No user interface can compensate for a poorly designed application.

Although we have no prescription for success, we know of some considerations without which failure is certain. The user interface designer must:

• Construct coherent conceptual models.

• Identify and develop use cases.

• Apply metaphors wherever practical—to facilitate learning and use of the user interface or to describe conceptual models.

• Use magic judiciously, to go beyond the metaphors in ways that do not clash with them.

There is no special order to these steps. We have to do them all repeatedly before they converge to a product.

You practiced these steps in the exercise on page 151. Given enough time, you would study usability too: observing users at work; presenting crude early mockups of windows to them for their feedback; and, once working prototypes are available, measuring the time for them to complete tasks.

In real projects, the difficulty of user interface design, indeed application design, is compounded by the often conflicting requirements placed on the application by different groups of users. Each group does things in its own way, or deals with its own cross-section of the objects, or sees the business from its own standpoint. Conflicting conceptual models are all around. This cacophony of demands makes it even harder to produce a coherent overall conceptual model and a first-rate user interface.

For a comprehensive treatment of the problem of designing user interfaces, see the book by Dave Collins [Collins 1995], which amplifies the theme only touched upon here, namely that a good user interface design is inseparable from a good system design. For the pervasiveness of metaphor in human cognition, see [Lakoff and Johnson 1980]. For several excellent essays on metaphor in user interfaces, see [Laurel 1990]. Two essays in that volume that challenge the value of metaphor are [Nelson 1990] and [Kay 1990]. The former is a diatribe against excessive use of metaphor and the latter emphasizes magic in overcoming the limitations of metaphor.

We have seen conceptual models that are metaphors, or definitions, or pictures. Here is one final example, from Nobel physicist Richard Feynman's perspective on physical laws: "A philosophy, which is sometimes called an understanding of the law, is simply a way that a person holds the laws in his mind in order to guess quickly at consequences" [Feynman 1967]. His "philosophies" help physicists anticipate experimental outcomes in precisely the same sense that coherent conceptual models help computer users anticipate the behavior of applications. Feynman's "philosophies" are yet another kind of conceptual model.

This chapter concludes our three-chapter tour of user interfaces. We turn next to the essential subject of polymorphism.

CHAPTER 14

Polymorphism

One of object-orientation's most vital properties is *polymorphism*. Polymorphism increases the extensibility and clarity of object-oriented code. It influences object-oriented design so much that many authorities treat it as a fundamental object-oriented principle, alongside the objects, classes, and inheritance we discussed in Chapters 1 and 2.

Polymorphism relates to several other ideas, including *subtyping* (Chapter 17), *type-checking*, and *dynamic binding*. We begin with dynamic binding, which is an idea that makes sense in either object-oriented or non–object-oriented contexts.

14.1 Dynamic binding

Alan Kay observes that postponing a decision until the last possible moment is one of the most fruitful and characteristic trends in the evolution of computing [Kay 1993]. Examples of postponement in computing history include linkers, relocatable programs, and virtual memory. Another is *dynamic binding*, which postpones selection of an operation until execution time.

Most traditional languages, like Pascal and FORTRAN, don't support dynamic binding: if you write **foo(x)** in those languages, the compiler (or linker) determines the exact function **foo** to be executed, then *compiles* the directions to find that function. If the program has more than one function **foo**, the compiler uses the rules of the language to pick one. When the program eventually executes, that one runs.[1]

---

[1] The special situation in languages like C or Ada where the compiler can pick among functions with the same name but different argument types, such as **foo(3)** for integers and **foo("hi")** for strings, is known as overloading. This is not an example of postponement because the *compiler* distinguishes the two functions by examining the argument types, long before the function executes. Overloading is emphatically not dynamic binding.

Dynamically bound languages don't preordain the function that executes. Instead, the function is selected while the program is already running, from possibly many functions named **foo**. It is often impossible to select the function or method any earlier, as this example in Smalltalk, which is dynamically bound, illustrates.

```
aCondition
        ifTrue: [y := 3]
        ifFalse: [y := #(5 7 eleven)].
y printOn: someStream.
```

Smalltalk has numerous **printOn:** methods—classes often define their own **printOn:** method to customize the way in which instances print or display themselves in textual form. (Recall the exercise on rendering any object into text, on page 56.) If it happens that the "true" path executes, the **printOn:** that executes should be the one appropriate for **3**; that is, for class **Integer**. If the "false" path executes, it should be the one for #(5 7 eleven); that is, for class **Array**.

The Smalltalk compiler cannot preordain the choice, for it can't predict which branch will actually occur at execution time. This is dynamic binding—the ability to postpone selection of the specific **printOn:** method until execution time. The more interactive an application is, the more situations arise in which the compiler can't know the function in advance, and the more unavoidable such postponements are.

14.2   Dynamic binding enables...polymorphism

Newcomers commonly assume that dynamic binding must work by way of conditional code that selects among the candidate methods, and is necessarily slow. Not always. The presence of conditional code and the speed of method selection depend on how a particular language system—the compiler plus the runtime environment—implements dynamic binding. Today's Smalltalk implementations are fast, and the different technique that C++ employs is even faster. (We'll see in Chapter 16 how C++ gets this speed by foregoing conditional code entirely.)

Here is one way to do dynamic binding. This technique is sometimes used in non–object-oriented languages, but we will see that it is unsatisfactory for object-oriented ones. Suppose your application has a user interface that will show each item in a mailbox. The items or "objects" could be memos, spreadsheets, or documents. You could use a conditional statement like CASE, SELECT, or SWITCH, depending on your language:

```
case y.type of
   m : showMemo(y) |
```

```
    s : showSpread(y) |
    d : showDocum(y)
end;
```

This is Pascal, but the same style works in any language, as long as the "type" information is available along with the "object" at the time the program executes. In this example, the programmer would have to build and maintain the extra "type" field. Now, if you can do it in non–object-oriented languages, you can also do it in object-oriented ones. Moreover, in Smalltalk the type or class of **y** is readily available just by sending the message **y class**. Nonetheless, Smalltalk or not, this is an awful way to do dynamic binding, for the following reasons.

First, performance. On many computers, conditional branches, especially those with many cases, are slower than straight line code. (Branches are less of a drawback nowadays on most RISC computers, because they can pre-execute code ahead of a branch while they evaluate the branch condition.)

Second, and more serious, is an engineering drawback. Sooner or later you'll want to extend the application to accommodate other kinds of objects—changing and enhancing software is inevitable. Let's say graphics could now show up in the mailbox, too. You would have to alter the case statement to accommodate another case (**g : showGraphic**); that much is unavoidable. Furthermore, if the same case statement occurs elsewhere, for example to show the items in a file folder, each such occurrence must be repaired, too. But the case statement is much more insidious than that. Not only do you show items, but you are also likely to mail them, or print them, or save them, or execute or read them. These operations involve nearly the same case statement, each of which must be altered, too. Searching for and altering all those statements is tedious and error-prone.

We would like to avoid having to repair client code—the code that uses our spreadsheet and memo objects—every time we add a new kind of object to our library of reusable components. We are willing to concede that adding graphics objects necessitates new library code, namely the **Graphics** class, but we hope that client code can benefit from these new objects without incurring widespread alterations.

The solution to this problem in Smalltalk looks like this:

```
y showIt
```

That's all. If you now add a class of graphic objects to your application, this line of code doesn't change. If the line occurs at several points in the client code, none of those occurrences changes, either. And if a similar line of code occurs to mail, print, save, execute, or read objects, those occurrences don't change, either. We have liberated client code from conditionals and in so doing immunized it against a whole category of invasive alterations.

Does the conditional really disappear? You may suspect me of merely factoring the noxious conditionals out of the client code and into just one conditional hidden inside a single **showIt** method. That approach is indeed possible. But it makes for a complex **showIt** method and is still one error-prone conditional too many. It is unnecessary and undesirable.

Here's how the object-oriented design works without any conditional at all. There are really *several* methods, all with the same name, **showIt,** one for each class of objects we're interested in: spreadsheets, documents, graphics, and so on. By asking the variable y to **showIt,** we are really asking the object that happens to lurk under y to **showIt:**

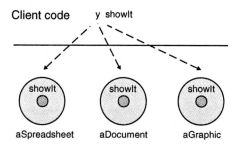

One of these objects lurks under y

Whatever kind of object that is, it responds directly with its *own* **showIt** method. There is no type testing and no branching. The running program doesn't even know what kind of object is there, and it doesn't care. It just trusts that the object understands **showIt.**

The fashionable name for this conditional-free style of programming is *polymorphism.* "Poly+morphism" is of Greek origin and means, "multiple+form." The variable y assumes "multiple forms," depending on the kind of object it happens to point to. Each kind of object administers its own **showIt** method, and so the response to the message y **showIt** effectively also assumes "multiple forms." Polymorphism—multiple forms—is a way to replace conditionals by classes, resulting in code that is easier to read and easier to modify.

14.3   A word on terminology

The concept of dynamic binding in object-oriented systems has two aspects: determining the object (and its type) and, having done so, looking up its chain of superclasses for the method. The latter often also goes, aptly and unambiguously, by the name *method lookup.* I use "dynamic binding" in the broadest and loosest sense, to cover both aspects. Many authors limit "dynamic binding" to one or the other; that is, either to type selection [Booch 1991] or method lookup [Meyer 1988; de Champeaux et al. 1993].

You can think of dynamic binding as a mechanism for postponing method selection, implemented in different ways by different object-oriented languages. Polymorphism, although it requires a dynamically bound language, is not a mechanism but a design technique for improving the clarity of our software. The relationship between polymorphism and dynamic binding is a striking example of the inseparability of design from implementation. You can't design polymorphically unless your language supports dynamic binding.

14.4   Exercise: polymorphism

❑ Suppose an importer wants to calculate the tariff on the motor vehicles she imports. Suppose her software must apply different calculations, depending on whether the vehicle is a truck or passenger car. What should the high-level design look like? Think of two designs.

14.5   Solutions and discussion

Solution 1. Define an abstract class **Vehicle**, and two concrete subclasses, **Truck** and **Car**. Define a method **Vehicle>>tariff** that does nothing. We called such a method "pure virtual" or or "subclassResponsibility" on page 64. Then define methods **Truck>>tariff** and **Car>>tariff** that apply the respective calculations for the two kinds of vehicles.

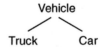

Solution 2. Define a class **Vehicle** with an instance variable named **type**. The method **Vehicle>>tariff** has the form:

```
type = 'truck'
        ifTrue: ["truck calculation"]
        ifFalse: ["car calculation"]
```

Object-oriented developers invariably think of the first solution first. People without object-oriented training, however, have recourse only to the second, which is actually not object-oriented. By now you know the drawback of solution 2: it is harder to maintain if and when other kinds of vehicles like motorcycles with different tariff calculations appear on the scene.

To summarize: The polymorphic, object-oriented design is extensible because the client code consists solely of:

```
v tariff
```

This line of code doesn't change, even if motorcycles are imported. Polymorphism uses classes instead of conditionals to solve the problem.

14.6 Exercise: Smalltalk's if-less-ness

Consider any code that sends the **ifTrue:ifFalse:** message, such as this sample:

```
X := ...

...
X ifTrue: ["true path"]
    ifFalse: ["false path"].
```

Think about the following questions without looking at any Smalltalk browsers. Then use a Smalltalk browser to verify your answers.

❑ In what class should the method **ifTrue:ifFalse:** be?

❑ What should the method **ifTrue:ifFalse:** do? In particular, should its code be conditional? And how many **ifTrue:ifFalse:** methods are there?

14.7 Solution

A plausible first guess for a class that implements **ifTrue:ifFalse:** is class **Boolean**. But the browser shows no such method:

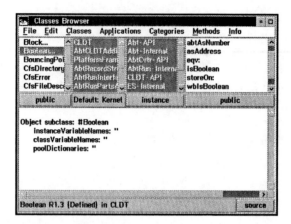

A closer look at class **Boolean**, however, reveals two subclasses named **True** and **False**. Examining class **True** first, we find among its methods an **ifTrue:ifFalse:**. Now, one might well expect to see some conditional code in the body of this method. But there is none:

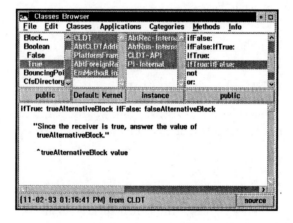

The evaluation of the "trueAlternativeBlock" is *unconditional*. That's because the receiver of the message, knowing itself to be the **true** object, has no need for the message's "falseAlternativeBlock." A **true** object ignores the false alternative and simply executes the true alternative.

Now, class **False** has a totally different method, albeit also named **ifTrue:ifFalse:**. The logic within *that* method unconditionally executes the "falseAlternativeBlock." After all, the **false** object knows full well that it has no need for the true alternative and summarily ignores it.

This situation seems paradoxical, at least on a superficial first glance. How can something as ostensibly conditional as a method named **ifTrue:ifFalse:** in fact execute no conditional code? The answer is exactly the same principle the **tariff** methods illustrated in the earlier exercise: subclasses can replace conditionals, as long as each subclass supports its own version of the method. Smalltalk just takes the principle radically far, down to the level of boolean objects.

14.8 Summary tip

As a rule of thumb, think twice about conditional statements in your code. Many of them may be opportunities for subclassing and polymorphism. "IF" statements disquiet object-oriented programmers. Unless you are certain never to expand them with additional cases, you should be as suspicious of them as as you are of the "GOTO" in conventional programming.

14.9 Commentary: performance

Performance is a peculiar topic. The things that people dispute heatedly and at great length are often the ones that matter least. Usually they are the things that are easy to measure—how many conditionals, how many levels of address indirection, a highly specialized benchmark, and so on.

What really matters—when static SQL can be an order of magnitude faster than dynamic SQL, or when searching a queue from the rear instead of the front can halve CPU time, or when a working set size exceeds virtual memory—isn't so easy to measure. Instead, these are matters for savvy design. The savvy designer grasps the problem at hand and has a mental arsenal of alternatives to apply to it, plus an intuition born of experience to weigh their trade-offs and anticipate which is best and by how much.

Keeping these caveats in mind, what are the performance implications of polymorphism in object-oriented languages? Its measurable effect reduces to the net of two opposing forces:

1 Fast: replacing conditionals by defining new subclasses.

2 Slow: method lookup. Looking up an inheritance hierarchy for the class that implements a method, no matter how fast, is still slower than calling a function whose location is known at compile time. The techniques that language implementors use to achieve acceptably fast lookup are covered in Chapter 16.

The danger with cold calculations of these forces is that they are likely to distract us from the main event. Polymorphism above all contributes to cleaner systems that are more mentally tractable. And designers can understand tractable systems and hypothesize ways to improve their performance. You can't write faster code unless you can understand it.

Benchmark experiments on early versions of the CHOICES operating system, developed in C++ at the University of Illinois, showed that it performed unfavorably against UNIX. A year later, benchmark results showed CHOICES to be consistently superior to UNIX. The developers cited two reasons for the improvement. The first was that performance bottlenecks were easy to fix because they were encapsulated—hardly a surprise, for encapsulation is the most flaunted of object virtues. The second was replacing conditionals by subclasses—polymorphism *can* improve performance.

14.10   Commentary: Smalltalk, C++, and type-checking

The expression *type-checking* means to try to detect occasions when an object is being used in circumstances that are appropriate only for objects of other types or classes. (Remember that we don't distinguish between the words *class* and *type*; that is, not until Chapter 17.) Sending a message to an object that doesn't understand it is a typical example of an error that object-oriented languages type-check:

```
Whale new + 2.71828
```

Because **Whale** instances do not understand arithmetic messages like + **2.71828**, Smalltalk will inform us of this type error with a walkback.

The type-checking rules in C++ and Smalltalk are quite different. Consider these Smalltalk statements:

```
R := Rectangle new.
T := Triangle new.
R := T.
```

Smalltalk variables like **R** and **T** point to objects. They have no allegiance to any specific type (class); they can point at one moment to an object of one type and at another moment to an object of a completely different type.

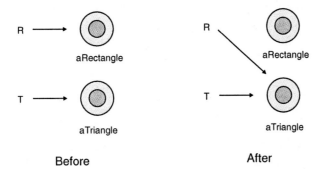

Before   After

The assignment statement **R := T** just switches **R** so that it too points to the triangle object. This is not a type error in Smalltalk.

Contrast this with the analogous situation in C++ (The assignment syntax in C++ is **r = t;**):

```
Rectangle *r;
Triangle *t;
...
r = t;
```

The C++ compiler, recognizing that variables **r** and **t** have been declared for different, presumably incompatible classes, detects right away that the assignment is an error. In effect, the type of object that a variable like **r** (or **t**) may point to is fixed once and for all by the compiler. Hence, any code that tries to use the variable for another type of object won't even compile.[2]

If you take this restriction literally—that C++ fixes the type of object that a variable can hold or point to—then you may wonder whether the polymorphic mailbox example illustrated on page 161 works in C++. In other words, you may worry that the variable **y** in **y showIt** (or in C++ syntax, **y->showIt();**) is constrained to just one kind of object. Fortunately not. In C++, if you declare **y** to be a pointer to objects of

---

[2] The C++ policy of detecting type mismatches early appeals to our instinct for safety. On the other hand, safety comes at a price. A program written in a language like Smalltalk where variables are untyped is quicker and easier to modify, and more flexible because its variables can accept more types of values. The debate for and against early type-checking is exhausting, emotional, endless, and rarely profitable to linger on. Suffice it to say that C++ and Smalltalk represent opposite poles in the debate, both with good reasons. Safety is important, and so too is flexibility.

type **T**, then the compiler will *also* allow **y** to point to objects of the subtypes of **T**! This is a remarkable, but intuitive and natural feature of the language. It says that it makes sense for a shape variable to refer to a rectangle object (or a triangle, or...). But the converse would be silly: to expect that a rectangle variable could refer to an object of any shape.

Similarly, an insect variable ought to be able to refer to any butterfly, but a butterfly variable ought not to be able to refer to an arbitrary insect. That's how object-oriented languages like C++ and Eiffel and Java work: a variable can point to objects of any of its subtypes, but it can't point to an object of its supertype(s).

Here's a concrete C++ example. First, declare rectangles and triangles to be subtypes of shapes, and (details omitted) supply various methods that override do-nothing methods in the shape superclass. These methods might calculate area or perimeter, for example.

```
class Rectangle : public Shape { ...
class Triangle : public Shape { ...
```

Next, declare variables of each of these types, and (details again omitted) make **r** and **t** point to a rectangle and triangle object:

```
Shape* s; Rectangle* r; Triangle* t;
...
```

Either of the following assignments is legitimate—an insect can refer to a butterfly:

```
if (...) s = r;
    else s = t;
```

On the other hand, an assignment like **r = s;** would be forbidden by the compiler—a butterfly can't refer to an arbitrary insect. Next, ask for the area of **s** with this message:

```
answer = s->area();
```

Which area method executes, the one for rectangles or the one for triangles? The right one. That is, assuming certain C++ niceties are observed in declaring **area**(), the area method for whatever **s** actually points to executes: if the conditional is true, then **s** points to a rectangle, and **Rectangle**'s **area**() executes; if the conditional is false, **s** points to a triangle, and **Triangle**'s **area**() executes.

That's how C++ supports polymorphism, as a compromise between the flexible dynamism of Smalltalk and the rigid safety of traditional type-checked languages. The same approach is used by other object-oriented languages—Eiffel, Java, Modula-3... —that oblige the programmer to declare types for variables. Smalltalk differs from all these because there is no way to declare a type for a Smalltalk variable; any variable can refer to any kind of object.

14.11   Commentary: the tomato in the mailbox

Suppose you're handling your postal mail. You discard the bulk mail, but you open your packages immediately. This is a fairly ordinary object-oriented problem. The polymorphic solution is to design a **Mail** supertype of both **Package** and **BulkMail** and write appropriate **handleMail** methods for each kind of mail. As we know, this solution sidesteps the need for runtime type testing ("if the object's type is **BulkMail**, then…").

You can't always sidestep runtime type testing, however. Suppose you find something in your mailbox that isn't an instance of a subtype of **Mail**, say a garden-fresh tomato from your neighbor. Does *this* problem have a polymorphic solution?

In C++, the answer is no. Polymorphism works only for types that share a supertype. Other than inventing an artificial supertype of both **Mail** and **Tomato**, your only recourse is for your program to ascertain at execution time that the object is a tomato and not mail, then send it a valid **Tomato** message. This difficulty motivated the ANSI C++ committee to add runtime type testing to the C++ standard. (See [Lea 1992] for practical uses of this feature.)

Contrast the situation with Smalltalk. Polymorphism works for tomatoes and mail, even though they are in unrelated parts of the class hierarchy. In other words, if you write a **Tomato>>handleMail** method that eats the tomato, client code like **y handleMail** works fine, whether **y** points to a package or a tomato. The Smalltalk variable **y** isn't constrained to any specific type(s). The Smalltalk developer doesn't need runtime type testing to solve this problem.

We can describe the polymorphism that Smalltalk supports—and C++ doesn't— as *implicit* polymorphism. People also refer to it variously as *ad hoc, signature-based,* or *apparent* polymorphism. This is a concept on which the terminologists have not yet had their last word. Implicit polymorphism is polymorphism that works for types of objects that may not share supertypes; explicit type relationships aren't necessary. It's polymorphism *across* type hierarchies instead of *within* type hierarchies.

Ordinary polymorphism—polymorphism within explicit hierarchies—is sometimes called *inclusion* polymorphism. The rules for any variant of polymorphism amount to the way in which a language determines whether it is okay to substitute instances of one class for instances of another. These rules have to do with measuring consistency between classes, a matter I'll tell you more about in Chapter 17.

To sum up, C++ supports only inclusion polymorphism, while Smalltalk supports both inclusion and implicit polymorphism. Where implicit polymorphism is necessary, the C++ developer reverts to runtime type testing. Thus, the need for runtime type testing is greater in C++ than in Smalltalk because of the absence of implicit polymorphism in C++. Ironically, Smalltalk makes runtime type testing easy (send any object the message **class**), but requires it less often. In any language, you should use runtime type tests sparingly. (Again, see [Lea 1992].) They are apt to introduce hard-to-maintain conditionals and are antithetical to the object-oriented style of programming.

❑   To emphasize this point one final time, decide whether this sample use of runtime type testing is desirable (Hint: it is not.) and what you would do to rectify it:

```
mailbox do: [ :m |

                m class = BulkMail
                        ifTrue: [ m discard].
                m class = Package
                        ifTrue: [ m open].
                m class = Tomato
                        ifTrue: [ m eat]

        ]
```

14.12   Commentary: multi-methods

Sometimes, the orthodox object model is not enough. For some problems, it is just awkward to conceptualize the solution as a method on an object. Sometimes a behavior involves two peer objects, and neither one particularly merits having sole responsibility for the behavior. For example, why model a dancing couple by writing a method on one favored partner that accepts the other partner as an argument? Wouldn't it be more natural to write a *multi-method* on both partners? Of course, there is no such thing as a multi-method in most object-oriented languages, including Smalltalk. The only commercial language with multi-methods is CLOS. What then do you do instead when confronted with this kind of problem?

The answer is a technique first published by Dan Ingalls [Ingalls 1986]. First, designate one of the dancers, say **x**, as a preferred target. Send it the message **dance: y**, passing along the other object, **y**, as an argument. Now, **x** will need the help of behavior on **y**, and so it redispatches a message **danceX: x** to **y** to invoke this behavior, passing itself as an argument, as illustrated here:

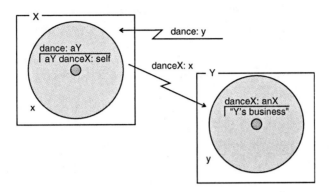

Note that we allow the two dancers to belong to different classes. Nothing prevents two disparate dancers from dancing, for example if **X** is **BalletDancer** and **Y** is **Swing-Dancer**. Also, don't overlook the significance of passing **self** as an argument to **y**: not only is **y** getting control, but **y** is getting full access to **x**. Thus, the objects **x** and **y** are as intimate as object-orientation lets two objects be.

Now, none of this discussion so far has a very polymorphic feel; it only conveys a strong sense of alternation of control, plus object-oriented intimacy. Polymorphism happens when we let a variable range over objects of different types, and we haven't considered that possibility yet. So let's add some variability. We could let either **x** or **y** vary, but to make things interesting, we'll let them both vary. We must then generalize the preceding sketch:

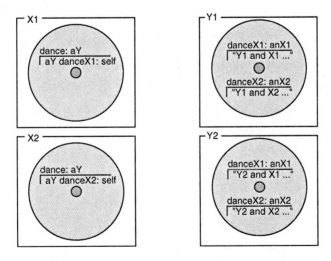

The message flow is the same as before—it starts with **x dance: y** and proceeds with a redispatch to **y** of a message of the form **danceX: x**. Only now we see four variations in which this dance may play out. But the implementation uses *no* conditional statements! We have an example of *multiple polymorphism*, where both the receiving variable **x** and the argument variable **y** are independently polymorphic, because either can refer to an instance of two classes.

Because the alternation of control resembles what occurs in a classical pas de deux, where the dancer and ballerina take turns upstaging each other, I call this object-oriented arrangement a *pas de deux* or a *duet*. But the name that occurs most often in the literature is *double dispatch*. By whatever name, this arrangement occurs widely in object-oriented systems, and is discussed again as a pattern in Chapter 18.

As a final aside, let's contrast multi-methods with the runtime type testing discussed earlier. Because C++ has traditional functions as well as methods, we could use a function of the form **dance(x, y)**, thereby more faithfully portraying the symmetry between the two real-world dancers. And because the C++ standard supports runtime type testing, this **dance** function can consist of if-statements like:

```
if ((BalletDancer*)(x) && (SwingDancer*)(y)) wild_combo(x, y);
```

which means, "if **x** is a ballet dancer and **y** is a swing dancer, then have them dance a wild combo." We would add a similar if-statement for every combination of dancer types that we cared about. This technique is an alternative to the double dispatch solution of dancing outlined above.

The symmetry of the function **dance(x, y)** in this approach is more attractive than double dispatch, which depends strongly on arbitrarily favoring one partner or the other. The runtime type tests, however, expose maintenance programmers to the instabilities of conditional code, which we have sought to avoid throughout this chapter. Moreover, the symmetric solution is not even possible in Smalltalk. Smalltalk has methods only. Therefore we must designate one dancer or the other as the primary object to carry the dance responsibility.

CHAPTER 15

Practicing polymorphism

Understanding polymorphism, which was our purpose in Chapter 14, is not as valuable as being good at applying it. This chapter is an opportunity for you to design an object-oriented, polymorphic solution to a real problem. This is the problem of undoing a user's actions. First, we need an application.

15.1   Design exercise I: a shape editor

Consider a simple application that lets the user create, move, or remove shapes. The kinds of shapes won't affect the overall design much, so let's agree to limit them to circles and squares. This application is a foundation for many families of commercial applications—graphical editors and simulators, network management tools, CASE tools, and video games.

❏ Use CRC cards to brainstorm about the essential classes and their responsibilities. Brainstorming works best as a social act, in a group of two to four peers. Hints:

  • Stick to the model. In other words, don't worry about the look and feel, or "view," of the application. This is largely an exercise in disciplining yourself to prevent the user interface from influencing your design. Design only the essential underlying classes—those which will work with any view at all.

  • Don't forget that container objects are ubiquitous in the everyday world, and are therefore likely to insinuate themselves into even a small design like this one.

  • If you find fewer than three classes, you definitely don't have enough to describe the application in an object-oriented way. If you can't find enough classes, try resorting to the trick of looking for nouns and verbs in the problem statement. Nouns may signify objects and verbs may signify responsibilities.

- Finding too many classes is just as undesirable. If you find more than about six, you're probably obscuring the essence of the design.

15.2   Solution and discussion

I will discuss the ideas that students typically try as they work toward a solution, following the same order in which they try them.

The most obvious CRC cards are ones for **Circle** and **Square** objects. It is also not much of a stretch to anticipate that an abstract superclass named **Shape** might be handy for gathering common expectations of circles and squares. For example, if we expect both circles and squares to be capable of movement, we can record that responsibility in the **Shape** class. Imagining further how we might eventually move a shape, we might even allow for an instance variable that captures the position of each shape instance. Our CRC cards would now resemble:

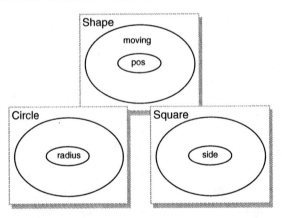

Instance variables specific to **Circle** and **Square** appear on their respective cards.[1] Because the application is supposed to "create, move, or remove" shapes, it is tempting to add "creating" and "removing" responsibilities to the **Shape** "doughnut" above; almost everyone considers this. However, I advise against adding either one, for these reasons:

---

[1] Orthodox use of CRC cards does not plunge to the level of instance variables. I use them here to indicate the way toward implementation a little further than is customary.

First, creating an object is not the object's responsibility. An object that doesn't exist yet can hardly create itself. Rather, as we have seen, creation is a responsibility of the object's class, by means of something like a **new** method. It is fine to write down this responsibility for creation, but not on the doughnut that represents an instance. Write it somewhere else, like the upper-right corner of the card, or the reverse side.

Second, writing "removes itself" on the **Shape** doughnut (or the **Circle** or **Square** doughnut) is disagreeable for two reasons. First, you are metaphorically asking the object to commit suicide, and programming objects don't want to do that any more than real objects do. Second, the expression "remove itself" implies a place from which the object is to be removed—remove it from *where*? We need to put our finger on this place.

According to the second hint, we need a container object. If you remove flowers, you remove them from a vase; if you remove books, you remove them from a library, or a bookshelf. What shall we call the container that holds our shapes? A common but undesirable answer is **Window**. A window suggests a user interface, and we do not want our design to be biased by user interface or view considerations. We want to emphasize the model aspects, so we need a more neutral word. I suggest **ShapeRoom**; you can probably do better, but **ShapeRoom** is good enough for us to proceed.

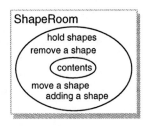

This container for the shapes is a handy place for recording several responsibilities: holding shapes, removing them, adding them, even moving them. The CRC card for this class now looks like the one on the right. This class is a talented container; it supports ordinary container-like responsibilities, but also somewhat more, like moving shapes within it. It does what we would expect of a shape editor; **ShapeEditor** could well be another name for it. An instance of this class—a model—will process messages from the user interface—a view.

Notice that the instance variable named **contents** suggests how **ShapeRoom** will fulfill its container-like obligations: this instance variable should refer to an instance of class **OrderedCollection**, or perhaps **Set**. In other words, a **ShapeRoom** buys an ordinary Smalltalk collection to hold its shape objects.

Also notice that "moving" appears on the card for **ShapeRoom** as well as the card for **Shape**. A **ShapeRoom** receives a message to move a specific shape to a specific point. The method in **ShapeRoom** that performs this function in turn sends a message to the specific shape to move itself to the specified point. This arrangement isn't unusual—a high-level move method on **ShapeRoom** collaborates with a lower-level one on **Shape** to get its job done.

Next, let's take a moment to review the topic of the previous chapter, polymorphism. Consider the presentation of the shapes on the user interface. This is nominally a responsibility of the view classes that I said we would not design here. Nevertheless, model classes must cooperate by making information about themselves available to view classes. We can call this responsibility of shapes "rendering." Each kind of shape will render itself in a way appropriate for itself; hence we should expect circles to render themselves differently than squares would. A view will not know or care whether a shape is a square or circle; it will simply trust the shape to render itself acceptably.

Thus, class **Circle** and **Square** will each have a method named, say, **render**, and class **Shape** will have a subclassResponsibility method with the same name. **Shape>>render** documents the obligation of each subclass to support rendering, but itself does nothing. As the application evolves, and additional classes of shapes emerge, each will require its own **render** method. In other words, shapes are polymorphic. Here, as in the examples of the last chapter, client code, in this case a view, will not be affected by introducing new classes of shapes.

15.3   Design exercise II: undo and redo

Now that we have an application, this simple shape editor, we want to make the user's actions undoable. *Undo* means reverting an interactive application to an earlier state. An application with strong undo support motivates users to explore unfamiliar features and provisional streams of thought because they know they can always revert to their point of departure if things turn out badly. If an application also lets its users *redo* what they've undone, so much the better. A few years ago it was unusual for interactive applications to support undo, let alone redo. Today, the opposite is true: almost all new applications support undo, albeit to varying degrees. But once you have been spoiled by an application with unlimited undo-redo, anything less is an anachronism.

❑ Design an enhancement to the shape editor that lets the user undo any number of his most recent actions. If possible, brainstorm with CRC cards and a small group of peers. Hints:

- A good object-oriented solution will handle multiple undos as well as it handles one undo. You might as well aim for unlimited undo. Don't get sidetracked into worrying about redo yet. After you solve unlimited undo, unlimited redo is a small extension.

- As always, if you have trouble getting started, look for nouns and verbs. They are especially telling in this problem.

- Four to seven classes is a good range for describing the solution. The number depends on the original application. It therefore pays to review the shape-editor exercise.
- You will need another appropriate container class.

15.4 Solution and discussion

The solution is an object-oriented classic; it also works for other interactive applications. It appeared early in the 1980s in the MacApp framework for Object Pascal developers, and proliferated thereafter. It has even achieved the status of a design pattern (Chapter 18).

The key to discovering the solution is the clause, "undo...actions" in the problem statement. Here, "actions" is a noun (!), and nouns are always plausible aspirants for objects. The verb "undo" then looks like a promising responsibility of an action object—actions should know how to undo themselves. Once you accept this much, unorthodox as it may at first seem, you have little choice but to sketch a card like the one on the right.

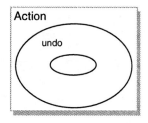

The trouble is that an action is a pretty nebulous idea, and so this card isn't very satisfying. That's where the original, concrete problem comes in. The shape editor had exactly three functions: create, move, and remove. Each of these is an action that the user may want to undo. That gives us three kinds of undoable actions or, in other words, three subclasses of **Action**. This is a perfect setup for an abstract class and three concrete subclasses:

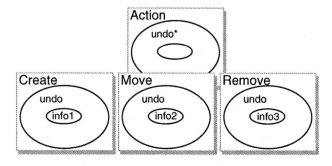

* = pure virtual, subclassResponsibility

info2 = information needed to undo myself (a move)

Undoing is a subclassResponsibility of the superclass—it does nothing—but a concrete responsibility of the three subclasses, each of which carries it out in its own way. They will retain any information (in the form of instance variables) they need to carry out their mission. For example, the only way a **Move** object can have the wherewithal to undo itself is if it knows the shape instance being moved and the position from which it came. Thus the information inside the **Move** instance pictured above consists at least of instance variables representing a shape and the shape's original position. (Look for these instance variables when you work with the code in the next section.)

To understand the life cycle of these action objects, imagine a sample scenario: move a circle, then move it again, then undo both moves. Each move will result in a separate instance of the **Move** class. These two instances must be stored in order, then recalled and undone in reverse order. A container of some kind is evidently needed, and because of the order reversal, a stack seems eminently suitable. Thus whenever the application moves the circle, it instantiates a **Move** object and pushes it onto the stack. When the user calls for one or more undo's, the application pops the **Move** objects off the stack one by one, and asks them to undo themselves. The **Move** objects are able to comply because they know the circle and its previous position. Summing up the design:

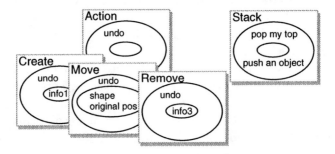

One loose end remains: how do you attach this design to the design of the original editor? Not much changes. The implementation of the "move a shape" responsibility of **ShapeRoom** must now instantiate a **Move** object and push it onto the stack. Similarly, the "add" and "remove" responsibilities of **ShapeRoom** instantiate **Create** and **Remove** objects, respectively, and push them onto the stack. **ShapeRoom** gets one additional responsibility, "undo." **ShapeRoom** carries out its "undo" responsibility by popping the top action from the stack, whatever the action may be, and asking it to undo itself.

Notice the implications of the clause, "whatever the action may be:" this is another polymorphic design. The room doesn't know and doesn't care whether the popped action is an instance of **Create, Move,** or **Remove.** For that matter, the room doesn't care what kinds of actions reside anywhere in the stack; it trusts only that they know how to respond to requests to undo themselves. Even if you should later extend the application with additional kinds of actions, the room won't care—not one jot of its code changes. This is an archetypal example of polymorphism's value.

Inexperienced designers usually feel tricked that something so verb-like as "move" turns out to be an object. Sometimes they feel that the solution is contrived. After all, in the original shape editor, "move" was a responsibility—more akin to a method than an object. That analysis remains correct and valid. It's simply irrelevant for the present problem—the undo problem has only a superficial relationship to the editor problem. The editor problem was about manipulating shapes, and so we designed shape objects. The undo problem is about manipulating actions, so we design action objects. Because actions are at the heart of the problem, they become the leading candidates for classes. The problem has shifted from shapes to actions, and the designer's attention had better shift along with it.

Finally, remember that real designs proceed in fits and starts and rarely arrive smoothly at a neat conclusion. Thus, a team of designers working on this problem for the first time should have hit a few dead ends and scratched out and discarded quite a few CRC cards along the way. Good design derives from failure.

15.5   Implementing undo

❑ Build a stack class named **StackBuy** by buying from class **OrderedCollection**. If the stack is empty, make **pop** return the **nil** object. If necessary, review the stack designs on page 100. Test **StackBuy** until you are confident that it works correctly.

❑ Build a stack class named **StackInherit** by inheriting from class **OrderedCollection**. Ideally, **StackInherit** and **StackBuy** should behave identically. That is, although their internals differ, a user or client shouldn't know the difference. (But remember the tradeoffs discussed on page 102. In Smalltalk, some behavioral differences are unavoidable.) Test **StackInherit** also.

❑ The code you are about to work with requires application **CwExamples** to be in your image. IBM provides this application with either the Standard or Professional product. (If you are using the Professional version and it does not appear in your Application Manager, pick the menu options *Applications > Available*, then select the **CwExamples** application. *Load* the most recent edition.)

❑ Obtain the file **student.aps** from http://www.claritycomputing.com/books/sod/files. This code implements a working shape editor, except that the undo feature is broken. File in the code by following these steps:

- Start from an Application Manager.
- Select any application. It doesn't matter which; any selection will activate the menus you'll need.
- Pick menu option *File In*.
- In the dialogue box, locate and select the file **student.aps**, and push *OK*.

❑ Select the application **ShapesApp**, double-click on it to expose its subapplications, and select and browse the subapplications **ShapesModels**, **ShapesUndoSupport**, and **ShapesViews**. Answer these questions:

- What are the names of the two main methods in the action classes? Read their code to reassure yourself that they are simple yet will do the job.
- What class and method instantiates a **Move** object? A **Remove** object? A **Create** or **Add** object?
- Why does **Move** have a third instance variable representing the target position?

❑ Try the class method **example** in both **TextualView** and **GraphicalView**. What is the problem? Fix it, using class **Stack** in the **ShapesUndoSupport** application.

❑ Verify that your own stacks, **StackBuy** and **StackInherit**, also fix the problem.

15.6 Summary

Most object-oriented solutions to this problem use the name **Command** instead of **Action**. By either name, this is one of the most exquisite applications of polymorphism in object-oriented design.

The solution is recognized as a design pattern, also called *Command* (page 217). Two noteworthy characteristics of the pattern:

1 *Small size.* The solution required dozens, not hundreds of lines of code.

2 *Minimal memory.* The application stores only the information indispensable for undoing (or redoing) an action. In many cases, like moving, this information amounts to just a few words of storage. By contrast, the non–object-oriented alternative that some people consider—saving the entire state of the application upon every action—consumes machine resources so rapidly as to render multi-level undo impractical.

This chapter completes your study of the object-oriented essentials. The rest of the book pushes into areas which beginners rarely see, but are part of the mental landscape of experienced Smalltalk developers.

CHAPTER 16

How object-oriented languages work

This is the first chapter in which we venture past the essential object-oriented principles. We begin by dealing with how object-oriented languages actually work, deep down inside. We will see that the look and feel of a language is shaped by these inner workings.

At one end of the spectrum is Smalltalk, noted for its incremental development style, its handling of memory concerns for the programmer, and its reflectiveness. (*Reflectiveness* or *reflection* is a software system's ability to examine and modify itself on the fly.) These are all consequences of a runtime engine, also called the Smalltalk virtual machine, which controls execution of every message and monitors computing resources.

At the other extreme, C++ relies on a conventional compile, link, and execute cycle. It is faster at runtime than Smalltalk and it links readily to foreign languages, but the price is a sluggish development feeling and memory bugs that sorely test a programmer's mettle.

You don't need to know the content of this chapter to program in Smalltalk or C++, but knowing it will go a long way toward explaining why your language and its environment behave as they do.

16.1 Virtual machines

A *virtual machine* is a synthetic computer. It behaves as a real machine would, if only there were such a machine. Because there isn't, people use a virtual machine to emulate the one they wish they really had. Virtual machines are interesting only because of what they execute. For a Smalltalk virtual machine, that something is called the *image*.

The image consists of all the objects in your computer, both the ones you create and the ones Smalltalk already provides.

Because "everything is an object," the image contains unusual objects like *compiled methods*. That is, whenever you write and compile a Smalltalk method, Smalltalk's compiler produces an instance of the class **CompiledMethod**. Each of these objects consists of *bytecodes*, which are the machine instructions that the virtual machine knows how to execute.

A running Smalltalk system therefore consists of these two pieces of software—a virtual machine running on your underlying computer hardware plus an image running bytecodes on the virtual machine. This is really a familiar notion cloaked in a fancy name. An interpreter—a BASIC interpreter, or a Pascal p-code interpreter—is also a virtual machine. Instead of executing the bytecodes in a Smalltalk image, it executes some other language, like BASIC or p-code. Sometimes people even refer to the Smalltalk virtual machine as the Smalltalk interpreter.

The difference between Smalltalk's virtual machine and other, simpler virtual machines (or interpreters) is sophistication. The Smalltalk virtual machine does more than merely execute one bytecode after another. It also manages processing and memory resources, much as a full-blown operating system does.

By the way, one side-effect of this arrangement, or of any arrangement based on a virtual machine, is a technique for transporting applications between computer architectures. If Smalltalk runs on one computer architecture, we ought to be able to make it run on another by rewriting only the virtual machine. The image should run as well on one virtual machine as another. The industry's early learning experience with Smalltalk came about in just this fashion. Early in the 1980s, Xerox PARC released the Smalltalk-80 image, along with the specification for its virtual machine, so that any computer manufacturer could run Smalltalk-80 on their own hardware, merely by writing a virtual machine. In those days a basic virtual machine implementation could be built in about one programmer-year.

The situation is a little more complicated today because many modern images contain objects that are specific to the underlying operating system or windowing manager. These objects exploit specific features of the platform, and their presence guarantees that the image cannot simply be moved to other platforms. IBM Smalltalk overcomes this difficulty by encapsulating these platform-specific objects under a layer of objects that is standard across all its platforms. As we saw in Chapter 12, the layer for user interface objects resembles the Motif standard. The layer for file-system objects resembles another UNIX standard, known as POSIX.1. IBMSmalltalk code that adheres to these standards is then portable from platform to platform.

Smalltalk-80, now known as VisualWorks, preserves the old tradition best: its virtual machine encapsulates all of the underlying platform; this arrangement decouples the image from the platform. Smalltalk-80 images are therefore highly portable. But because they are oblivious to platform-specific widgets, user interfaces don't have the look and feel of the platform they are running on. (ParcPlace-Digitalk has stated its intent to base its combined VisualWorks/VisualSmalltalk offering on the Smalltalk-80 virtual machine.)

16.2   Method lookup

Method lookup, also called *method dispatch,* selects the right method to execute among all the methods in an object's class and superclasses. Smalltalk's virtual machine performs this task by way of a component known as the *message handler* (or *dispatcher*).

At the moment of each message, and no sooner, the message handler decides which method the virtual machine should execute. It cannot, as conventional compiled languages can, decide the method at compilation time. In fact, Smalltalk is such a dynamic system that Smalltalk code could modify methods, or add or remove them, at any time, even immediately prior to executing them. Thus, any message can potentially affect the environment of classes and methods in which subsequent messages execute. Conventional languages can't do this; it would be akin to recompiling and relinking changes to your program in the midst of executing it.

Now, one proposal for handling this last-minute lookup could be to store a dictionary of method pointers for each object, as illustrated here for an object of class **Point**:

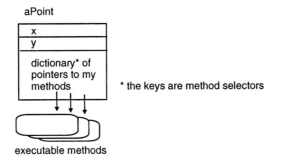

This hypothetical dictionary must be constructed carefully: if a method occurs in both a superclass and subclass, the dictionary entry should point to the overriding one in the subclass.

To resolve a message to this point instance, the message handler locates the message's selector among the dictionary's keys and executes the associated method. This proposal doesn't solve the prickly matter of messages to the special variable **super**, which breach the normal lookup and may access overridden methods.

Moreover, this proposal imposes unnecessary bloat on every object. It burdens an object as lean as a point with pointers to all the methods of **Point** and its superclass **Object**. That's many dozens of pointers, and they are all repeated over and over for each of possibly multitudinous point instances in an application. Clearly unacceptable. To remedy this problem, Smalltalk arranges matters in the following uniform way. (This is only a conceptual picture—the actual details vary between Smalltalk dialects. IBM Smalltalk for example conforms to the spirit but not the letter of this picture.)

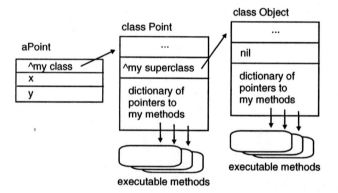

Each instance has just a pointer to its class. The class (**Point**) carries a dictionary of its (instance) methods, plus a pointer to its superclass (**Object**), which in turn carries a dictionary of its own (instance) methods. If there are more layers of classes in the hierarchy, the pattern repeats: each class object carries its own dictionary of methods, plus a pointer to its superclass. The dispatcher merely chases through the chain of dictionaries until it finds the method it seeks. If the method is absent from all the dictionaries, the familiar "does not understand" walkback appears. Notice the flexibility: the methods and the dictionaries may be altered at any time; the dispatcher dutifully chases through the current chain of dictionaries no matter how recently such alterations have occurred.

This approach minimizes storage consumption—each point carries its own private instance variables, plus one pointer to its class. But its performance is suspect—iterative searches up the chain would be intolerably slow. Smalltalk therefore resorts to two venerable performance tricks, caching and hashing. Hashing is a way to place each entry in a table at a magic offset that can be computed ("hashed") directly from the entry. Because every entry then resides at a predictable offset, table lookups can proceed directly by computing the offset at which an entry ought to reside. If the entry isn't at the offset, it isn't in the table. (I've oversimplified a little—hashing algorithms also have to handle the potential for collisions when the magic offset computed for two different entries is the same.) Because Smalltalk dictionary objects are designed with hashed lookups, instead of more naive binary or sequential lookups, search times are nothing like our worst fears.

Actually, searching through the method dictionaries is rarely necessary. Because a message that occurs once tends to recur in the near future, Smalltalk maintains a cache of recently sent messages, and the dispatcher looks in this cache first before beginning the laborious search up the superclass chain. The effect of a method cache is sizable. According to [Krasner 1984], an appropriate method cache can have hit ratios as high as 95 percent, decrease method lookup time by a factor of 9, and improve overall system speed by 37 percent.

Method lookup in C++ works without any kind of engine or dispatcher. It still relies on a table, called a *virtual function table* or *v-table*, for each class. But these tables are simply lists of pointers, not dictionaries with powerful lookup facilities as in Smalltalk. Imagine a music synthesizer application, where **Piano** and **Oboe** are concrete subclasses of the abstract class **Instrument**, and all instruments support methods (*virtual functions* in C++ parlance) to tune themselves (to some intonation and pitch) and to play (a note). The v-table for **Piano** looks like this:

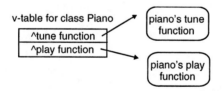

When the C++ compiler encounters a message to tune a piano (**piano->tune()** in C++ notation), it generates code to execute the function found by the first pointer in the v-table. If it encounters **piano->play()**, it generates code to execute the function found by the second pointer. The v-table is stable; unlike in Smalltalk, there is no prospect of introducing or removing methods at execution time. Thus, this generated code is unconditional; the compiler determines once and for all the location of the function to be executed. No dispatcher ever gets involved.

So far, this table is fairly unremarkable. The oboes, however, make life interesting. For **Oboe** also has a v-table, and it has exactly the same structure as **Piano**'s. That is, its first pointer points to the tune function for oboe and the second points to the play function for oboe. The compiler carefully builds all v-tables for subclasses of **Instrument** in this parallel way.

Now consider a polymorphic variable **instrument**, which could point to *either* a piano or an oboe.

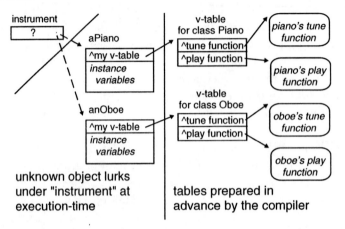

unknown object lurks
under "instrument" at
execution-time

tables prepared in
advance by the compiler

Which of the two play functions executes in response to a message of the form **instrument->play()**? The *right* one. The C++ compiler, knowing that **Oboe** and **Piano** are subclasses of **Instrument**, has crafted the two v-tables to have a parallel structure—the function pointers are in the *same* order in both tables. When the compiler encounters the expression **instrument->play()**, it unconditionally generates code to execute the method found by the *second* pointer in the table—even though it is quite unable to anticipate what kind of object **instrument** will point to when the code eventually executes. If the object turns out to be a piano, the second pointer points to piano playing; if the object turns out to be an oboe, the second pointer points to oboe playing. Either way, the second pointer is the right one, and the appropriate function will execute.

Let's recapitulate the two salient points about method dispatch in C++: it works flawlessly without a runtime engine, and the executing code is free of conditionals. All else being equal, you should expect C++ programs to run much faster than Smalltalk programs. All else is rarely equal in the real world, though, and performance is never this simple.

As one example, two of my friends—one partial to C++ and the other to Smalltalk—got into a dispute about speed and settled it by benchmarking a loop of method dispatches. To the chagrin of my C++ friend, the Smalltalk code was just as fast. The reason? They happened to be using a 16-bit operating system in which the v-tables were in a different memory segment than the objects. As a result, segmentation faults occurred on every function call, and this overhead swamped the speed benefit of the v-table scheme. This is an unusual example, but it illustrates an important performance principle, namely that astute programming almost always matters more than the programming language does.

Performance aside, here are other by-products of the method lookup implementations we've been discussing. *Reflection*, Smalltalk's ability to examine and fundamentally alter its own semantics while it is executing, is impossible in the traditional compile, link, and execute world of C++. Moreover, the instantaneous (re)compilation of a Smalltalk method—Smalltalk's exploratory development gestalt—is possible precisely because the runtime engine decouples the calling of methods from their compilation. The Smalltalk programmer can compile messages at will, and not worry whether methods exist to respond to them until the instant before they're called.

By contrast, adding or removing a C++ method requires recompilation of potentially many v-tables to preserve their parallel structure. And although we know that polymorphic client code does not need to be rewritten, it must still be *recompiled* to account for new offsets to the pointers in the tables. This recompilation overhead discourages exploratory programming. On the other hand, C++ cooperates readily with foreign languages, while Smalltalk's runtime engine gets in the way of calling into or out of the Smalltalk image.

16.3 Memory management: a brief history of garbage collection

A Smalltalk programmer doesn't manage storage for her objects. In particular, when she's done with an object, she doesn't worry about reclaiming the memory occupied by the object. Instead, a component of the virtual machine known as the *garbage collector* monitors memory and ascertains when it can safely reclaim the memory occupied by an object.

Consider this question: how many point objects are present in your Smalltalk system? The answer is easy to determine. I can count them by *displaying*:

```
Point allInstances size
```

The answer on my system at this moment is *13*. If I allocate a new point:

```
X := Point new
```

and count again, I get one more, *14*. If I now *execute*:

```
X := 'Casablanca'
```

the global variable **X** refers to a string instead of the point. The point has been orphaned—although it was once accessible through the variable **X**, it is now completely inaccessible—and is therefore eligible for garbage collection. If I count again, Smalltalk reports *13*, the original number of points. The garbage collector has reclaimed the memory occupied by the newest point. Here is the progression of events:

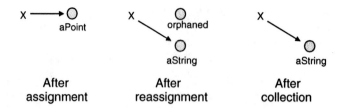

Garbage collection in Smalltalk contrasts sharply with memory management in C++ and many other compiled languages that permit a program to acquire chunks of memory while it executes. Because C++ has no garbage collector, the programmer must carefully and explicitly reclaim an object's storage at the appropriate moment. The dangers of entrusting this responsibility to the programmer are well known: freeing an object's memory too soon invites another object into the space, corrupting the original object's data. And failing to free memory soon enough exposes the program to running out of room for additional memory allocations. These are among programming's most nightmarish bugs; they often manifest themselves as catastrophic crashes that occur well after the event, considerably complicating debugging.

On the other hand, a garbage collector is a program that runs continually, consumes CPU cycles, and, being beyond the programmer's control, can become especially active at inopportune moments. Critics observe that an airplane's control system or a nuclear power plant's monitoring system can ill-afford to pause while a garbage collector decides to shift into high gear. The traditional debate goes like this:

- Pro: Only a garbage collector can safeguard against application crashes induced by subtle and inevitable errors in memory design.

- Con: Only a programmer can fine-tune memory management for high-performance applications. In particular, a garbage collector's sporadic intensification makes it unacceptable for real-time software.

Next, by examining how garbage collectors work, we will gain insight into the lives and deaths of objects. This is a useful study regardless of your position in the (endless) debate on the merits of garbage collection.

Most early garbage collectors, prior to the mid-1980s, were variants of either *mark-and-sweep* or *reference-counting* collectors. A mark-and-sweep collector makes two passes through memory. The first pass begins at one or more *anchor* objects that the virtual machine knows it needs (like the *activation stack* in Smalltalk, which contains all executing methods and the objects they refer to).

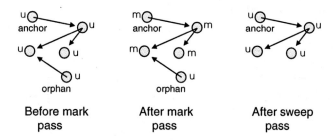

| Before mark pass | After mark pass | After sweep pass |

The anchor object is "marked"—let's say a bit is turned on—and then all objects the anchor refers to are also marked, and then all objects these objects refer to are marked, and so on recursively until no more objects are reachable. At the end of this mark pass, objects that remain unmarked must be inaccessible and are therefore garbage objects, eligible for reclamation. A second pass sweeps through all the objects, reclaiming space from unmarked objects and turning off the mark bit on all others, preparing them for further collections.

A major drawback of this scheme is its burstiness—the collector may not often go into action, but when it does, the rest of the system freezes while it makes these two exhaustive passes through memory. The user experiences a long pause during which nothing seems to happen.

Reference counting isn't bursty; a reference-counting collector does some book-keeping *every* time a pointer is set or reset. The collector maintains a count of the number of references to each object. If a count ever drops to 0, that object must be inaccessible, and the collector immediately reclaims its storage:

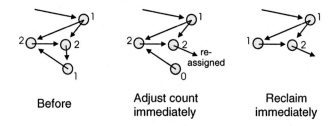

| Before | Adjust count immediately | Reclaim immediately |

Reference counters eliminate the distracting pauses of mark-and-sweep collectors. On the other hand, reference counters never rest, so the overhead of maintaining the counts degrades performance continuously. Reference counters also overlook *dead cycles*. For instance, a pair of objects may refer to each other but still be isolated from the rest of the system; their counts will each be 1, hence they are not reclaimable, even though they are genuine garbage. Reference counting by itself is therefore insufficient to collect all garbage correctly. Nevertheless, the earliest Smalltalks used reference counting because it is straightforward to implement and it eliminates pauses.

Another famous older collector, sometimes called a *Baker collector* [Baker 1978], addresses shortcomings of both preceding schemes. It suffers neither reference counting's susceptibility to dead cycles, nor mark-and-sweep's two full passes through memory. A Baker collector partitions memory into two halves, known as *semi-spaces*. All new objects are allocated in one of the semi-spaces, designated the *active* one. The collector occasionally flips spaces, making the other one active. But before opening up the new active space to additional object allocations, it makes one pass through the old semi-space, starting from an anchor, just like a mark-and-sweep collector. And just as in a mark pass, it recursively reaches only all the live objects. Instead of marking them, however, it immediately evacuates each one by moving it into the new semi-space. In the object's original place, it leaves a *tombstone* with a forwarding address to the new location, just in case other objects come looking for it later during the pass. At the end of this single pass, all live objects have been evacuated into the new active space; the detritus in the old semi-space is garbage and requires no further processing.

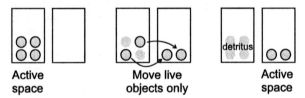

Active   Move live   Active
space   objects only   space

In due course another flip occurs, in the opposite direction. Notice that as a result, each flip enjoys an entirely clean semi-space into which objects are moved and allocated. I'll say more about the benefit of this cleanliness in a few moments.

The Baker collector has a cunning wrinkle: with a little care, the flip can proceed *incrementally*. That is, new object allocations can begin before the flip finishes; the collector can make these allocations in the new active space while it continues to evacuate live objects from the old space. The one danger is that one of the newly allocated objects may point back to a (not yet evacuated) object in the old active space; such a pointer will be incorrect at the end of the flip. To safeguard against this condition, the collector must move the unevacuated object immediately, ahead of schedule. Once this precaution, known as *scavenging*, has been taken, the Baker collector is truly incremental and, like the reference counter, overcomes the burstiness of a mark-and-sweep collector.

One undesirable property shared with mark-and-sweep collectors remains—Baker collectors process live objects over and over again. The profusion of live objects in Smalltalk—from 15,000 in a small Smalltalk system to more than 278,000 in the image I'm using at this moment—makes this a considerable burden. If only we had a way to overlook objects that are particularly durable, thereby sparing us the overhead of repetitious reprocessing. This observation brings us to *generation scavenging*, which late in the 1980s became the de facto standard for Smalltalk garbage collection.

Generation scavengers depend on the empirical observation that most objects perish quickly. New objects—points, arrays, sets, rectangles, blocks...—are created like mad in running Smalltalk systems, used briefly, then orphaned. The garbage collector must process these objects, but we would like it to ignore as much as possible the other tens or hundreds of thousands of longer-lived objects.

A scavenger begins just like the Baker collector, but every time it flips an object, it also increments the object's *generation count*. An object that survives *n* flips will be *n* generations old. The scavenger deems objects that survive to some threshold age, let us say three generations, venerable enough to move to a privileged area, called the *tenured area*.

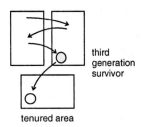

third generation survivor

tenured area

Once tenured, objects are no longer subject to repetitive garbage processing. Thus, short-lived objects are efficiently collected by Baker flips, and long-lived objects are promoted eventually to the tenured area, where they are left quietly alone. The opportunities for varying the basic scavenger design are evidently multitudinous—how many generations to allow before tenuring (63 in the original VAX implementation), how to process a tenured object if it perishes, whether and when to age tenured objects into successively more securely tenured areas.... A good generation scavenger consumes as little as 3 percent of CPU time, compared to 9 to 20 percent for the older techniques. For a sampling of scavenging schemes, see [Lieberman and Hewitt 1983; Krasner 1984; Samples et al. 1986; Ungar and Jackson 1988]. In particular, [Krasner 1984] recaps the history of the early VAX Smalltalk-80 implementations through more and more sophisticated garbage collectors—first mark-and-sweep, then Baker, and finally a generation scavenger.

16.4   The irony of garbage collection

The remarkable irony about garbage collectors is that their reputation for consuming processing cycles is half wrong. Some of them also *save* cycles. Curiously, these savings have nothing to do with cleaning up objects; they occur at the other end of an object's life, when its memory is first allocated. The savings have to do with the clean spaces I mentioned earlier.

A side-effect of schemes like the Baker collector and the generation scavenger is that object allocations occur in one large, contiguous chunk of free memory. Memory has no holes, no gaps that must be computed and accounted for. This absence of "fragmentation" considerably simplifies allocation; finding space for a new object is a mere matter of returning the location of the beginning of free memory and then advancing this beginning by the size of the object. New objects simply go right after the last object in memory.

By contrast, the heaps found in C, or Pascal, or C++ are full of holes and gaps. Memory allocation schemes must rely on one or more chains of holes. Each object allocation entails a search through these chains for space of adequate size, followed by adjusting the chain to reflect the space relinquished to the new object. Searching and managing these chains takes time, which is why fragmentation is the enemy of efficient object allocation, and conversely why clean spaces enable fast object allocation.

Thus, garbage collection, which purports to worry about the end of an object's life, can in fact expedite its birth. The effect is measurable: adding a garbage collection scheme for a C++ application's objects can sometimes *improve* the performance of the application. Regardless of the performance implications, the main benefit of garbage collectors stands: by automating storage reclamation they reduce the incidence of memory design errors.

16.5   Commentary: why not garbage collect C++?

If garbage collection is so beneficial, why can't it be retrofitted onto any language? Garbage collection is possible in Smalltalk because all objects have a uniform structure known to the virtual machine. Everything is an object, and every object's memory layout begins with a standard three-word header, consisting of a pointer to the object's class, some flags, and the object's size. (Each word is four bytes.) After these three words come the object's instance variables, one word per instance variable.

Knowing this regularity, the memory manager (i.e., the garbage collector) can figure out where an object begins and ends, and most critically, where the objects it points to are. Any garbage-collection scheme needs this information. Unfortunately, in a language like C++, the contents of an object are arbitrary. Within the memory of an object is a jumble of information—data, pointers, even other objects directly embedded inside. A memory manager cannot know where all the pointers are, and so it cannot find the objects pointed to. That kind of information is in the semantics of the program, where it is inaccessible to a hypothetical virtual machine. Hence, you will find that all object-oriented languages with garbage collectors—Smalltalk, Eiffel,

CLOS, Java…—adopt a uniform object structure. C++ is as flexible as can be, hence lacks this uniformity; it therefore precludes garbage collection of arbitrary objects.

For the definitive discussion on the desirability of and prospects for garbage collection in C++, see [Stroustrup 1994].

16.6   Smalltalk deviates from uniformity

Even Smalltalk, insistent as it is on uniformity, has its limits. Methods, for instance, are written in Smalltalk and call other Smalltalk methods. Carried on indefinitely, this recursion would be hopelessly circular. Some Smalltalk methods must be expressed in something other than Smalltalk. These methods are called *primitives*. They are typically written in a language like C, compiled, and packaged into a "dynamic link library" (on Windows or OS/2), from which they may be called by a Smalltalk method. An example is integer multiplication. The method **SmallInteger>>*** reads:

```
* aNumber
    "Answer a ... "
    <primitive: VMprSmallIntegerMultiply>
    "... more code ..."
```

The very un-Smalltalk-like expression **<primitive: ... >** is the call to a special function outside of Smalltalk. (The code following the primitive executes only if the primitive call fails.)

Primitives need not be limited to low-level methods like multiplication. Because a primitive is essentially a way to call a foreign language from Smalltalk, it can also be used to access functions that Smalltalk doesn't provide, or to replace a slow Smalltalk method with a faster version coded in another language. Primitives are the means by which Smalltalk issues calls to outside services like database managers or communication programs.

Another area in which Smalltalk is not uniform is its storage model. Most objects conform to the standard structure I discussed in the preceding section; that is, three header words followed by the object's instance variables. But objects such as small integers—those which fit with room to spare in a 32-bit word (or 16 bits, in some implementations)—are created and used so commonly in Smalltalk that the overhead of the standard structure would be grossly inefficient. Smalltalk therefore dispenses with the header for these objects and stores the whole object in one word. This special treatment for small integers and other small objects saves both time and space. But it introduces an irregularity into the virtual machine.

Smalltalk goes further with its special treatment of small integers. Not only are they stored in a different format, they are also stored "in-line." Here's what I mean: ordinarily you would expect assignments like **X := someWhale** and **Y := 149** to establish pointers to a whale and integer object, respectively. Indeed, the word in memory specified by **X** does contain a pointer to a whale object. But the word specified by **Y** contains the small integer **149** itself, not a pointer to **149**. Thus the layout of memory inside the image might look like this:

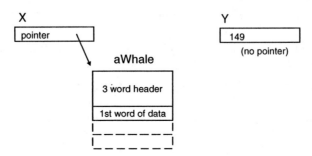

Accessing small integers directly, rather than through a pointer, is much more efficient for the virtual machine. But how does the virtual machine know whether a word is a pointer to an object (**X**) or the object itself (**Y**)? It recognizes the difference by using a flag bit, such as the first bit in the word. If the bit is turned on, the word represents a small integer. Otherwise it represents a pointer to a conventional object. (Actually, several other special small objects are distinguished by specific bit patterns too: characters, the **true** and **false** objects, and the **nil** object. They are known collectively as *immediate* objects.)

You will never observe any of these storage conventions at the Smalltalk level. These are strictly private conventions for use by the virtual machine. Smalltalk continues to deceive the developer into believing that, "Everything is an object, and all objects are treated uniformly."

While we're on the subject of economy, realize that even packing individual character objects into a word apiece squanders a lot of space, namely three bytes of every four. This waste is particularly excessive when, as is the case more often than not, they occur together, as in a **String** object. For strings too, the Smalltalk virtual machine deviates from uniformity for the sake of efficiency. The characters in a string occur in successive bytes, right inside the string object, illustrated in these alternative memory layouts for the string **'juice'**:

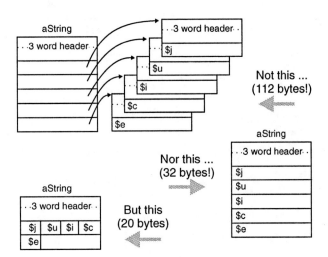

Smalltalk offers other specialized formats for storing the instances of a class. Most classes simply use the standard structure of three header words followed by a word per instance variable. But you can specify the other formats to use at the time you define your classes—you will see how in the coming exercises.

16.7 Exercises

Inspecting classes

❑ You know how to find the superclass of a class using Smalltalk's browsers. Try it in another way by using inspector(s) to find the superclass of **Date**.

❑ Use inspectors to find the bytecodes—numbers like **132, 36** ...—for the method **dayOfYear** in the class **Date**. Begin by inspecting the class **Date**; in IBM Smalltalk, inspect down through the instance variable **methodsArray** rather than **method-Dictionary**.

Object memory layouts

❑ Although the memory layout of objects is strictly the business of the virtual machine, you can see intimations within Smalltalk that the instances of some classes are treated differently than others. For example, the classes like **String** that store their data in consecutive byte-sized objects answer **true** to the message **isBytes**. To see how many such classes there are, *inspect* this expression:

```
Object allSubclasses select: [:sc| sc isBytes].
```

❑ How does Smalltalk know whether to lay out objects of a class in the usual way, or in the compressed form that strings use? To answer this question, browse the definition of an ordinary class like **Rectangle**, and compare it to the definition of **String**. Confirm that ordinary classes are created by the old standby:

```
subclass:instanceVariableNames:classVariableNames:poolDictionaries:
```

What method does class **String** employ? This is the method that informs the virtual machine that it should use the compressed-memory layout for strings.

❑ How many other conventions does Smalltalk have for laying out objects? Hint: Locate the class that implements the class definition messages above and look for similar methods.

Counting instances

❑ To estimate the number of classes within your Smalltalk image, *display*:

```
^Object allSubclasses size.
```

For reasons that you will understand when we discuss metaclasses in Chapter 20, this estimate is about *twice* as high as it should be.

❑ You can count the number of objects in your Smalltalk image by *displaying*:

```
|count|
count := 0.
Object allSubclasses do: [:cl | count := count + cl allInstances size].
^count
```

But try this experiment overnight—it may take hours. That's because the **allInstances** method invokes a full-blown garbage collection, and we are invoking it once for every class.[1]

---

[1] In IBM Smalltalk you can get a quicker but less precise count by using **basicAllInstances**, which does not invoke garbage collection. You can sharpen this count by clearing the garbage once in the beginning with the message **System globalGarbageCollect**. Nevertheless, be prepared to wait a while.

Non-uniformities in Smalltalk's compiler

Not all messages are equal. That is, Smalltalk's compiler recognizes a few special messages and generates optimized code for them. You can rewrite and recompile those methods in any way you like, but your code, whatever you write, will be ignored.

❑ To demonstrate this curiosity, recompile the **ifTrue:** method in class **True** after inserting **self halt** into its body. Then *display*:

```
7 = 7
    ifTrue: [ 'Breezing through the halt' ].
```

The same short circuit applies to all the other common boolean messages, like **ifTrue:ifFalse:**, **ifFalse:**, etc. Another noteworthy message that the compiler intercepts in this fashion is **==**.

Technical aside: The only way to circumvent the compiler's optimization and force your rewritten method to execute is to invoke it indirectly. The usual technique is to use variants of the method **perform:**, as in:

```
7 = 7 perform: #ifTrue: with: [ 'Hit my halt' ]
```

16.8 Summary

Every implementation choice in an object-oriented language is a tradeoff. If method dispatch is fast, compilation will be slow. A garbage collector will reduce the number and severity of bugs, but degrade performance. A compiler optimization speeds up a corner of the language, but at a loss of consistency in the language. An image can be portable, but it won't enjoy the platform's native widgets. Virtual machines make interactive debugging a snap, but complicate life with foreign languages.

This interplay between a language's definition and its underpinnings shapes the whole texture of the programming system—its responsiveness, its reflectiveness, the degree of its coupling to other languages and systems, even the design techniques that are most suitable in it. Smalltalk—the product of one combination of all the choices—is a respectable point in the space of object-oriented languages.

We now shift from the guts of object-oriented languages to a conceptual predicament that awaits practicing object-oriented designers.

CHAPTER 17

Two kinds of inheritance

Next in our series of beyond-the-basics topics is the distinction between a type and a class. Until now we've blurred this distinction: I've encouraged you to think that inheritance is simply synonymous with the AKO (A-Kind-Of) concept. Seasoned designers, however, cringe at this oversimplification.

17.1 Beauty and the beast

Consider two classes, **Rectangle** and **Square**, in any object-oriented environment. Don't worry about Smalltalk; the first four sections in this chapter are independent of the object-oriented language. Here are rectangle and square instances:

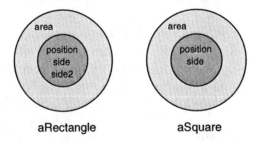

aRectangle   aSquare

Each has a method for calculating its area and instance variables to identify its position (let's say the upper-left corner) and the length of its side(s). We won't worry about rotation—all our squares and rectangles will have vertical and horizontal sides only.

Now, a design problem: should **Rectangle** be a superclass of **Square**? Or vice versa? Two perfectly defensible opinions are:

1 Squares are special kinds of rectangles, namely those which have sides of equal length. Every schoolchild knows this fact. Therefore, **Square** should be a subclass of **Rectangle**.

2 We expect a subclass to inherit everything from its superclass and, generally, to add further traits. Butterflies have all insect traits, plus more. The picture above clearly shows that a rectangle has the traits of a square, plus one additional instance variable. Therefore, **Rectangle** should be a subclass of **Square**.

Before you get excited about one point of view or the other, let me tell you once and for all that there is nothing wrong with either argument. The dispute is unavoidable: there are two reasons for subclassing, and they aren't always compatible. (And if one finds neither reason compelling, one can always design *neither* class to be a subclass of the other; this is a valid third alternative.)

Imagine two object-oriented programmers, one a *consumer* of a class hierarchy and the other the hierarchy's *producer*. The consumer wants to reach over and use ("buy") the classes in the hierarchy with minimal confusion. He doesn't want surprises; he expects the hierarchy to be an intuitive AKO hierarchy, and he definitely doesn't want to examine any underlying code or instance variables. Like the schoolchild, he expects **Square** to be a subclass of **Rectangle**. The consumer values external *consistency*.

The producer or developer of the hierarchy, on the other hand, cares how well the *insides* of objects work. She has two reasons for subclassing **Rectangle** from **Square**. First, her job is simpler because she automatically inherits the instance variables **position** and **side**, and just adds an instance variable for **side2**. (Of course, she must override the **area** method to calculate the product of **side** and **side2**.) Second, she worries that if she subclasses in the other way, every square inherits an extra instance variable (**side2**) it doesn't need; if a graphics application uses thousands of squares, it will waste a lot of memory. This developer values *practicality*.

The dilemma, then, is this conflict between consistency and practicality. You cannot inherit at the same time for the sake of an attractive appearance on the outside and for the sake of code reuse and machine constraints on the inside. A class hierarchy cannot at once satisfy its consumer and its producer.

We need to sharpen our vocabulary. The term for the first kind of hierarchy, the one that is externally attractive ("beauty"), is a *type* hierarchy. When that's the focus, we use the words *type* and *subtype*. AKO, which implies consistency, is really subtyping.

The second hierarchy, the one favoring internals ("the beast"), goes by the familiar words *class* and *subclass*, and frequently the expression *implementation inheritance*. Of course, in practice you often see the word "inheritance" by itself. Generally, when experts draw fine lines and say just "inheritance" they mean implementation inheritance. To minimize the risk of confusion in this chapter, I will avoid using "inheritance" by itself unless the context is unambiguous—it will either be "subtype inheritance" or "subclass (or implementation) inheritance," or simply "subtyping" or "subclassing."

The object community first recognized the troubling presence of these two distinct forms of inheritance in 1986. (See [Snyder 1986; Lalonde et al. 1986].) Efforts to wrestle with the trouble produced several evocative synonyms:

Subtype Inheritance (Beauty)	Subclass Inheritance (Beast)
Subtyping	Subclassing
Specification inheritance	Implementation inheritance
Visible inheritance	Invisible inheritance
Essential inheritance	Incidental inheritance

For details, see [Snyder 1986; Sakkinen 1989; Wegner and Zdonik 1988]. By whatever names, it became clear that the subtype/subclass distinction was an inescapable fact of object-oriented life.

17.2   Why types matter: polymorphism

The type (beauty) of an object is the means by which a consumer programmer recognizes an object's applicability to some problem. For **S** to be a subtype of **T** (imagine **Butterfly** and **Insect**, or **Square** and **Rectangle**), the external description of **S** ought to be consistent with that of **T**. And if so, you would expect to be able to use an instance of **S** anywhere in a program where the program expects something of type **T**. This property is called *substitutability*: an instance of a subtype may be substituted wherever something of the supertype is expected and the program will still work. Thus anywhere a rectangle works in an application, a square also works; the application musn't fail because someone has substituted a square for a rectangle. This is what we mean by saying that **Square** is a subtype of **Rectangle**.

The converse, however, is false. If an application depends on a square, say to form the faces on the dice for a game of craps, an arbitrary rectangle just won't do. Thus **Rectangle** is not a subtype of **Square**.

This freedom to substitute instances of a subtype sounds suspiciously like polymorphism, and indeed that's just what it is. In polymorphism, the program is unaware of the actual type of the object lurking under a variable—any subtype will do. The subtype relationship specifies what is substitutable, hence the permissible range of polymorphic objects. To put it bluntly, substitutability and polymorphism amount to the same idea.

Another way to think about substitutability is to think about variables **s** and **t** of types S and T, respectively. Freedom to substitute an S instance wherever a T instance is expected justifies assignments of the form **t := s**. This is the same rule we saw for C++ (page 168). An insect variable may refer to a butterfly, but not conversely.

All the following terms, then, are allied: *AKO, subtype, substitutable, consistent,* and *polymorphic.* All represent beauty, which is different from the notion of a *subclass.* From now on we need to respect this distinction.

17.3   Commentary: an aside on subsets

A type generates a set. (Or at least something very much like a set. Mathematicians and logicians would quibble about using the word "set" here. I alluded to this fussiness on page 13.) For example, the type **Butterfly** generates the set consisting of all the butterfly objects that might ever be created.

Following this reasoning further, if S is a subtype of T, then the set generated by S is a subset of the set generated by T. That's because we have agreed that subtyping means S is consistent (AKO) with T, which implies that S's objects satisfy whatever T's objects satisfy. In other words, S's objects constitute a subset of T's objects. In everyday language, butterflies constitute a subset of insects and squares constitute a subset of rectangles.

Although subtypes generate subsets in a natural way, it would be reckless to assert the converse, that by taking any arbitrary subset of the supertype's objects, with methods defined to be the same as the supertype's methods, we'd get a subtype. That's because methods that make sense on the superset might not make sense for the subset. For example, suppose rectangles have a "squish" method that doubles their length and halves their width. Squares, although forming a legitimate subset of the set of rectangles, can't be squished. Squares then wouldn't understand the same messages that rectangles do, and so in the presence of squishing, they wouldn't constitute a subtype.

Conclusion: Subtypes naturally generate subsets, but subsets do not necessarily define natural subtypes.

17.4   Commentary: what does "consistency" mean?

Intuitively, we understand subtyping to mean preserving the hierarchy's external consistency. But so far we do not have a precise definition of "consistency." For instance, birds fly, but penguins don't. Would we want to say that penguins form a subtype of birds or not? Are penguins consistent *enough* with birds to warrant being a subtype?

What conditions should their **fly** method abide by to be consistent with the **fly** method for birds?

More rigor is evidently desirable. We'd like an objective test for consistency. Unfortunately, no one test exists. The candidates range from the weakest condition, where it doesn't take much to be consistent, to the strongest, most rigid condition, where it's extremely difficult to be consistent.

Here are four candidates, covering the spectrum from weakest to most rigid. In order of increasing strength, we'll call them *anarchy, conformance, behavioral consistency,* and *rigidity*:

- *Anarchy.* S has at least all the message selectors that T has, and possibly more, but there are no limits on what the method bodies themselves do. For example, if **Bird** has a **fly** method, then the subtype **Penguin** must too. But **Penguin>>fly** may answer *No!* while **Bird>>fly** answers *Yes!* Yet more flagrant, **Penguin>>fly** might answer a special error object or generate a walkback, informing you that you should not have sent the message in the first place. The effect would be to *cancel* the **Bird>>fly**. The possibilities for **Penguin>>fly** being unlimited, anarchy barely deserves to be called subtyping. Yet it is what Smalltalk allows. Smalltalk imposes no restrictions on what a subtype method does. This is such a weak form of consistency that one could say in good conscience that it isn't in the spirit of subtyping at all. And it is often said that Smalltalk programmers don't really subtype; they subclass.

- *Conformance.* We now depart from Smalltalk; conformance can be checked only by a language whose variables have types and as we know, Smalltalk's do not. Nevertheless, as an object designer, you can still *think* about conformance, and knowing about it can improve your designs.

  Conformance has to do with the consistency of the types of arguments and return values of methods. I will discuss the most widely accepted definition. First let's adopt the convention that the word "subtype" includes the type itself. A type then is always a subtype of itself, and also a supertype of itself.

  S will conform to T if its methods follow certain rules. The gist of these rules is to force each method to "deliver more" and "require less" than the corresponding method in T. By delivering more and requiring less, S's instances will be more accommodating. Therefore S's instances can be substituted wherever T's instances are called for.

  That's the outline; now the specifics. We need to think about the return types and argument types of a method. First, the return type.

  Consider methods for laying eggs, **Duck>>lay** and **Bird>>lay**. **Bird>>lay** returns an instance of **Egg**, and **Duck>>lay** returns an instance of **DuckEgg**. Thus **Duck's** method returns a more specific type of object than **Bird's** method does—ducks deliver more than birds do when they lay. We say that the return type of **Duck>>lay** *conforms* to the return type of **Bird>>lay**.

The official wording is: for the return types of a method **m** to *conform*, the type of object returned by **S>>m** must be a subtype of the type returned by **T>>m**. (Remember that the types of the returned objects may be equal, too.) The right-hand side of this schematic illustrates the possible objects returned by **T>>m** (**Bird>>lay**) and **S>>m** (**Duck>>lay**). (Ignore the left-hand side for now.)

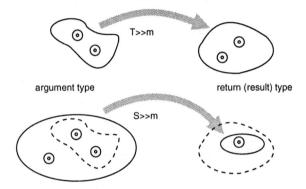

Notice that fewer objects may be returned by **S>>m** than **T>>m**—only duck eggs, not all eggs. That is the key. The objects returned by **S>>m** are more specific; they represent a subtype or subset of the objects returned by **T>>m**.

That's the rule for conformance of return types—it's drearily straightforward. The rule for argument types, however, has a twist. We will need a little extra notation: **S>>m(P)** means that the method **m** accepts an argument of type P. We are going to define what it means for the types P and Q of the arguments of the method **S>>m(P)** and method **T>>m(Q)** to conform.

Consider **Piano>>play(Pianist)**; in other words, the play method for pianos requires an argument, namely a pianist. Think about the **ConcertGrand** subtype of **Piano**. Who can play a concert grand? In other words, what condition should we impose on the argument type of **ConcertGrand>>play(___)**?

It is tempting to argue that the argument type ought to be the **Virtuoso** subtype of **Pianist**. But this impulse turns out to be dead wrong, at least for this interpretation of conformance. That's because we want our rules to guarantee substitutability, and if we demand that only a virtuoso can play a concert grand, then the concert grand will not be substitutable for the piano! (For example, imagine the piano in my living room being played by a pianist. We want to roll in a concert grand to replace it and for the living room to continue to operate normally. Well, it won't if we suddenly require a virtuoso instead of a pianist. The only way for the substitution to work is if the concert grand may also be played by a pianist, or even possibly a more general type of individual, like **Person**.)

Paradoxically, to guarantee substitutability, I have to make my **Concert-Grand>>play(___)** method accept a *supertype* of **Pianist** as an argument! This rule makes the software consistent, although it may not do much for musicality. (A design technique known as *multi-methods* preserves the musicality of this problem. The idea is to treat **Piano** and **Pianist** as peer classes and to imagine a "method" that operates on *both* objects at once. This outlook differs from our customary object-centric perspective, where we always have a preferred object. For a discussion of multi-methods, see the commentary on page 170.)

Thus conformance of argument types works in the opposite direction from conformance of return types. The official definition must be: for the argument types of a method **m** to *conform*, the type of an argument of **S>>m** must be a supertype of the respective argument of **T>>m**. (Again, the types may be equal, too.) Looking back at the left half of the schematic above, you can see that **S>>m** (**Concert-Grand>>play**) accommodates more possible arguments than **T>>m** (**Piano>>play**). The arguments that **S>>m** accepts represent a supertype or superset of those that **T>>m** does.

Putting everything together into a definition of subtype based on conformance, we can say that for **S** to be a *subtype* of **T**, **S** must have all **T**'s methods and possibly more, and for any method **m** in both **S** and **T**, **S>>m**'s return and argument types must conform to **T>>m**'s. (Notice that this definition is recursive: the subtype relationship between **S** and **T** is cast in terms of the subtype relationships of arguments and returns. Recursions need a condition to get them started or stopped, and we started this one by declaring that any type is a subtype of itself.)

Here's another way to express this definition, using some jargon that has caught on in the C++ community but which originated in the mathematical discipline known as *category theory*. Return types follow a *covariant* rule—they vary in the "same" direction as **S** and **T**. That is, if **S** is a *sub*type of **T**, then the return of **S>>m** must also be a *sub*type of the return of **T>>m**. Argument types follow a *contravariant* rule—they vary in the "contrary" direction from **S** and **T**. That is, if **S** is a *sub*type of **T**, then an argument of **S>>m** must be a *super*type of the respective argument of **T>>m**. Briefly then, **S** is a *subtype* of **T** if **S** has all **T**'s methods and possibly more, and any methods in common follow covariance in their returns and contravariance in their arguments.

This subtyping rule—conformance—reflects a theoretical ideal whose essential appeal is substitutability. Each language defines its subtyping rule in its own way, usually not in accordance with the ideal. In Smalltalk, conformance is irrelevant because of the typelessness of Smalltalk's variables. Even among languages whose compilers check for the types of arguments and returns, few (see the upcoming table) adopt the ideal.

For example, Eiffel's rule for consistency of argument types is the *opposite* of what we've discussed—covariance instead of contravariance. Eiffel's rule has been the subject of vigorous debate (see [Cook 1989]). Its rationale is that covariance of argument types is in practice more useful than contravariance. **Concert-Grand>>play(Virtuoso)** should conform to **Piano>>play(Pianist)** because practicality (musicality) should prevail over any lofty desire for consistency (substitutability). **ConcertGrand>>play(Person)** may be theoretically sound, goes the Eiffel argument, but it has no practical value.

- *Behavioral consistency.* By behavior, I mean the semantics of methods; that is, what they do rather than merely their names or selectors or signatures. The spirit is the same as for conformance: for **S** to be a subtype of **T**, **S>>m** should require less (behaviorally) and deliver more (behaviorally) than **T>>m**.

  How can we specify a method's behavior? The customary technique is to use *preconditions* and *postconditions*. These mean just what they say: preconditions consist of what the method expects prior to its execution (i.e., what it requires) and postconditions consist of what it guarantees when it finishes (i.e., what it delivers). Therefore, requiring less and delivering more simply mean *weakening* the preconditions and *strengthening* the postconditions.

  Thinking about of preconditions and postconditions for your methods is good discipline, even though all you can do about it in Smalltalk is record the conditions informally in comments. Computer scientists don't have a practical way to formally specify and validate preconditions and postconditions anyway. So there is nothing shameful about documenting methods with informal preconditions and postconditions in their comments. Only Eiffel among the commercial object-oriented languages has even rudimentary support for checking this kind of consistency.

- *Rigidity.* The strongest possible form of consistency would be to categorically forbid alternate implementations of a method. For an object-oriented developer, this is an academic, useless notion. **S** could only add brand-new methods to **T**'s methods. Penguins could add any number of methods to bird methods, but penguins could not have their own **fly** method. Instead they could only reuse the **fly** method from birds. Penguins must then fly like any other bird, an unsatisfactory condition. No object-oriented language is this rigid. Prohibiting alternate implementations entirely would produce an unacceptable object-oriented language.

Now let's relate these theoretical ideas to the rules for consistency in actual object-oriented languages. The table below describes these rules for several languages. Think of them as the rules that determine when polymorphism or substitution works. The first column indicates whether substitutability requires an explicit implementation inheritance relationship between S and T; that is, a declaration of S as a subclass of T. The remaining columns describe how far each method S>>m may deviate from the method T>>m.

		When S is substitutable for T (polymorphism)		
	Must S subclass from T?	For S>>m to be consistent with T>>m		
		Return types	Argument Types	Behavioral Conditions
C++	Yes	Covariant	Must agree	n/a
Eiffel	Yes	Covariant	Covariant	May weaken preconditions or strengthen postconditions
Emerald	No	Covariant	Contravariant	n/a
Java	No	Covariant	Must agree	n/a
Modula-3	Yes	Must agree	Must agree	May raise fewer exceptions
POOL-I	No	Covariant	Contravariant	May have more "properties"
Smalltalk	No	No restriction	No restriction	n/a
Theoretical ideal	No	Covariant	Contravariant	May weaken preconditions or strengthen postconditions

Polymorphism in C++ was originally conservative: any change to the declared types of arguments and returns waived polymorphism. But the ANSI C++ committee took a small step toward conformance in 1993 by allowing covariance for return types, as shown in the table.

Note that only the research languages Emerald and POOL-I support ideal conformance—covariance in return types and contravariance in argument types. For further information on the type systems of the languages in the table, see: [Stroustrup 1991; Meyer 1992; Black et al. 1986; Sun 1995; Cardelli et al. 1992; America 1991; Goldberg and Robson 1983].

17.5   Consistency and Smalltalk

What has this discussion of topics like conformance to do with Smalltalk, where variables don't have types in the first place? Well, just because the designer can't express these ideas in the Smalltalk language doesn't mean she is incapable of thinking about them. It would be a peculiar designer indeed who was oblivious to the concept of consistency. And that is the nub of this chapter: to warn you that as a Smalltalk developer you will have to reconcile your idealistic thoughts about consistency with the absence of means to represent these thoughts in your software. You have just one inheritance mechanism, and the path of least resistance is to use it for subclassing.

Beginners are mostly motivated by AKO (subtyping), but gradually, as they become familiar with classes and their workings, they begin to inherit for the sake of reusing the code they find—they subclass. In the end, expert Smalltalk programmers use inheritance frequently for subclassing. The reason is simple. In Smalltalk, more than other object-oriented languages, when you inherit, you inherit *everything*—all the instance variables and all the methods. You get access to all the insides, whether you want them or not. It's a producer's sandbox.[1]

The Smalltalk developer, hobbled by having to inherit all the insides, has no way to define a type hierarchy. The limitation is grim, but not as grim as it sounds. Often, class and type hierarchies are the same or nearly so, which explains why many Smalltalk developers survive without knowing the difference. Often, but not always. What would we see if we masked Smalltalk's class hierarchy and looked instead for subtype relationships?

William Cook did this experiment for the collection classes in Smalltalk-80 and found...an entirely different hierarchy! [Cook 1992] In the next exercise, you'll replicate his experiment.

---

[1] *Technical aside:* By contrast, C++ offers more control over inheritance. *Private members* and *private inheritance* in C++ limit what subclasses can access and what consumers of the subclass can access. These features distinguish what a class inherits for the sake of its own implementation from what it inherits for the sake of its appearance to the consumer—a step toward separating subtyping from subclassing. Java goes further. It supports two distinct notions—conventional classes plus *interfaces*. An interface specifies a set of method names. The programmer can develop separate class and interface hierarchies, associating specific classes with specific interfaces at will. And as you may have guessed, polymorphism (substitutability) in Java depends on an object's interface, not its class.

17.6   Exercise: Smalltalk's container "types"

Consider these container classes: **Array**, **Bag**, **Collection**, **Dictionary**, **Set**, and **String**. (A bag is like a set, except that an element can occur more than once in a bag; you cannot add an element twice to a set.) Our goal is to arrange them into a reasonable type (AKO) hierarchy. To do so, we have to examine public selectors that are appropriate for consumers of these classes. Here is a representative list—**size**, **at:**, **at:put:**, **includes:**, **<**, **indexOf:**, **remove:**, **removeKey:**, **add:withOccurrences:**. This is a somewhat contrived subset of methods—a complete assessment would entail *all* public methods—but we want to keep the exercise manageable.

We also have to settle on some definition for consistency. Let's use a simple one: **S** is a subtype of **T** if **S** has all the selectors of **T**, *and they all work*. This is a little more fastidious than the anarchic subtyping rule (page 202), because we are saying that we don't want to count methods that issue an error. A deliberate error in a method tells us that the developer must want to invalidate the method. We called this condition a *cancellation*. Also, some methods aren't explicitly cancelled, but still don't work right. One example of a method that fails a lot is **at:**, which is defined in **Object** but fails in most subclasses.

❑ For each class, tabulate its valid selectors. You should use browsers, but I encourage you to supplement your browsing by executing experimental messages like **Array new size** that will test whether the **size** method is supported by the **Array** class. It should take some time to do a thoughtful analysis. After you determine which classes support which selectors, arrange the classes into a plausible type hierarchy.

17.7   Solution and discussion

Here is what I found by snooping into these collection classes. Your results should be the same. In fact, because these classes are all standard Smalltalk classes, you should arrive at the same results no matter which dialect of Smalltalk you use. (The plus (+) means that the method is valid for the class.)

	size	*at:*	*at:put:*	*includes:*	*<*	*indexOf:*	*remove:*	*remove Key:*	*add:with Occurrences:*
Array	+	+	+	+		+			
Bag	+			+			+		+
Collection	+			+					

	size	*at:*	*at:put:*	*includes:*	*<*	*indexOf:*	*remove:*	*remove Key:*	*add:with Occurrences:*
Dictionary	+	+	+	+				+	
Set	+			+			+		
String	+	+	+	+	+	+			

To analyze the first column, I found that in IBM Smalltalk, **Array**, **Collection**, and **String** successfully inherit a **size** method from **Object**. But **Bag**, **Dictionary**, and **Set** don't. Instead, each overrides **Object>>size** with its own **size** method. Nevertheless, by one means or another, all six classes enjoy a working **size** method. Each class therefore gets a + in the first column. (In other dialects of Smalltalk, the **size** method comes from somewhere else in the class hierarchy, and different intermediate classes and cancellations and reimplementations occur along the way. No matter. You will still find that all six classes enjoy a working **size** method.)

For the second and third columns I found that **Array** successfully inherits **at:** and **at:put:** from **Object**, and that **Dictionary** and **String** provide their own overrides. The other classes—**Bag**, **Collection**, and **Set**—inherit **at:** and **at:put:** from **Object** too, but the methods actually produce walkbacks. Thus only **Array**, **Dictionary**, and **String** get a + in the second and third column.

Continuing carefully in this way, I completed the rest of the table. Again, you should arrive at the same results from any standard dialect of Smalltalk, even though the details of your route may differ. From the table, we can propose a *type* hierarchy like the diagram below.

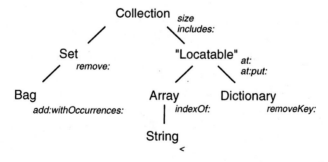

Each type is labeled by the message selectors that pertain to it and its subtypes. Notice the fictitious type **Locatable**. This is a convenient type into which we can factor the selectors **at:** and **at:put:**, which service **Array** and **Dictionary** and their subtypes.

17.8 Exercise: Smalltalk's container "classes"

Consumers appreciate the type hierarchy above because it is easy to locate the classes they want to buy; it's an intuitive AKO hierarchy. Unfortunately, the hierarchy you see in Smalltalk is different. It's a producer's hierarchy—the beast—optimized for those who built it, not for those who hope to find its classes in intuitive locations.

❏ Use a browser to sketch the actual class hierarchy in Smalltalk.

17.9 Solution and discussion

The IBM Smalltalk *class* hierarchy we derive directly from a browser is:

An innocent consumer, expecting an AKO hierarchy, is shaken by this one. Sets and bags are unrelated and arrays and strings have lost their intuitive AKO relationship. Why?

Sadly for the consumer, these classes were built by producers in ways advantageous to themselves. The consumer doesn't know it, but bags are built with dictionary-like objects inside them, so they don't need to inherit from sets. Strings are stored in a unique, compact way (remember the figure on page 195), so they don't inherit from arrays. And so on.

These internal design decisions, which the consumer doesn't want to know about, nevertheless affect the structure of the class hierarchy. Class hierarchies set AKO expectations for consumers, even if, as here, they are not AKO hierarchies. This is the unfortunate by-product of this chapter's theme: Smalltalk has only one hierarchy, which cannot serve two incompatible masters, subclassing and subtyping. The collection hierarchy you see through Smalltalk's browsers is a subclass hierarchy, not the subtype hierarchy you would wish to see. The type hierarchy is conceptually present, but for practical purposes it is invisible. We had to work hard to ferret it out.

Incidentally, the *class* hierarchy derived from a ParcPlace-Digitalk Smalltalk browser doesn't help, either:

This hierarchy fails to capture the natural type relationships in an additional disconcerting way—**Dictionary** inherits from **Set**. The producers chose this design for implementation reasons: encapsulated within a set is an array, which dictionaries inherit for their own private purposes.

An early exposé of the type versus class dilemma in Smalltalk appears in [LaLonde et al. 1986]. For a thorough analysis of Smalltalk collection classes, see [Cook 1992].

17.10   Summary

Objects have outsides and insides. When we think that a square is well known to be a special kind of rectangle, we are thinking of its customary behavior—its outside. When we think that a square has just one side instance variable and a rectangle has two, we are thinking about how they are constructed inside rather than how they present themselves to their users. The sad truth about most object-oriented languages today, including Smalltalk, is that they don't make the same distinction that our minds do; they muddle subtyping with subclassing.

It is subtyping, not subclassing, that determines polymorphism. We can accuse Smalltalk, with its typeless variables, of having an unusually forgiving type system (look back at the table on page 206). Smalltalk enforces no discipline on the formation of type hierarchies, whereas other object-oriented languages go to great pains to check type relationships for consistency.

As compensation, according to the first column in the table, Smalltalk supports what we called implicit polymorphism (page 169). This polymorphism doesn't depend on declared relationships between the classes. If two classes support the same messages, they are consistent, even if they are in unrelated parts of the class hierarchy. If **Puddle** and **CarBattery** both support **jump** and **drain**, Smalltalk regards them as substitutable types, and so they may act polymorphically with respect to each other. Looking back at our analysis of Smalltalk collections, **Bag** is a subtype of **Set**, so a bag may be polymorphically substituted for a set, even though they are unrelated by inheritance.

17.11   Commentary: standardizing Smalltalk

Our analysis of the collection classes in the exercises above raises an interesting question: are the incompatible collection class hierarchies of the ParcPlace-Digitalk and IBM dialects a roadblock for standardizing Smalltalk? The ANSI committee's answer is a resounding "No." Its current approach to the problem is to standardize Smalltalk's type hierarchy rather than its class hierarchy. This is a progressive departure from the traditional Smalltalk mentality of subclass-based inheritance.

Notice how the ANSI approach fits with collection classes: I mentioned in the solution to the exercise that the result of the type analysis for the dialects is the same. That is, the collection *type* hierarchies from ParcPlace-Digitalk and IBM agree even though the collection *class* hierarchies don't. And it is the type hierarchy that matters to consumers. The type hierarchy represents their intuitive understanding of the behavior of objects, and it governs the objects they can use polymorphically in place of other objects.

A major attraction of any standard is the prospect of portable code. If we want to port our Smalltalk code from one ANSI standard dialect to another, we will have to follow one essential guideline when we write the code: we should only buy, not inherit from standard classes. By buying, we use only the standardized interfaces of the classes. On the other hand inheriting, even from standard classes, is sure to cause trouble because inheritance couples our subclasses to the nonstandard insides of classes (beast) instead of their standard outsides (beauty).

Also keep in mind that only part of an application is likely to be portable. The ANSI standard will focus on foundation classes—containers, magnitudes, streams, and so on. These are the basic building blocks for any Smalltalk application, but a real working application uses many other classes that are unlikely to be standardized. User interface classes are the first obvious omission because, as we know, these differ dramatically among vendors. But they are followed by persistence and database classes, communication classes, and so on. The best we can hope for is trouble-free portability of model code between standard dialects; the rest of an application will take work.

CHAPTER *18*

Design patterns

Having now thought quite a bit about objects and programmed with them in Small-talk, you are in a position to tackle a higher level of abstraction—design patterns. Patterns occur in every activity; software isn't special. A good chess player doesn't think through all possible combinations of moves; that is mathematically beyond reach.[1] Instead, he draws on his mental respository of positions or *patterns* to limit the number of combinations he explores. Having this personal repository of patterns distinguishes the expert from the novice, whether the subject is chess or software.

Just as the chess player's patterns come from positions he has played plus ones those he has studied in other games, the designer's patterns consist of those she has discovered on her own plus ones she has seen in other people's designs. My purpose in this chapter is to give you an edge by priming your personal repository of design patterns with proven patterns from other people's designs.

Think of an object-oriented design pattern as a grouping of objects or classes that recurs in good designs.[2] These groupings are signs of a natural evolution toward larger-scale reuse: in its early years, the object community focused on what made a good object or class, and now it turns to the question of what makes a good grouping of objects or classes. Our first example (page 215) is a pattern that has already occurred three times in this book, in the form of the **Account** and its transaction log, the **AddressBook** and the contacts in it, and the **ShapeRoom** and its shapes. This pattern is a *smart container*

---

[1] Even chess-playing supercomputers like Deep Blue, which won a game against world champion Gary Kasparov, use "patterns" to augment their raw computational power. For example, a computer might use a heuristic such as, "a castled king affords greater protection than an uncastled one." *Heuristic* is a fancy word for a rule of thumb, which is also not a bad way to think of a pattern.

[2] To some people, a pattern is or implies a great deal more. See the commentary at the end of this chapter (page 240) for an indication of these more profound understandings.

because, for example, an address book contains contacts, but it is also smart enough to search by company or zipcode, to dial a contact's phone number, and so on.

The patterns in this chapter are ones I particularly enjoy. All designers have their own favorites, formed mostly of those that have helped them solve nasty problems. Erich Gamma, Richard Helm, Ralph Johnson, and John Vlissides have organized twenty-three patterns into a catalogue, now a standard reference book [Gamma et al. 1995]. You will eventually develop your own idiosyncratic catalogue, based on the patterns that pertain to the problems you encounter.

Because these are *design* patterns, don't expect the Smalltalk code in this chapter to be entirely spelled out. A pattern is a reusable design, not reusable code. The descriptions include enough details to imagine how each pattern can help solve a problem, but to fully apply a pattern to your problem, you will still have to invest some of your own energies. In so doing, you will probably uncover variations on the basic techniques outlined here.

18.1   Notation

We need some notation to help convey the essence of a pattern. Here is an example of what we'll use, based mostly on OMT [Rumbaugh et al. 1991].

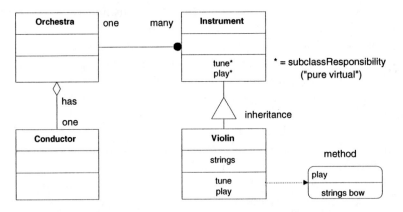

The three-part rectangular boxes are classes; the top part is the name of the class, the bottom lists pertinent methods, and the middle contains pertinent instance variables. The triangle means inheritance and the diamond means aggregation. A dark circle indicates a *relationship* or *association* that involves possibly many instances of a class, such as the many instruments in an orchestra above. When we need to depict the logic of a method, we'll use a rounded box, as for **Violin>>play**. And we continue to mark subclassResponsibility methods with asterisks, as we have done since Chapter 5.

These notations are a far cry from a full-bodied design methodology notation, but they are enough to get us started.

I mentioned in Chapter 6 the gray area between aggregations and containers. A similar gray area exists between aggregations and one-to-many or one-to-one associations. An aggregation is a particularly strong kind of association, one in which the designer feels that "part-of" is an apt description. But what one designer calls an ordinary association, like the one-to-many relationship between orchestra and instruments illustrated above, another may choose to call an aggregation. This second designer would have used the diamond notation to indicate that instruments are *part-of* an orchestra, or an orchestra *has* instruments.

Two designers could also quibble over the relationship between orchestra and conductor. One could argue for an ordinary one-to-one association; the other for the more special aggregation, as illustrated above. These are judgment calls. The decisions are influenced by the problem you are solving (which doesn't help here because I have not yet presented any problems). For example, a problem on simulating a conductor's schedule and duties might warrant reversing the relationship entirely and declaring that a conductor *has* an orchestra:

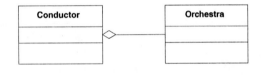

These nuances remind us that design is an inexact craft, but they won't matter for this chapter. We need notation only to illuminate concepts and avoid ambiguities.

18.2   Smart container (aka collection-worker)

Let's begin on familiar ground, by reviewing the common design for a checking account, an address book, and a shape editor. They all look like this:

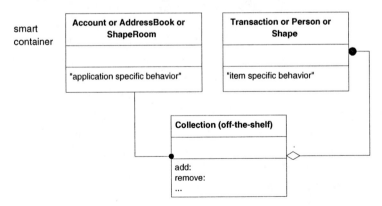

Class **Account** is conceptually like a container, because it "contains" transactions, yet it is smart in the sense that it processes transactions and adjusts its balance. The actual container is a built-in container from Smalltalk, in that case an instance of **Sorted-Collection**. Similarly, class **AddressBook** basically contains person objects, but it has behavior (for managing contacts) that goes beyond what any of Smalltalk's built-in collection classes can do. And class **ShapeRoom** conceptually contains shapes, but it can move them around and even undo the user's actions.

In all three examples, the job of adding, removing, and holding on to the pertinent items goes not to the smart container but to some built-in Smalltalk collection class. The smart container only *appears* to contain its items. Peter Coad calls this "the fundamental pattern" or the *collection-worker* pattern; it is the base for most of the patterns in his book [Coad et al. 1995].

18.3 Reification

Reification is a broad term that means to turn something that doesn't seem to be an object into an object. It is so broad that it is not quite fair to call it a design pattern. If anything, it is a meta-pattern, out of which other design patterns emerge.

The most striking examples of reification occur when the designer treats a method or verb-like idea as an object. You have seen a classic example in the undo exercise on page 176, where commands or actions became classes of objects. We will revisit this particular reification in the next section.

As a matter of fact, any time an activity or behavior starts out as a method, but over time you sense that it has rather complicated variants, then that activity is a good candidate for a class, and the variants are candidates for subclasses. That is what happened in the undo situation. Specific kinds of actions—moving, creating, and removing—became subclasses. We reified each operation into a class of its own.

Another common example is searching. At first blush, searching a repository of objects is plainly a job for a method. But pretty soon one realizes that the act of requesting a search can be a rich activity; there may be all manner of ways of specifying a search. This discovery leads pretty quickly to reification: one defines a class called **Search** with instance variables that represent the various arguments describing the criteria for a search. A search object immediately becomes handy if you want to search again, with slightly different criteria. And the next thing you know, you want to search for different kinds of objects in different repositories, so you define separate subclasses of **Search** for each such kind of object. The innocuous verb-like act of searching has blossomed into several potential classes.

You'll notice that once you reify something into a class, its principal public method often turns out to have a really routine name, like **undo** for the **Command** class. In the **Search** example, the name is likely to be **execute** or **doIt**. The method then gets reimplemented polymorphically in each concrete subclass so that every kind of **Command** knows how to **undo** itself and every kind of **Search** knows how to **execute** itself. This observation illustrates a rule of thumb: *reification begets polymorphism.* Whenever you reify from a method to a class, you are likely to enjoy the benefits of polymorphism.

Although the most dramatic reifications start from a method, not all do. One common form starts from a relationship between two classes of objects: introducing a **StudentCourse** class to manage the intricacies of the many-to-many relationship between **Student** and **Course** classes counts as a reification. For example, grades and attendance are better encapsulated within an instance of **StudentCourse** than within either an instance of **Student** or **Course**. This form of reification is known as an *association class*, and information such as grades and attendance are known as *link attributes* [Rumbaugh et al. 1991].

Reifications can also start from larger-scale activities than a method. For example, [Jacobson et al. 1992] suggest that an entire use case can be an appropriate candidate for an object. When they reify an activity, be it a whole use case or a more modest activity, they call the resulting object a *control object*. In other words, a control object is a reification of an activity. (These control objects should not be confused with the controller objects of MVC.)

In general, reifications exhibit the evolution of a design from plain beginnings to object-oriented respectability. A draw method eventually becomes a **DrawingTool** class; a conversion method for translating, say, an MM/DD/YY string format into a date object eventually becomes a **Converter** class (**AbtConverter** in VisualAge); operations for copying bitmaps eventually become the **BitBlockTransfer** class (**BitBlt** in VisualWorks); and so on. The essential lesson of reifying is that when things start to get complicated in a design, the experienced designer steps back and considers the possibility of introducing a brand-new kind of object. One can almost say that reification *is* object-oriented design. As you study the command pattern again, look at it in this spirit.

18.4 Command

You have solved the undo problem before; now let's cast it into the form of a pattern—the *command* pattern.

❑ How would you complete this design for undoing actions or commands?

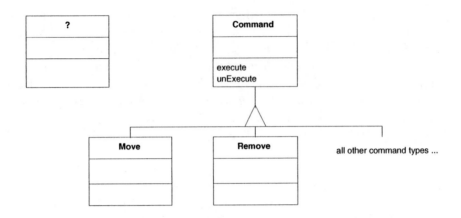

Solution: We review the earlier discussion (beginning on page 177), using now different names. Both **Command>>execute** and **Command>>unExecute** are subclassResponsibility (pure virtual) methods in the **Command** class, and they have concrete realizations in each of **Command**'s subclasses. To maintain a chronology of the command objects, we need a **Stack** class. A **Stack**'s LIFO (last-in-first-out) policy ensures that the most recent command will be undone first. The result is:

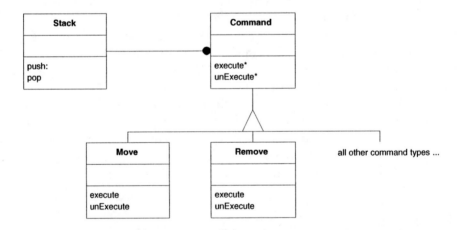

Not only does this illustrate the command pattern, but you should appreciate that formulating a **Command** class in the first place is an archetypal example of reification. The crucial discovery of the undo solution was to accept that so verb-like an idea as *move*, or *remove*, or *command* is, for the undo problem, an object.

18.5   Factory method

It often happens that one class depends crucially on another for certain services. For example, in a client/server system, the class that transfers customer data back and forth between a database server and a Smalltalk client (typically called the **CustomerBroker** class) needs the **Customer** class whenever it creates a new customer object. Or a **Calculator** class in an office desktop application needs a standard **CalculatorWindow** class when it presents itself on the screen.

Early in an application's life cycle, the designer inevitably realizes that other pairs of classes have the same relationship: **OrderBroker** needs **Order** when it creates a new order object, or **Phonebook** needs **PhoneWindow** when it presents itself. This situation often leads to code that looks like this:

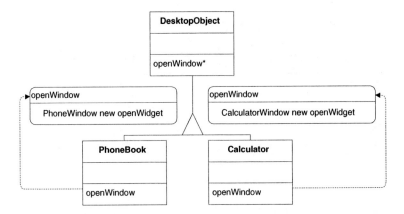

Notice the small but troubling redundancy: the messages ...**new openWidget** appear twice, in exactly the same form.

❑ This redundancy calls for a simple but dramatic improvement. We should try to factor the common ...**new openWidget** code out of the subclasses and elevate it to the superclass **DesktopObject**. But how?

Solution: Just write the code for **DesktopObject>>openWindow** in the only way that makes sense: **self windowClass new openWidget**. Here the **windowClass** method must be deferred to the subclasses. That is, each subclass must support a **windowClass** method that returns its associated class. The result is:

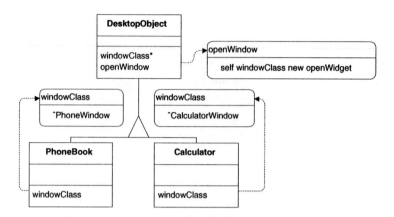

This pattern is known as a *factory method*, mainly because it frequently occurs when an object manufactures an instance of an associated class. Note the pattern's minimalism: each class and each method does only what it makes sense for it to do, and no more.

This pattern is an excellent indicator of the quality of any design involving abstract classes. It occurs in the life of a design only after the designer has spent some effort architecting clean relationships between classes. Conversely, if you don't see the pattern anywhere, it can be an indication that classes and their relationships have been haphazardly laid out.

18.6   Objects from records

The *objects from records* pattern is more specialized and intricate than the others in this chapter. It solves today's most fundamental client/server problem, moving back and forth between typical flat, relational databases on a server and objects at a client work-station.

A record, as programmers have always understood it, is simply a string of bytes that is subdivided into distinct fields. Historically, records were strips of data fitting end to end in a file or a "dataset." Today we commonly encounter records in the form of rows of a relational database table. Sometimes, in complex client/server applications, the bytes in a record may be assembled at the server from several database rows or other sources. But no matter where the data comes from, the essence of a conventional record is still just a string of bytes:

1223334444	Odysseus	10 Polyphemus Way	Ithaca	Greece	...
id	name	address	city	country	...

Although there is nothing novel about a record, it is so much an intrinsic part of a
typical server that it (or something like it) must play a leading role in any mechanism
for exchanging data between a server and an object-oriented client. Historically, programmers first solved this problem by translating each field in the record into a corresponding instance variable:

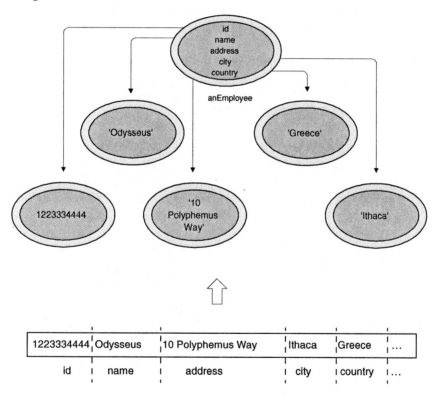

This translation generally occurred as soon as the record arrived from the server,
and it was performed sometimes by the **Customer** and sometimes by another object
(such as a **CustomerBroker**). The record had then served its purpose and became an
unwanted appendage.

This approach had some drawbacks. It is always important in an object-oriented design to distribute behavior into the classes for which the behavior makes most sense. That a business object class like **Customer** is responsible for translating low-level byte representations into objects exceeds our normal expectations of a "customer." A "broker" is a somewhat better candidate, but a broker ought to focus on locating and retrieving information from wherever it happens to reside, whether a local database or a remote server, which is a different function than translating between byte representations and objects.

Moreover, the "record" object's role is so passive that it hardly deserves to be called an object. We like our objects to have interesting behavior, and the record above is merely an inert data structure. All these drawbacks repeat in the opposite direction when the application needs to send an updated customer object back to the server. As an additional difficulty, users sometimes decide not to proceed with an update but would rather restore the customer object back to its original state. Since an instance variable can't hold two values at the same time, the original one and the updated one, this design doesn't maintain enough information to revert the customer object.

The pattern *objects from records* addresses these drawbacks by making the record an integral part of the customer object and also giving the record the responsibility for translation. The record objects will resemble a traditional record, but will be quite a lot smarter. In its simplest form, the record object encapsulates the data, its layout within the record, and the conversion or translation between bytes and objects. A customer object doesn't even need instance variables. Of course, it still needs getter and setter methods, but these can communicate directly with the underlying record instead of with instance variables. The design looks like this:

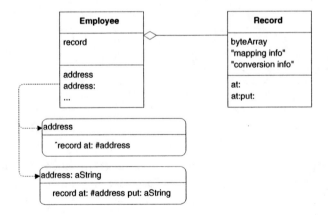

"Mapping information" consists of the bookkeeping needed to map names of fields like **#address** to positions and lengths in the byte array. "Conversion information" is the information needed to convert each field of the record to and from primitive objects such as strings and integers.

That summarizes the basic pattern. For the reader who is interested in the details, here is a closer look at class **Record** and its collaborators. In addition to a **ByteArray** that contains its original raw data, we may as well cache the results of each field conversion if and when a conversion occurs. The cache saves having to convert again if the field is accessed a second time. It also provides a serendipitous slot in which an updated value may be stored via **Record>>at:put:**. If the user commits the update, the cached values are copied onto the original byte array, and if the user reverts or rolls back, the cached values are simply cleared.

Thus, a more complete design is:

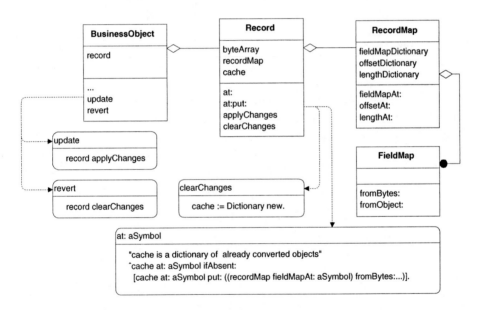

You should consider this pattern for any client/server application involving a non–object-oriented server. It decouples problem domain objects from server data structures and minimizes the overhead of converting to and from objects. The basic form may be embellished in several practical directions. For example, you can automate the generation of getters and setters, or you can automatically generate record maps from whatever defines the records—COBOL copybooks, C structures, or SQL statements. And if you lament the absence of instance variables—which you shouldn't too deeply, since the essence of an object is its behavior rather than the particulars of how it stores its data—you can resurrect them for use as a cache; conceptually this amounts to transplanting the cache from the record object to the business object.

This pattern may become obsolete someday, if legacy relational databases vanish and object-oriented distributed computing becomes common through facilities like the Object Management Group's specification for distribution (CORBA) or object databases (such as GemStone, ObjectStore, Tensegrity, and Versant). In the meantime, *objects from records* remains a fast, clean way to exchange information among computers across a network.

18.7   Proxies and ghosts, I

A *proxy* stands in the place of an actual thing. Proxies, like objects from records, occur in client/server designs. That's because an object, or even more to the point, a collection of objects, may be quite large, and it may be impractical to materialize the entire object or collection from the server. Instead, the client manipulates proxies for the objects, and only if the user needs the whole object does the application materialize it. Now, when the object finally does materialize, its proxy may behave in one of two ways. It can either forward messages to the object, so that in effect the proxy is transparent, or it can transform (or "morph") itself into the object, so that the proxy disappears. We'll discuss the second kind of proxy in the next section.

The first kind, sometimes called a *handle-body*, looks like this:

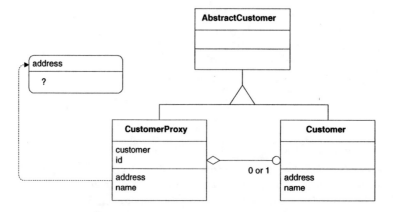

The "handle" is the proxy and the "body" is the customer. The hollow circle means that the proxy has either zero or one customer object, depending on whether or not its underlying customer object has been materialized.

❑ What should the code for the method **CustomerProxy>>address** do?

Solution: It should check to see if the **Customer** has been materialized, and if not, it should materialize it. Then it should forward the **address** message on to the **Customer**, like so:

```
address
          "Answer my address"
          customer isNil
                    ifTrue: [customer := "materialize the customer"].
          ^customer address
```

This trick of initializing an instance variable only at the moment you discover you need it is known as *lazy initialization*. One hopes that most customers will not be needed by the client, and so the space and time for materialization will occur for relatively few customers.

Finally, how does the proxy know the right customer to materialize? It must know one more crucial tidbit, namely, some key that identifies the customer for which it is the proxy. This key is generally a unique identification number stored with each customer in the server database. The full design is then:

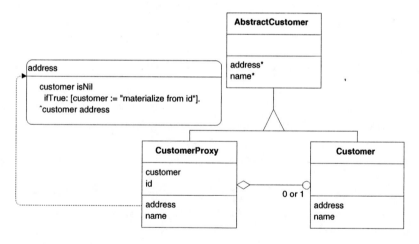

As a crowning touch, we have remembered to add subclassResponsibility methods to the abstract class. Although not mandatory in Smalltalk, it is always a good practice to use them to indicate that the programmer must provide a concrete overriding method in each subclass (page 64).

18.8   Proxies and ghosts, II

The second kind of proxy is called a *ghost*. Consider this diagram:

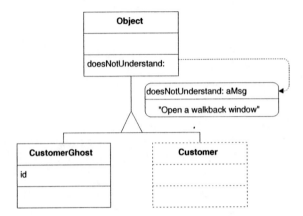

As for any proxy, the ghost must contain at least enough information in the instance variable **id** to uniquely identify the object it represents. **Object>>doesNotUnderstand:** is the familiar error message that executes whenever a message is not understood by an object. The essence of the ghost pattern is for the ghost to override this error.

❑   Unlike the handle-body proxy in the previous section, the ghost does not support an **address** getter. What then should it do if it receives the message **address**?

Solution: Normally, the inherited **doesNotUnderstand:** would execute, and a walk-back would follow. To provide a more satisfactory response to the **address** message, we override the usual **doesNotUnderstand:**. Instead of announcing an error, this version of **doesNotUnderstand:** will begin by materializing the customer. With a customer object now in hand, a conventional handle-body proxy would merely redispatch the **address** message to the customer.

But this being Smalltalk,[3] we will do something extraordinary: we will transform (morph) the ghost into the customer. That is, the ghost object of a moment ago will become an entirely different kind of object, namely the customer object. To morph an object in Smalltalk, we will need a special method named **become:**. Finally, we'll redispatch the **address** message to **self**, which by this time refers to the customer and not the ghost.

---

[3] This is the only Smalltalk-specific pattern in the chapter.

The method in its entirety looks like this:

```
doesNotUnderstand: aMessage
    "I, as a ghost, do not support aMessage. I will materialize a
    customer, morph myself to it, and then try aMessage again."
    |customer|
    customer := "materialize the customer"
    self become: customer.
    ^aMessage sendTo: self. "re-dispatch!"
```

Note how the redispatch in the last line treats **aMessage** as an object. In Smalltalk, everything is an object, including messages. Even in other dialects, where the form of the redispatch varies slightly, the essential truth remains intact: a message is an object too.

The overall pattern is:

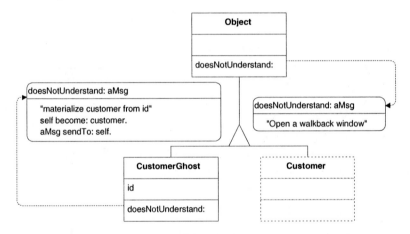

The happy outcome of all this activity is that where there was once a ghost that understood nothing, there now stands a customer that understands **address, name,** as well as every other customer message. Thus all future message sends will be successfully and immediately handled by the customer.

Technical note: It is only fair to say that this attractive design can have one drawback. In some Smalltalk implementations, where objects refer directly to other objects rather than through a table of object pointers, **become:** can be much slower than the virtually instantaneous method executions you are accustomed to. The degradation occurs because the virtual machine must locate all references to the ghost and reset them to point to the customer. You should therefore run some simple performance tests before adopting this pattern.

18.9   Dependency (aka broadcasting, model-view, observing, publish-subscribe)

Remember that in a well-designed user interface, views are directly aware of models, but not conversely. All a model can do is broadcast **update** messages to its views (or more generally, to its dependents), and the views then issue any specific inquiries to the model that they deem appropriate. This lopsided communication recurs often enough in object-oriented systems that it warrants recognition as a design pattern, called the *observer* or *dependency* pattern. In the model-view situation that you are most familiar with, views are the *observers* or *dependents*, and models are called *subjects*.

Here is the basic scenario:

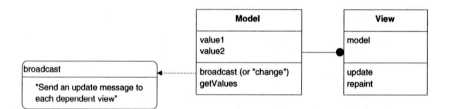

In Chapter 11 we discussed a variety of ways to implement the dependency relationship. The model may have a concealed instance variable, or there may be a shared dictionary somewhere that maintains the dependents of every model in the system. The specific implementation is unimportant for this discussion. By whatever means, the view receives an **update** message.

❏ What should **update** do?

Solution: It should query the model for the values it cares about and then reflect these possibly changed values into its display, roughly along these lines:

```
update
    "Obtain current data, then redisplay myself"
    model getValues "and process them".
    self repaint.
```

The result is:

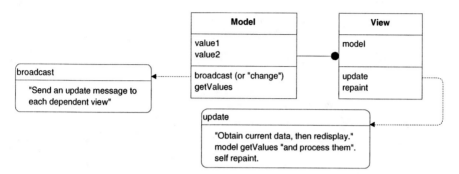

As we learned in Chapter 11, the essential benefit of this pattern is that the model functions independently of the number and kind of views. Models then can represent the conceptual objects of the problem without being burdened by user interface considerations. Views, on the other hand, concentrate on rendering information. They know their models and how to extract the information they care about from them.

Notice that "observer" is a misnomer for view or dependent because modern views, in absorbing the additional responsibility of MVC controllers (Chapter 11), are not just read-only objects. They respond to user inputs and may set values in their models as well as get them. However intrusive this "observation" is, models remain oblivious to their views, which is the most important theme of the pattern.

In general, the dependency pattern is the right way for an object to notify unknown numbers and kinds of other objects (its dependents) about changes in its state. For example, a traffic light simulation might notify all vehicle objects that it has changed to green. Or a palace vault might broadcast an alert to various security devices and stations if its entry has been breached. In fact, the whole idea of event notification, such as an operating system notifying windows that a mouse event has occurred, fits into the scheme of this pattern. (Also, with all broadcasts it is reasonable to pass some information along as an argument, such as the coordinates where the mouse event occurred, or a severity indication like "this event is a dire emergency.")

In the pattern's sharpest form, the broadcast consists of an arbitrary cluster of messages, with different clusters triggered by different events. See page 120 for a discussion of this form of the pattern.

18.10   Solitaire (aka singleton)

A computer should hold no more than one instance of some kinds of objects. Examples include objects that manage resources such as windows, or memory, or time. Another example, from distributed or client/server applications, is a broker object which obtains objects from the server and keeps track of those it has already obtained.

The problem is to design the protocol for constructing and accessing an instance of a class in a way that minimizes the possibility of inadvertently constructing a second instance. Here, for example, is an undesirable solution:

```
TheBroker := Broker new.
...
TheBroker getObjectWithId: '1234'.
```

For one thing, we have introduced a global variable **TheBroker**, and global variables are as a rule a bad idea. Global variables present the temptation of writing, elsewhere in the application,

```
OnlyBroker := Broker new.
```

which creates a second broker, or just as disastrously,

```
TheBroker := Broker new.
```

which loses the first broker together with its knowledge of objects it has already obtained from the server.

The *solitaire pattern* eliminates the global variable and its risks:

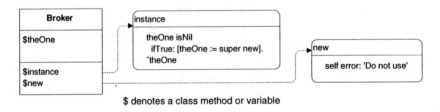

$ denotes a class method or variable

❑ What should you write to obtain an object from the server?

Solution:

```
Broker instance getObjectWithId: '1234'.
```

Lazy initialization in the class method named **instance** assures us of the same instance of **Broker**, whether this request is the first or a subsequent one. As an additional precaution against accidentally creating brokers, note that the **new** method has been disabled.

Typical client/server systems involve more than one class of objects. Because the logic that materializes each class of objects may differ, or different classes may require different servers, it is usually appropriate to define a separate broker for each class. **Broker** is then an abstract class with specific broker solitaires like **CustomerBroker** and **AccountBroker** as subclasses.

Technical aside: When **Broker** has subclasses, a class variable for **theOne** is not as suitable as a Smalltalk *class instance variable*. Each subclass inherits its own separate, unshared copy of a superclass's class instance variable, in which the subclass's separate broker may reside. Class variables don't have this property. Instead, all subclasses share a class variable defined by their superclass—not very helpful if you want each to have its own separate broker.

18.11 Duet (aka pas de deux, double dispatch)

Those few occasions when a "function" just doesn't seem to be a method on a single object, but rather ought to be a "method" on two peer objects, can cast the whole applicability of object-oriented programming in doubt. Our modern, object-centric view of the world is too narrow for these situations.

For example, is **play** a method in class **Instrument** that takes a **Musician** as an argument? Or is it a method in class **Musician** that takes **Instrument** as an argument? Or is it something else, an operation on a *pair* of objects? If the situation calls for an operation on a pair of objects, we use the *duet* pattern. The most interesting application of this pattern occurs when **Instrument** and **Musician** both have subclasses, because **play** then becomes an operation that is polymorphic on both of its arguments. (Refer to the commentary on multi-methods on page 170 for an example and discussion.)

A basic example of duets is arithmetic, where the asymmetric interpretation of **a + b** (**a** receives the message; **b** is "just" an argument) rattles Smalltalk newcomers. From our earliest functional schooling, we developed faith in the symmetry of the operation **a + b**. We psychologically want addition to be an operation on two objects—a multi-method—rather than a message to one of them. But Smalltalk, being a "pure" object-oriented language, cannot oblige.

Only CLOS among commercial object-oriented languages supports genuine multi-methods. In Smalltalk we can synthesize an arithmetic multi-method with this duet:

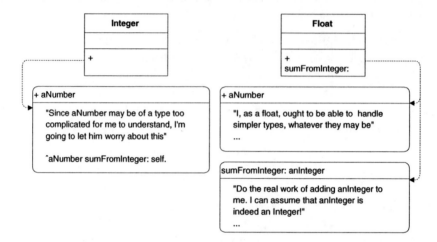

You can use **+** to add an integer and a float *in either order.* But only one of them—the **Float**—can do the real work. If the other—the **Integer**—is asked to do the job, it automatically sends a message to the **Float**, announcing that it is an integer seeking assistance from the **Float** to do the arithmetic.

This pattern is a "duet" because it makes the participants seem like peers. It is a *double dispatch* or *pas de deux* because of the dramatic transfer of control and passing of **self** as an argument to the other object.

For the programmer who implements the pattern, the important outcome is the elimination of conditional tests. The integer does not check anything; it immediately and unconditionally sends the message to its argument, announcing that it is an integer in need of aid. As we've learned from studying polymorphism, one of the best ways to simplify software maintenance is to write code without conditionals.

For the consumer programmer, the important outcome is conceptual simplification: it doesn't matter which of the two objects he sends the **+** message to. In effect, **+** is, from his perspective, a non–object-oriented operation. It also doesn't matter what types of objects participate in the operation. He can add any combination of **Float**, **Integer**, or **Fraction** without a second thought.

❑ What happens if the **+** message is merely used to add two integers together, rather than the more complicated scenario of an integer and a float?

Solution: **sumFromInteger:** still executes unconditionally, but it is now sent to an **Integer**, so the **Integer** class had better implement **sumFromInteger:** as well. Fortunately, this is a reasonable expectation—an integer ought to be able to add another integer to itself.

Although duets are a clean way to implement arithmetic, and VisualWorks and to a lesser extent VisualSmalltalk use them for arithmetic, IBM Smalltalk does not. For speed, IBM Smalltalk implements arithmetic directly in its virtual machine.

18.12   Lawyer (aka object handler)

Often, two kinds of objects work together, but neither should be complicated by direct knowledge of the other. We have seen this situation in many-to-many relationships (page 217), and we are now about to see it in one-to-one relationships.

Consider an icon object and the model object that it stands for. In the spirit of model-view separations it would be unseemly to give the model object knowledge of a visual object like its iconic representation. Also, an icon is such a simple visual object—roughly a bitmap—that we would not expect it to know how the user interface happens to associate some model object with it.

We wish to decouple the two objects, yet on the other hand we would like to keep the model informed about the icon's experiences. For example, if in a graphical editor the user drags an icon representing a graphical element to a different location, we would expect the coordinates of the graphical element to change. Neither the icon nor the graphical element alone has this responsibility. So we construct a third object, called an *object handler* or *lawyer*, which knows both the icon and the graphical element [Collins 1995].

The user interface then manipulates lawyers instead of icons. Through lawyers, the user interface can communicate indirectly with either party a lawyer represents, be it the icon or the underlying object. The pattern looks like this:

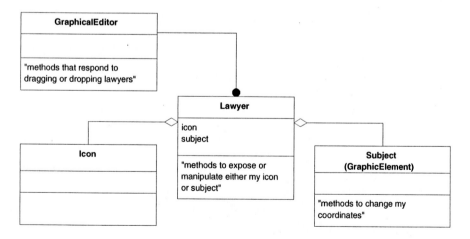

Updating the coordinates of a graphical element is a relatively simple service of one lawyer—the lawyer merely mediates between the icon and the graphical element. This lawyer is an example of the *mediator* pattern [Gamma et al. 1995]. Lawyers make especially good livings by talking to other lawyers; this is the relationship we examine next.

Consider icons again. The usual visual feedback that occurs as a result of dragging one icon over another depends only on the types of the objects represented by the icons. For example, the feedback will indicate that you cannot drop a file icon onto a calculator icon, but that you can drop it onto a printer icon. This has nothing really to do with the underlying objects; the user interface can compute the feedback from the icons alone. But suppose a sophisticated user interface must provide more refined feedback, such as an indication that you cannot drop a file icon onto a printer icon if the printer object is off-line. This feedback depends on the state of the underlying printer object and therefore cannot be determined solely from the icons.

❏   What objects can make this determination?

Solution: We have ruled out the icon objects, since they are oblivious to the state of their associated objects. But lawyer objects can make the determination because they know about the icons (is the file icon over the printer icon?) as well as the underlying objects (is the printer on-line?). Thus the file lawyer can negotiate with the printer lawyer to determine the appropriate feedback. Here are the relationships and responsibilities:

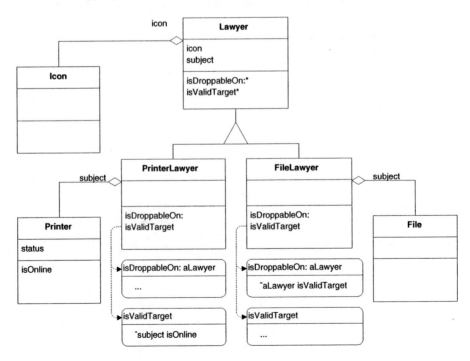

Let's step through the interactions. Suppose the user has positioned the file icon over the printer icon. Since the user interface manipulates lawyers rather than icons, it asks the file lawyer whether it is droppable on the printer lawyer. To answer the question, the file lawyer asks the printer lawyer whether it is a valid target, which the printer lawyer in turn determines by asking its subject the printer whether it is on-line. Depending on the response, the user interface will display either a "cannot drop" or an "ok to drop" indication.

Without delegating the negotiation to the two lawyers, we would have had to write and maintain messages flowing directly among all four principal parties—two icons and two model objects. Lawyers simplify the interactions in direct manipulation user interface designs just as observers or model-view separations simplify the interactions in windowed user interface designs.

This pattern is not just about user interfaces. The essential lesson is that whenever two objects are in one-to-one association with each other, the association becomes a prospective object in its own right. This object—a lawyer—reifies the association. In our example, the lawyer reifies the association between an icon and the object the icon represents. The striking additional twist in our example is that two lawyers can go on to negotiate with each other.

18.13 Composite

The *composite* pattern is the workhorse of recursive relationships. Whether you are nesting graphics or exploding a bill of materials or processing a parse tree, the composite lets you apply some operation to every object or node in the structure.

Suppose you want to calculate the cost of a complex product like a telescope. The telescope consists of a basic scope and an eyepiece. In turn, the basic scope consists of a tube and an objective lens, the lens has glass plus a sophisticated fluorite coating.... We can represent any such product with this recursive design:

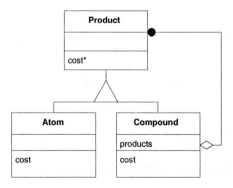

The picture shows us that a compound product consists of any number of other products, each of which could be either atomic or another compound product. **Product** is an abstract class. It cannot calculate its cost and it has no instances. **Atom** is usually also an abstract class; in our example, it has irreducible subclasses like **FluoriteCoating**, each of which can calculate its own cost.

❑ What is the Smalltalk code for **Compound>>cost**?

Solution: The instance variable **products** is a collection (say, an **OrderedCollection**), so **cost** should simply iterate over each product in the collection, ask it for its cost, increment a total, and respond with the final total. The entire pattern is thus:

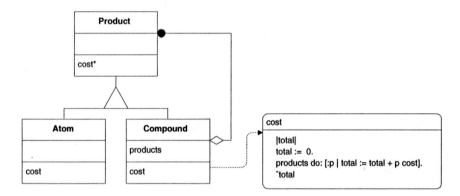

The composite pattern is simple and elegant. What helps account for its appeal is how the polymorphic **cost** method acts in a different but unimpeachably apt way for each class.

The composite pattern is the basis for more specialized patterns, such as the next one.

18.14   Visitor

The *visitor* pattern blends features from two of the preceding patterns, namely the duet and the composite. The composite pattern is attractive as long as the action that must be performed at each node is a straightforward polymorphic message like **cost** above. When the action shows signs of blossoming into a complex method involving other far-reaching objects, the composite solution loses its appeal.

Problems having to do with language translation or program compilation fall into this category. As a translator iterates through the nodes of a parse tree, it may require knowledge about a foreign language. This knowledge probably isn't encapsulated within the parse tree. A node object from an English sentence knows its syntactic role in English, but shouldn't have to know about foreign words and syntax.

Here is a sample problem. Bear with me while I remind you about some grammar lessons from school. The first thing a translation program does is the same thing you did when you diagrammed sentences. It generates a parse tree.[4] The sentence, "The cat chases a dog," results in this parse tree:

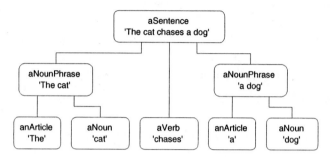

We want to eventually produce the French sentence, "Le chat poursuit un chien," from this tree. Each node in this tree is an object, but they are instances of several classes. The leaf nodes along the bottom row are called **Terminal** nodes. Thus there are three subclasses of **Terminal**, namely **Article**, **Noun**, and **Verb**. The non-leaf nodes are **NonTerminal** nodes. The subclasses of **NonTerminal** are **Sentence** and **NounPhrase**. The inheritance hierarchy for these classes looks enticingly like a composite:

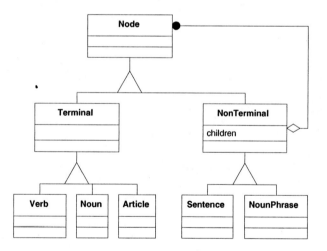

---

[4] There are many ways to generate a parse tree, the simplest of which is known as *recursive descent*. The mechanics of generating a parse tree by this or any other means will not concern us; we are interested in what you can do *after* you have the parse tree.

But if we try to apply the composite pattern, recursively sending a **translate** message to each node object, we face the drawbacks alluded to above. First, the tree is an English parse tree, and its nodes shouldn't have to know any French. (If they did, the design could not be reused for translating English into, say, Chinese.) Second, translation is more subtle than just translating leaf nodes one by one. Translating the noun *cat* to *chat* affects the translation of the preceding article *the*—the gender and spelling of *chat* imply that the result should be *le* (and not *la* or *l'*). Unfortunately by the time the **translate** message arrives at *cat*, the preceding word has already been translated. To translate correctly, we evidently must involve the **NounPhrase** class, and if we insist on using the composite pattern we will have to add complex, French-specific logic to its **translate** method.

❑ How can we decouple these French-specific complications from the English-based node classes?

Solution: Invent a new class that reifies the **translate** method. That is, instead of writing a complex, French-specific **translate** method on each node, define a class called **Translator**. An instance of **Translator** *visits* each node. Upon each visit, it is asked to perform some operation, which is why the pattern is called a *visitor*. It looks like this:

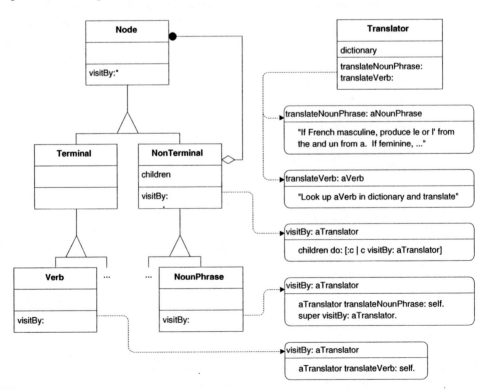

The burden of translation has been lifted from the humble node and placed on the back of the able-bodied visitor. **Translator** will have an instance variable for storing a language-specific translation dictionary. The complex **translate** method has been replaced by the **visitBy:** method, which merely dispatches a message back to a translator object, passing **self** (the node) as an argument. The translator object can then do whatever it wants with the node. Any complex logic, such as translating the gender and article of a noun phrase, resides in the translator instead of the nodes of the parse tree. Note the similarity to a duet: the message to the translator announces the type of object being passed (**translateNounPhrase:** or **translateVerb:**), just as our duet did (**sumFromInteger:**).

This pattern also makes other translator classes feasible (**EnglishToFrench**, **EnglishToChinese**...). The English parse tree doesn't change at all; to translate to another target language, the parse tree's nodes are simply visited by a different translator. The visitor pattern neatly factors behavior into classes for which the behavior is most suitable. By not cluttering the parse tree with extraneous information, it is easier to reuse for other language translations. The visitor pattern is a fitting finale to this chapter because it extends two fundamental patterns—the composite and duet—and illustrates again the value of reification.

18.15   Conclusion

Since there are infinitely many ways to group objects or classes, it's not constructive to call every grouping a pattern. A grouping deserves to be called a pattern only if doing so is useful for designers. As for what constitutes "usefulness," here are some informal criteria:

- The grouping is based on metaphor(s) or other recognizable ideas. This, together with the next criterion, helps designers remember the pattern.

- The grouping has an evocative, memorable name. Among object-oriented designers, pattern names are a lingua franca for quickly exchanging ideas about how to solve a problem, or understanding how a piece of software has been structured.

- The grouping resembles a micro-architecture. In other words it is not an ad hoc assemblage of objects, but an assemblage that conveys a coherent sense of function, structure, and aesthetics.

Once you know a few design patterns, you will start to recognize opportunities for applying them. It's like a chess player who studies openings or a guitarist who learns a few chords. Sooner or later they are likely to have an opportunity to use them.

Here is a summary of the patterns we've studied:

Applicability	Pattern	Sample problems
Big object and small objects	Smart container	History log, address book, ...
Heavy verbs	Reification	Converters, Search, Command, ...
Interactive applications	Command	Undo/redo
Redundant code	Factory method	One class routinely uses another
Flat or relational data	Objects from records	Client/server materialization
Too many large objects	Proxy and ghost	Remote computation
One-way observation	Dependency	MVC, alerts, events, callbacks
No more than one instance	Solitaire (singleton)	Brokers
Functions instead of methods	Duet	Multi-methods
One-to-one associations	Lawyer	State-based visual feedback
Nested objects	Composite	Drawings, bill-of-materials
Language translation	Visitor	Translators, code generators

You will find general treatments of all but smart containers, reification, objects from records, duets, and lawyers in [Gamma et al. 1995]. For more on smart containers, see [Coad et al. 1995]; for objects from records, see [Wolf and Liu 1995]; for duets see [Ingalls 1986]; and for lawyers (object handlers) see [Collins 1995].

18.16 Commentary: history

The idea of a software pattern can be traced as far back as the mid-1970s, when Adele Goldberg and Alan Kay at Xerox PARC realized that novice programmers couldn't solve hard problems, no matter how wonderful the programming language. The novices could comprehend the language well enough, but they couldn't be expected to know the design techniques that might be expressible in the language. This discontinuity is analogous to a child who can read and write English, but is too young to have digested the wisdom of great literature. To provide some conceptual building blocks above the raw language, Goldberg and Kay introduced *design templates*, which are a forerunner of today's design patterns [Kay 1993].

Kent Beck and Ward Cunningham discussed a small, potent set of software patterns in 1987 [Power 1988]. But the interest in patterns really burgeoned at Bruce

Anderson's architecture handbook workshop at OOPSLA '91.[5] Articles on patterns began to appear a year later [Coad 1992; Eggenschwiler and Gamma 1992; Johnson 1992]. The landmark catalog appeared at the end of 1994 [Gamma et al. 1995]. Ralph Johnson organized the first conference on the subject of patterns in software in 1994 [Coplien and Schmidt 1995].

Software patterns have become so fashionable that they run the risk of overexposure. Just as almost anything may be construed as a metaphor (page 146), almost anything may be construed as a pattern. Thus, many "patterns" are too narrow and arcane to be of much use to the general computing public, and many articles that would be interesting in their own right have been unnaturally cast into a pattern format. Nevertheless, plenty of promising, unexplored territory remains for patterns in software.

Before programmers got excited about software patterns, the architect Christopher Alexander and his associates published a series of books, starting with [Alexander et al. 1977; Alexander 1979], on the use of patterns to build living spaces for people. Alexander suggested that his catalog of 253 patterns could be a basis for everything from laying out a community down to deciding the décor for a room. His patterns, like good software patterns, are metaphoric ("City country fingers"), memorable ("Light on two sides of every room"), and architectural ("Perimeter beams"). His work inspired the early software-pattern investigators.

Alexander wanted to go far beyond merely applying proven patterns to the act of building. He wanted the resulting living space to have what he called, "the quality without a name." Patterns were just a means to this end. Unfortunately, this zen-like quality admits no definition. By and large, people agree on some few dwellings and communities that have the quality, and they agree that most dwellings and communities don't. It is the same with software. Programmers can generally agree that certain software is masterfully designed, but they encounter such software rarely.

In the years following publication of Alexander's books on patterns, he realized that patterns alone did not ensure that the results would have "the quality without a name." (He knew it as early as 1977, but the depth of the insufficiency became apparent only after disappointing experiments.) Revisiting the chess analogy: knowing and applying chess patterns improves one's game, but rarely does a beautiful chess game happen. The key to attaining this quality in software (or any endeavor) has not been discovered. For an appreciation of the depth of the problem as it pertains to rhetoric and philosophy, read [Pirsig 1974], and for a discussion of how Alexander hopes to solve it for architecture and what his ideas mean to software, see the series of articles [Gabriel 1993–1994].

---

[5] OOPSLA is the annual conference on "Object-Oriented Programming, Systems, Languages, and Applications."

CHAPTER 19

Frameworks (one hearty example)

Object-oriented *frameworks* are as fashionable as patterns, and developers everywhere try to build them. Like patterns, so many things are now called frameworks that the meaning has gotten blurry, making it tough to appreciate their importance.

A framework is a general skeleton for a software application. More than one application may be built around the same framework, but they will all be shaped by the basic structures and mechanics of the framework, as though frogs of different appearances and appetites could be shaped from the same frog skeleton. To build frogs you use a frog framework; to build snakes you use a snake framework.

In technical terms, a framework is a body of code that is reusable across different projects. An example I've already talked about is the original MVC framework for user interfaces. MVC consists of the abstract classes **Model**, **View**, and **Controller** and the interactions among them. The most famous of these interactions are the broadcasts that a model issues. Practically every application developer in Smalltalk-80 reuses MVC by inheriting from one or more of these three abstract classes.

On the other hand, not every reusable library of classes qualifies as a framework. For instance, no one calls a library of container classes a framework, nor does anyone call a library of user interface widgets a framework. What's the difference? For one thing, a framework like MVC imposes a structure on an application, whereas a library of containers or widgets doesn't.

Another difference is what Erich Gamma calls the *Hollywood Principle*:[1] "Don't call us; we'll call you." Programmers are accustomed to writing calls to the functions in a library. (We say programmers call an *API*, for *application programming interface*.)

---

[1] Erich says that programmers at Xerox PARC coined this usage.

The Hollywood Principle inverts this relationship: the programmer writes code that the framework calls. The programmer will have to know in advance what the framework is going to call—his code must conform to the framework's expectations. These being object-oriented expectations, the framework will include some abstract classes for which he builds subclasses and overrides subclassResponsibility (pure virtual) methods. Using a framework always involves subclassing from abstract classes; using an ordinary library of container or widget classes usually does not.

In other words, a framework specifies missing elements. When you supply these elements, the framework makes them operate together as a working application. By supplying different elements, you can create a different application. A framework provides all the machinery for an application except the application itself.

The best way to understand the idea of a framework is to study an example. We are going to tour some highlights of a framework that provides the machinery for developing client/server applications. This framework simplifies construction of Smalltalk applications that use non-object data from computers across the network. A framework like this one accounts for a substantial part of the overall effort in developing a client/server application; the cost and expertise needed to develop this support from scratch exceeds the cost of developing the application's model and view objects.

19.1   Problems

Any framework for supporting Smalltalk at the client and non-object data at the server must address some fundamental problems. You can think of these problems as the basic use cases of client/server computing.

- *Materialization:* Transforming traditional, non-object data, usually in the form of records in a file or rows in a relational database, to and from objects that an object-oriented language can process.

- *Identity management:* Ensuring that at most one version of an object resides at the client workstation. In other words, materialization should not produce a second copy of an object if the object has materialized once before.

- *Searching:* Looking for one or more objects that match some criteria.

- *Updating:* Changing the state of objects at the client workstation and cascading those changes back to the appropriate server. (The problem of creating a new object and saving it is similar.)

This drawing summarizes the problems:

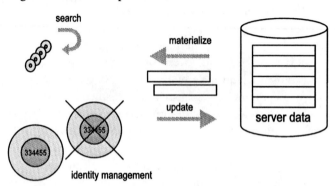

Imagine now that a programmer has been handed a client/server framework, and is developing an application for, say, bankers who watch over loans. We want to understand what he must do about each of the problems above. To understand what follows, you will need to know just a few facts about relational databases:

- Data are stored in tables. The columns or fields of a table have names, such as "LoanNumber," "OutstandingAmount," and "Collateral." And each row in a table contains related data, such as a specific loan's number, its outstanding amount, and its origination date.

- The standard language for manipulating relational data is *SQL*, the *Structured Query Language*. All relational database systems support *dynamic SQL*; a dynamic SQL statement must be reinterpreted by the database every time it is issued. Some database systems also support a form of pre-compiled SQL, which, once compiled, is bound to the database and can therefore execute faster than dynamic SQL. An example of this kind of SQL is IBM's *static SQL* for its DB2 family of database systems. (You won't need to know the details of the SQL language to understand this chapter.)

19.2   Materialization

The heart of any client/server application is materialization—the act of producing objects at the client workstation from some form of flat, non–object-oriented data at the server.

What the framework does. The framework uses the *objects from records* pattern (page 220) to convert flat data (records) to and from objects. An abstract class named

BusinessObject represents the objects produced by the pattern, and another abstract class named **Broker** encapsulates the algorithms for sending and receiving records to and from the server.

The design of a broker depends on the overall client/server architecture. One broker can issue dynamic or static SQL calls to the server; another can use a communication protocol like APPC or TCP/IP to issue calls to procedures or programs that execute at the server to process the data. In other words, some brokers are *SQL brokers* and others are *transaction brokers*. Because the private behavior of these brokers differs, the framework has different abstract classes for them. (See the commentary on page 254 for more on broker varieties.)

Let's assume that the application designer decides to use the class of brokers that supports static SQL. The name for this abstract class is **SQLBroker**. This class collaborates with another abstract class called **DBPackage**, which houses the package of static SQL statements that gets bound to the database.

The framework must know that a specific combination of broker, package, and class of business objects works together—it won't do for a **LoanBroker** to try to materialize a **Customer** object, for example—so it declares subclassResponsibility methods named **Broker>>objectClass** and **Broker>>package** that link these classes.

What the programmer does. He builds concrete subclasses of the abstract classes, say **LoanBroker, LoanPackage,** and **Loan,** and links the classes with these methods in **LoanBroker:**

```
objectClass
        "Answer the class of business objects I broker"
        ^Loan
```

and:

```
package
        "Answer the the package of SQL statements I need"
        ^LoanPackage instance
```

The framework then ensures that these classes will work together correctly to materialize loan objects.

❑ Explain the function of the **instance** message in the method above.

Solution: There should be only one instance of **LoanPackage** at the workstation. Packages are therefore solitaires (page 230) and **instance** is the (conventional) name of the class method that returns the unique instance of **LoanPackage**.

Here are highlights of the classes involved in materialization:

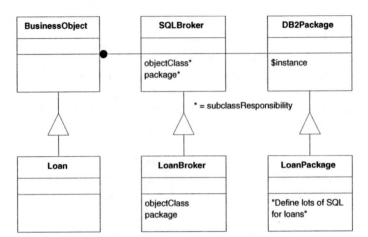

You might recognize the methods **objectClass** and **package** as examples of the factory method pattern (page 219). The factory method is the bread-and-butter pattern of framework building.

19.3   Managing object identity

A built-in peril of client/server systems is the materialization of two separate objects that represent the same business object. This circumstance exposes the user to the risk of independently changing both copies, which would be a serious breach of object identity. (Remember the discussion of object identity, beginning on page 73.)

How could such a thing happen? Suppose a loan object materializes as a result of searching for all loans with more than $50,000 outstanding. Imagine that some time later a second search for all loans to some tycoon materializes the *same* loan. Unless the application was designed carefully, two loan objects at the client workstation now represent the same loan. To complete the misadventure, suppose the banker updates the wording of the collateral ("…log cabin, running water, screened-in porch…") in one and extends the payment terms in the other. Now neither loan object has the data the banker intended, and no matter which loan(s) are committed back to the server, confusion results.

What the framework does. A **Broker** contains a dictionary of all the objects it has materialized. Each entry in the dictionary has for its key a unique descriptor for the object and for its value the object itself. Thus if 100,000 loans are stored in the server database, and the **LoanBroker** has materialized 29 of them, 29 entries will be in the **LoanBroker**'s dictionary. Each of them consists of a key—probably the loan's loan number—and a value that is the loan object itself.

If the banker requests another loan object, the framework checks whether the loan's loan number is one of the 29 keys already in the dictionary. If so, it must not materialize another copy, for that would produce the unpleasant scenario above.

To make all this work, the broker evidently needs to know what to use as a key for its business objects. Therefore the **BusinessObject** class has a subclassResponsibility method called **identityKey**. The broker uses this method to manage the entries in its dictionary, and in particular to determine whether a business object is already in the dictionary.

What the programmer does. He writes a method **Loan>>identityKey** which simply returns the loan's loan number. The framework does the rest.

What else the framework does. The other side of the coin is cleaning up: when should the framework *remove* entries from the broker's dictionary of materialized objects? The framework can't afford to ignore removal because after prolonged use, a broker's dictionary of objects may grow so large as to overrun the workstation's memory. The challenge is for the framework to recognize when a business object is no longer needed by the application; that is, when no other business objects or views in the application refer to the object. At that moment the object can safely be removed from its broker's dictionary.

This challenge sounds suspiciously like a garbage collection problem (page 187). But not quite, for we have an additional, circular twist: the Smalltalk garbage collector won't recognize the object as garbage until the broker's dictionary releases its reference to it; on the other hand, the dictionary dares not release the reference until it knows that the object is garbage.

Fortunately, the latest major Smalltalk releases extend memory management with a feature called *weak references*. A weak reference to an object is a reference that doesn't matter to the garbage collector. Ordinary references are *strong* references; these are the references that the garbage collector uses to know that an object is still needed.

The idea is to design brokers to use weak references instead of strong ones so that the brokers don't stand in the way of the garbage collector. For this a broker must use a special dictionary known as a **WeakDictionary**—this and other collection classes whose names are prefixed by "weak" are the only kinds of objects that can refer weakly to other objects. The garbage collector doesn't care if a weak dictionary has a reference to an object; after all, it's not a strong reference but a weak one.

In the example above, suppose the weak dictionary has its 29 entries, each consisting of a loan number and the corresponding loan object, when the user decides to close all views that are open on one of the loans. There are now no strong references to this loan object, but the one weak reference from the weak dictionary remains. Weak references don't stop the garbage collector; it considers the object to be garbage, reclaims its memory, and finally removes its reference from the weak dictionary. We have achieved the desired effect: by using the **WeakDictionary** instead of an ordinary **Dictionary**, the broker automatically releases an object once no application objects refer to it.[2]

What else the programmer does. Nothing more than the **identityKey** method he has already written, since all the logic of weak references in the **LoanBroker** will be inherited from **Broker**.

Here are the highlights of identity management:

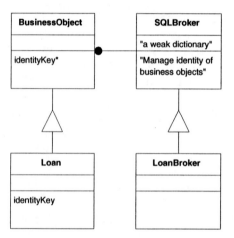

19.4   Searching (filtering)

Searching for things is a basic human activity. Sometimes we know exactly what we are looking for and we just want to grab it (the loan with loan number 334455), and sometimes we want to look at a collection of things (all loans with more than $50,000 outstanding).

---

[2] This problem has solutions other than weak references, but none are as satisfying. They all involve keeping track of references to business objects, which amounts to replicating the work of a garbage collector. A C++ version of this framework, lacking garbage collection, hence also weak references, would have no choice but to tackle this sizable and delicate job.

What the framework does. Let's begin with the first case, where the user or application knows a key that identifies the desired object. The **Broker** provides a concrete method with a name like **objectWithKey:,** which takes the key as an argument and returns the business object having that key.

What the programmer does. He does *not* override **objectWithKey:** in his broker subclasses because the code can be written once with complete generality in **Broker**. On the other hand, he will find many occasions for *invoking* this method.

For example, suppose every loan object contains a customer number. That is, a loan object contains the key identifying the customer that took out the loan. While examining a loan, the user may want to also examine the customer. So the user clicks some button, and the programmer's code responds to the click by sending the **objectWithKey:** message, carrying the customer's key as an argument to the **CustomerBroker**, which responds with the customer.

Or the programmer may have designed proxies for customer objects (page 224 ff.), and imbued the proxies with getters that supply only enough information to display them in a list widget. By and by the user wants to see the full customer object behind one of them; this proxy then sends the **objectWithKey:** message to the **CustomerBroker**. Since the proxy knows the customer number for the customer it stands for, the message carries this key as its argument.

Here are the highlights of these two scenarios for grabbing full customer objects:

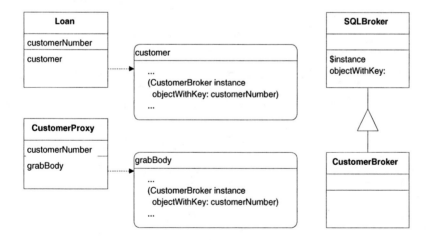

The moral of this story is that frameworks not only demand that the programmer override subclassResponsibility methods, but they also make available concrete methods that the programmer will want to invoke. Notice that the programmer doesn't need to examine any tricky code such a method may contain; he trusts that the framework got it right. Another way to say this, using some jargon, is that frameworks are characterized largely by *white-box reuse*, but they also provide some *black-box reuse*. (See page 253 for more on these terms.)

What else the framework does. The other kind of search sometimes goes by the name *filter*: the framework accepts a description from the user and filters the server for all the objects that match the description. This is an interesting problem for the framework designer because it is an opportunity to introduce two classes of objects that are not initially obvious. (Remember that such discoveries are known as reification. See page 216.) The first is an abstract class named **Search**; this class encapsulates the descriptions of the objects being sought. The second is **BusinessObjectList**, which is what a search returns.

Search objects solve a basic usability problem: after seeing the results of the search, the user often wants to adjust the description of the objects in some small way and search again. Because the framework retains the **Search** object, it is an easy matter for the user to access the original description, modify it, and reissue the search.

A **BusinessObjectList** is as good as an **OrderedCollection** for populating list widgets because it is designed to support the main methods of **OrderedCollection**—as far as list widgets can tell, a **BusinessObjectList** and an **OrderedCollection** are polymorphic. But **BusinessObjectList** also supports behavior that solves a client/server performance problem: in practice, a search may return so many objects that either the time to move all the data from server to client is unacceptably long or the objects consume too much of the client's memory. The search object therefore asks the server to limit the number of matching objects it returns, say to the first 50 business objects, and then creates a **BusinessObjectList** to hold these objects. If the user wants to see the next 50, the **BusinessObjectList** scrolls, which really means that it asks the search object to retrieve the next 50 matching business objects from the server. Thus a **BusinessObjectList** holds a limited number of the objects that match the search description, but it is smart enough to replenish itself with the others as needed. Because it is not the whole list but can access the whole list, we can call it a *virtual list* that must *mega-scroll* to reach all its business objects.

What the programmer does. He builds concrete subclasses of **Search** such as **LoanSearch**, and customizes **LoanSearch** to handle the search criteria that matter for loans.

The highlights of filtering or searching are thus:

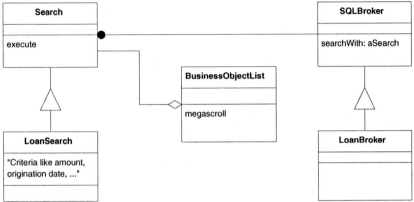

Note that a search object must collaborate with a broker to actually retrieve objects from the server. Also note that a **BusinessObjectList** must know the search object that produced its contents so that it can re-execute this search when it mega-scrolls.

19.5 Updating

An application that allows the user to update data at the server must support two basic scenarios:

1   The user makes changes and commits them,

2   The user makes changes, thinks better of them, and wants to discard them.

What the framework does. Because the user wants to be able to revert a business object to its original state, the framework must retain the object's original data somewhere. The *objects from records* pattern (page 220) that we are using for materialization provides storage for both the original data and the user's changes. The pattern accommodates a **Byte-Array** of data plus a cache of converted sub-objects. (The drawing on page 223 shows one implementation, with both the byte array and cache stored in the record object.)

The **ByteArray** houses the original data and the cache houses current objects, whether they are objects cached by conversions from the **ByteArray** or modifications to these objects made by the user. Only when the user commits the changes in the cache does the framework convert the cached objects to raw data in the **ByteArray** and send the data back to the server. If the user instead discards the changes, the framework simply empties the cache, which effectively presents the original **ByteArray** as the current data.

What the programmer does. This is another example of black-box reuse. Assuming that the user can click buttons for committing or reverting, the programmer writes code that responds to click events by invoking **Loan>>update** or **Loan>>revert**, respectively. These methods are actually inherited from **BusinessObject,** and so the framework does the rest.

Here are the highlights of the design for updating and reverting:

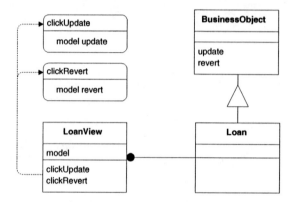

In keeping with the model-view or observer pattern (page 228), the view's loan is represented here by an instance variable named **model.**

19.6　Summary

The programmer who uses a framework is in something of a straitjacket. He loses some of programming's traditional freedom of choice. Because of the Hollywood Principle, his first thought is not, "I'll begin by laying out some logic," but, "Where am I *compelled* to begin?"[3] Since we are talking about object-oriented programming, he answers this question by looking for the framework's abstract classes and their subclassResponsibility methods.

---

[3] The Hollywood Principle illustrates a programming trend: application programmers are writing more and more code that conforms to expectations or guidelines from elsewhere. Another example of this trend is the handlers you wrote in Chapter 12 to respond to events and callbacks. Yet another is the hook methods that are object-oriented counterparts of user exits in early mainframe systems programs (see the aside on page 66). Since you are not obliged to write handlers or hook methods, these represent a variation on the Hollywood Principle in which you don't have to be there when the call comes. On the other hand, subclassResponsibility methods are obligatory—you had better be there when the call comes or you will be in trouble.

Object-oriented frameworks have other characteristics:

- A framework provides *white-box reuse*, as well as the more familiar *black-box reuse* you get from calling an API or using a library of container classes. A framework user must understand the abstract classes and what is expected of their subclassResponsibility methods, whereas a container user just calls encapsulated **add:** and **remove:** methods. White-box reuse follows from the Hollywood Principle: the framework will have expectations when it calls your code, and it is your job to look into the framework far enough to understand what those expectations are. They may be as straightforward as making sure you override a method named **foobar**, but whatever they are, you must understand them.

- Learning to use a framework takes effort. You can't do white-box reuse until you learn the abstract classes and their subclassResponsibility methods. Because the abstract classes interact with one another, you generally have to learn more than one class before you begin writing your application. Black-box reuse, on the other hand, usually occurs one class at a time. You are likely to use a **Set** today and a **SortedCollection** tomorrow; you don't have to understand interactions between them.

- Developing a framework takes time. You can't know a framework is reusable until you've used it on more than one project—that's the definition of reusability—so it takes at least twice as long to build a framework as to deliver a project. A framework gradually improves as it is refined on successive projects. The client/server framework outlined in this chapter has evolved over several years from really crude beginnings, and it continues to improve, with no end in sight.

- Developing a framework is hard. If it is going to simplify the application programmer's job, it must do all the things he doesn't want to do. For a client/server framework, these things can include conversions between databases and objects, communications and transaction management, event processing and window management, usability, and even performance optimizations. Technical difficulties that are not specifically part of the business problem are better left to a reusable framework than agonized over by each application programmer.

For background on the conceptual and practical considerations in client/server computing, see [Orfali et al. 1994]. The principles governing the client/server framework touched upon in this chapter are the subject of [Wolf and Liu 1995]. The actual framework is known as *MFW (materialization framework)*. However, the ideas, names of classes and methods, and algorithms here are simplified for clarity and do not coincide literally with their counterparts in MFW, nor does this chapter cover the full scope of the framework.

Object-oriented frameworks can deal with any aspect of computing: *Common-Point* consists of myriad related C++ frameworks for dealing with problems ranging from graphics to document-editing to National Language Support to I/O device drivers [Lewis et al. 1995]. *Accounts* is a Smalltalk framework for building business applications that maintain general ledger accounts, inventories, investment accounts, and the like [Johnson 1995]. *MacApp* is a framework for producing applications having the Macintosh look and feel using either C++ or Object Pascal [Schmucker 1986; [Lewis et al. 1995]. And *MVC* is, as historians say about certain landmarks, the oldest continuously operating framework in the world.

19.7   Commentary: varieties of brokers

The number of kinds of brokers in the computing world is enormous. They are at the heart of every distributed computing architecture.

Brokers that operate with server programs and exchange standard information units—records, CORBA objects, Network OLE objects…—are known as transaction brokers. Transaction brokers are compatible with relational databases: if the server data are relational, the server programs convert the data to and from standard information units. Transaction brokers partition logic between computing nodes; distributed systems based on them therefore decouple clients from servers, which enhances a system's long-term flexibility.

From the point of view of a client application, a broker object functions much like an object database: it retrieves objects, updates them, manages concurrent access to them, and so on. If you think of brokers and object databases interchangeably, then it is not hard to imagine object databases as an alternative approach to distributed objects. Thus you should expect object databases to compete with transaction brokers for dominance in client/server and distributed object computing.

Despite the benefits of transaction brokers, SQL brokers are more popular. They can produce working applications quickly because they don't require additional programs to be written in a foreign language at the server. On the other hand, they require a relational database at the server, and they couple the client tightly to the structure of the relational tables—the antithesis of the spirit of encapsulation. In the long run they will remain useful for proofs-of-concept and prototypes, but transaction brokers will displace them for extensible, high-performance applications.

19.8   Commentary: buying outdoes inheriting (sometimes)

Frameworks prove that there is an essential niche in the world for inheritance and white-box reuse. Moreover, we are all conditioned to savor the appeal of inheritance—creating a specialized object by inheriting from some class that provides function close to what we need. Inheritance is one of the most touted techniques in object-oriented programming and is so easy to do that we are liable to overdo it. Over time, however, good designs inherit less and buy more (Chapter 9). That is, we gradually realize ways to reduce white-box reuse in favor of black-box reuse.

Here is an example. A loan object's data are different from a customer object's, so the fields in their underlying records, as well as their sizes, are decidedly unlike. It is therefore tempting to create two subclasses of class **Record**, namely **LoanRecord** and **CustomerRecord**, each of which supports appropriate field-by-field accessors, such as **atCollateral** and **atCollateralPut:** for a **LoanRecord**, and **atName** and **atNamePut:** for a **CustomerRecord**.

This straightforward design works, but is unattractive. First, it proliferates classes, necessitating a separate record class for each class of business object. Second, the inheritance is not fundamentally behavioral; rather it is based on inert data attributes like the loan's collateral description and the customer's name. Interesting objects ought to be characterized more by behavior than data. In fact it seems here that each subclass is accompanied by an entire family of methods that have nothing in common with the rest. No methods are reused, shared, or overridden, and none are candidates for subclassResponsibility methods. The final and perhaps most alarming indication is that these record classes form an inheritance hierarchy with no polymorphism in sight.

These indications encourage us to consider an alternative, non–inheritance-based solution. We consider then a single concrete **Record** class and design it to be configurable so that its instances can serve either a loan or a customer. Although the records for loans and customers have disparate sizes and contents, we design them to be behaviorally identical. Specifically, their essential public selectors are **at:** and **at:put:**, where the first keyword parameter is the name of a field, such as **#Collateral** or **#Name**. In this way we rid the design of an entire hierarchy of record subclasses, trimming countless methods as well as classes from the application. This inheritance-free design agrees with the *objects from records* pattern (see the figure on page 223).

Here are two other examples of this progression away from inheritance-based designs:

- Pluggable views let programmers configure widgets instead of having to create subclasses of them (page 140).

- Early object-oriented exception-handling mechanisms laid out class hierarchies of exceptions, even though the essential behavior of all exception objects is the same. Hence recent exception schemes (including IBM Smalltalk's) use instance hierarchies of exceptions. This scheme nips in the bud a potential flurry of class building.

Lest these arguments induce you to *avoid* inheritance at all costs, remember that inheritance designs remain desirable as long as you find polymorphism in them. Thus the shortcomings outlined above do not apply to the key abstract classes we visited in this chapter, such as **BusinessObject** and **Broker**. You will find lots of overridden methods and polymorphic behavior (methods **Broker>>objectClass** and **Business-Object>>identityKey**, for example) in the subclasses of these abstract classes, which should reassure you that this inheritance-based design is entirely appropriate and worthwhile.

CHAPTER 20

Metaclasses

We have now learned about polymorphism, patterns, frameworks, and the rest of the customary object-oriented topics. This brief chapter offers a respite from those mainstream topics and a final excursion for readers who are curious about just how far Smalltalk goes to celebrate its consistent view of objects. Along the way it answers a simple but perplexing question: "Where is method **new?**" It is possible to program competently in Smalltalk for years without understanding the answer, but the answer is an opportunity to discover the abstruse world of *metaclasses*.

20.1   Facts about metaclasses

We begin with a challenge: since a Smalltalk class is an object too, it must be an instance of something. What? Each class is an instance of its own *metaclass*. If you think of classes as factories, then you can think of metaclasses as the factories that produce ordinary factories like **String**, **Date**, **Stream**, and **Whale**.

Metaclasses have two unusual characteristics:

1   Every class is the only instance of its metaclass. In other words, each metaclass has exactly one instance, no more and no less, and that instance is an ordinary class.

2   Metaclasses have no names. This explains why you won't see them in any browsers. How then do you see them in Smalltalk? The same way you see the class of any object in Smalltalk—by sending the object the message **class** and displaying or inspecting the result. Thus, just as displaying **2.7182 class** produces *Float*, displaying **Whale class** produces the metaclass of **Whale**. But how would Smalltalk display this metaclass? After all, I have said that metaclasses have no names. The answer is barely satisfying: Smalltalk only displays *Whale class*. That is, Smalltalk

only parrots the original message. Disappointing or not, this is how Smalltalk informs us that the result of a message is a metaclass.

❑ Predict the result of *displaying* each of the following expressions. If you are uncertain, try the experiments.

```
'melatonin' class
String class
Penguin new class class
Bird class
Bird class allInstances size
```

Solution: Your answers should be *String, String class, Penguin class, Bird class*, and *1*.

Having come this far, you will naturally wonder, "Isn't a metaclass an object too? If so, musn't it also be an instance of something?" The answer is indeed yes, a metaclass is an object, and the something it is an instance of is a class whose name is **Metaclass**. In effect, **Metaclass** is the factory that produces *all* the metaclasses we have been talking about. **Metaclass** then must be quite large.

❑ How many instances of **Metaclass** are there?

Solution: The instances of **Metaclass** are the metaclass objects, and we know there is precisely one for each ordinary class. Therefore there are as many instances of **Metaclass** as there are ordinary classes in Smalltalk. In the version of VisualAge I am now using, that amounts to about 2100 instances. You can count the metaclasses in your own system by *displaying* **Metaclass allInstances size**.

Notice that **Metaclass** has a name. It is an ordinary class! Its instances just happen to be these peculiar objects known as metaclasses.

20.2   Inheritance

❑ *Display* the result of each of these expressions.

```
Integer superclass
Penguin superclass
Penguin new class superclass
Penguin class superclass
```

Solution and discussion: The first two responses are dull: *Number* and *Bird*. But the result of the last two messages is important news about the inheritance of metaclasses. The responses, *Bird* and *Bird class*, tell us that the superclass of **Penguin**'s metaclass is **Bird**'s metaclass. Invent and experiment with other examples involving classes and the superclass message. Your experiments should confirm that whenever **A** is a subclass of **B**, **A**'s metaclass is also a subclass of **B**'s metaclass. More eloquently, *inheritance of metaclasses parallels inheritance of classes.*[1] We mustn't forget this discovery, so let's give it a name, say, *Rule P* (for *Parallel*).

20.3 Method new

Since a class is an object, it has ordinary methods, just as other objects do. Ordinary methods would be called instance methods, but for classes we have been using a special name for their methods, namely *class methods*. Thus, "class method" is merely a convenient label for referring to an instance method of the class's metaclass. It is easier to talk about "a class method for **Whale**" than "an instance method for **Whale**'s metaclass, **Whale class**."[2]

❏ Of all the class methods you will ever need, **new** is the most important. Suppose you write a class method **new** for **Bird**, and you don't write one for **Penguin**. What method do you expect the message **Penguin new** to execute? Why?

Solution: From our past experience, we expect the **new** method for class **Bird** to execute. That's because we believe that class methods are inherited. But now we have a reason for this inheritance: a class method is really a metaclass instance method, which like any instance method can be inherited from its superclass. But the superclass of **Penguin**'s metaclass is **Bird**'s metaclass (Rule P), so if **Penguin**'s metaclass has no **new** method, it inherits the **new** method from **Bird**'s metaclass.

This logic is pretty satisfying. Class methods are inherited because of Rule P. But here's the shocker. Suppose you don't write any **new** methods in the **Animal** hierarchy at all. What method do you expect the message **Penguin new** to execute? Everyone's first guess is a plausible one—the **new** class method in **Object**. But there is no such method! Class **Object** has no **new** method selector, either instance or class.

We will have to push a little further to find the default **new** method in Smalltalk.

---

[1] Or, *the superclass of the metaclass is the metaclass of the superclass.*

[2] Similarly, since a class is an object, it has a right to its own instance variables. These instance variables have a special name too: they are known as *class instance variables*. Thus, "class instance variable" is the convenient label we use to refer to an ordinary instance variable of the metaclass. We needed class instance variables for the solitaire pattern on page 230.

20.4   The full picture

We are going to assemble a schematic diagram that shows the conceptual relationships between instances and their classes and classes and their superclasses. You have seen the convention before, on page 17, but here it is again in a nutshell:

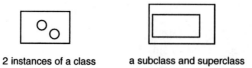

2 instances of a class   a subclass and superclass

The relationships between ordinary instances, their classes, and superclasses look like this:

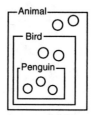

The parallel relationships for classes as objects, their classes, and superclasses look like this:

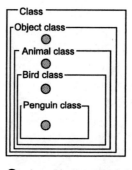

class objects are shaded

Each metaclass has exactly one instance; these instances are classes and are shaded to distinguish them from ordinary instances. From bottom to top they are **Penguin**, **Bird**, **Animal**, and **Object**. Notice the appearance of a class named **Class** that conveniently contains all the class objects. The picture shows that every class is a **Class**, which is a reassuring but unremarkable fact.[3]

---

[3] You encountered the class named **Class** in another context, while solving the exercise on object memory layouts on page 195.

Finally, the metaclasses are objects in their own right, and they all reside in a class named **Metaclass**. You can think of the metaclass objects depicted from bottom to top as **Penguin class, Bird class, Animal class,** and **Object class.**

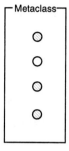

○ metaclass objects are striped

And here is the result of assembling all these schematics into a whole:

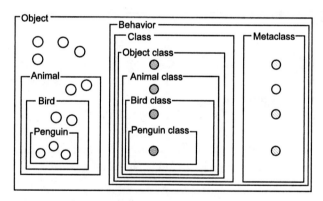

○ an ordinary instance

◉ a class as an instance (the only instance of its metaclass)

○ a metaclass as an instance

One of the side effects of this diagramming technique is that if all 2100 or so classes in VisualAge were represented in one diagram, each class would appear twice, once as a rectangle to indicate its subclass/superclass relationships and once as a shaded circle to indicate what it is an instance of. Similarly, every metaclass would appear twice, once as a rectangle and once as a striped circle.

Notice that one additional class has appeared—**Behavior**. **Behavior** is a superclass of both **Class** and **Metaclass**.[4] As its name and position in the hierarchy suggest, it gathers all the behavior that we would expect for class-like objects.

Behavior is in fact the answer to the question that began this chapter: the default method **new** is an *instance* method in **Behavior**. A glance at the diagram shows that this is an excellent location for **new**. For if none of the animal metaclasses implements a **new** method, inheritance up the metaclass hierarchy in the center of the diagram shows that the lookup for the message **Penguin new** will eventually arrive at **Behavior**, where the default **new** will execute.

In addition to **new**, what other instance methods could plausibly reside in **Behavior**? Well, any method that makes sense for all the class-like objects. By browsing class **Behavior** you will find alluring methods like **allSubclasses**, **allSuperclasses**, **instVarNames**, **methodDictionary**, as well as ones you've already used like **new** and **allInstances**.

20.5 Recapitulation

Smalltalk is pure. "Everything is an object," and every object is an instance of some class. Even an object like a class or metaclass is an instance of some class. The diagram above records these instance-of relationships as circles within rectangles. Whether a circle represents an ordinary instance, a class as an instance, or a metaclass as an instance, it is still an instance of some class, represented by the rectangle enclosing it.

The diagram also records subclass relationships as nested rectangles. Any class-like object, whether a class or a metaclass, also occurs in the diagram as a rectangle. And its superclass occurs as the immediately surrounding rectangle.

The left and middle columns in the diagram illustrate Rule P, that metaclass inheritance *parallels* class inheritance—that the superclass of the metaclass is the metaclass of the superclass. A *class* message like **Penguin new** is really an *instance* message of the metaclass. In the absence of any overriding implementations of **new**, it executes the default *instance* method **new** found in class **Behavior** at the top of the metaclass hierarchy.

---

[4] In IBM Smalltalk and VisualWorks have yet another class—**ClassDescription**, which is a subclass of Behavior and a superclass of both **Class** and **Metaclass**. Its purpose is administrative, and so it would add nothing to the present discussion.

20.6 Exercises

It is a simple matter to verify any relationship in the diagram by experimenting with an appropriate message. For example, the diagram asserts that **Penguin**'s metaclass is a subclass of **Bird**'s metaclass. To verify an *inheritance* relationship like this, use the **superclass** message. Thus, you would *display* **Penguin class superclass** and expect a result of **Bird class**.

Similarly, to verify an *instance* relationship, such as the diagram's assertion that **Penguin**'s metaclass is an instance of class **Metaclass**, use the **class** message. Thus, you would display **Penguin class class** and expect a result of **Metaclass**.

❑ Conversely, the diagram can help predict the result of the messages **class** or **superclass**. Use the diagram to predict the result of *displaying* each of the following messages. Of course you can also verify your answers by running the experiments:

```
Bird new class
Bird new class superclass
Bird class
Bird class superclass
Animal class superclass
Object class superclass
Bird class class
Animal class class
Object class class
Behavior class
```

❑ The diagram is incomplete. A large Smalltalk image contains hundreds of thousands of live objects instead of the 19 shown here. Where in the diagram would each of these objects, represented as plain, shaded, or striped circles, be?

- A whale instance
- A string instance
- **Whale**
- **String**
- **Whale**'s metaclass
- **String**'s metaclass
- **Metaclass**
- **Metaclass**'s metaclass

You can verify your answers by experimenting with the objects above, starting by sending each of them the message **class**.

CHAPTER 21

Why developing software is still hard

The whole job of software development remains about as hard as ever. Every aspect is hard: making sense of requirements, designing good classes, building coherent user interfaces, writing extensible code. Objects add an exciting flavor to the enterprise, but object-oriented development efforts often don't achieve their goals, and many end up as downright failures. What goes wrong?

21.1 Misconceptions

Object-oriented software development is not the bed of roses that many expect. This section challenges some of the popular misconceptions, and should adjust your expectations to a realistic level.

Object-oriented development is easier to learn and do

Reality: The Smalltalk language is easy to learn because it is so small. But the language by itself doesn't do much. It is powerful only in conjunction with the hundreds of foundation classes and thousands of supporting classes that are part of today's Smalltalk products. You will have to learn many of these classes before you can write clean Smalltalk code. This takes time and practice.

It also takes time to become proficient in applying the ideas in this book—designing with containers, polymorphism, patterns, and so on. Everyone has the innate ability to understand and talk about objects, but not everyone will work long and hard enough with them to become a good designer. Look at it this way: object-oriented development increases our toolkit of techniques, which gives us more ways than ever to make a mess. Without the maturity that comes with experience, it is harder than ever to pinpoint desirable solutions in this enlarged universe of possibilities.

Inexperienced programmers are better with objects

A popular misconception about object-oriented programming, particularly Smalltalk programming, is that it is detrimental to have had conventional programming experience, because bad habits acquired from this experience will have to be unlearned. The extreme form of this misconception is that it is better never to have programmed than to have been corrupted by conventional programming languages. Thus, the argument goes, an object-oriented project can succeed better with inexperienced programmers than it would with experienced ones.

Reality: The evidence suggests otherwise. Programming experience is advantageous for learning object-orientation.[1] And projects that move ahead, meet their milestones, and satisfy users and managers, are staffed by knowledgeable programmers—the more expert, the better. Expert programmers excel at the whole infrastructure of software development—connectivity, databases, versioning and configuration management, testing, procedural logic, requirements gathering—all of which were essential to software development before objects were popularized and none of which have been obsolesced by objects. And expert programmers learn objects faster, appreciate their ramifications, and sense how to apply them to problems at hand.

Object-oriented projects are more successful

Reality: An object-oriented project is no more likely to succeed than any other project. Out-of-touch leadership, misplaced optimism, complacency, the wrong tools, and all the rest are just as likely to afflict an object-oriented project as any other. Successful projects need business acumen coupled with technological knowhow, and you can find these qualities in conventional projects as well as in object-oriented ones.

Object-oriented applications enjoy reuse

Reality: A project enjoys reuse if a coherent framework is in place. A framework's abstract classes help developers avoid redundancy. But frameworks are hard to build,

---

[1] See the study of several hundred students in [Liu et al. 1992].

especially for the first problem that the framework is meant to address. Thus reuse within one project is not automatic.

Reuse of objects across projects is also not automatic. Plug-compatible objects are rare. Under the pressures of software development, it is hard enough to make an object work well for the product it is designed for, let alone for one it isn't designed for. The fellow who built the first fire didn't worry about building one in the rain until later. The first one demanded all his attention.

When reuse occurs across projects, it is commonly in the form of a framework that was successful on another project. A good framework's abstract classes stand a chance of being applicable to multiple projects. Eventually we will also succeed in assembling corporate or industry libraries of concrete classes, but only for problems that we understand thoroughly—old problems. New problems demand new solutions, for which there is nothing yet to be reused. Meanwhile, your most reusable asset is your design: code is less valuable than the thinking that went into its creation. Recast in the vocabulary of this book, an organization's real assets are the conceptual models of objects and patterns that its people hold. Therefore, for some time yet, the organization will be better off with the people than the code.

Performance depends on the language

Reality: Performance is popularly ascribed to the programming language: assembler and C++ are fast; LISP and Smalltalk are slow. But the effect of programming languages on performance is smaller than the effect of design. A good Smalltalk design is faster than a bad C++ design, and vice versa. Design therefore matters more than the language.

Be especially wary of the performance of distributed objects. These are typically objects that are portable enough to operate in either a Smalltalk or a C++ environment. We measured the performance of one such object to be 70 times slower than its native Smalltalk counterpart. Extreme generality is almost always as costly as it is seductive.

If it's demo-able, it's do-able

Reality: A demo is the tip of the iceberg. The hard, time-consuming work comes after, and under the demo, in producing robust, fast distributed or client/server support. Making objects persist across a network is tough. (See the border problem on page 267.)

Here's a rule of thumb: from the time the software operates fully, including accessing samples of actual data in a local database, allow half again as much effort to deliver the final product. In other words, a fully operational requirements release, which appears to a user as the final product, consumes only 40 percent of the effort. It is important to get this message across to everyone who is waiting for the final product, or else you stand the risk of disappointing your sponsors. What they can touch and see doesn't change for most of the development cycle.

GUI builders make it easy

Reality: GUI builders alleviate tedium. They are a pleasurable addition to our bag of software tools. But they don't make model-view separations automatic and they divert us from the profoundly challenging task—design. (Remember Chapter 13.)

"I design in Smalltalk"

Reality: Smalltalk programming is unusually close to design, but it is not the same as design. If you are working at a blackboard, whiteboard, with CRC cards, or somewhere else away from your computer, you are clearly designing. Good design is often a social activity. Very often, hard design problems succumb when you try to explain the difficulty to someone else, and some inconsequential remark triggers an idea that pays off.

Nevertheless, much of the time you spend in front of a Smalltalk system is honest design time. Designing is weighing alternatives, including discovering them in the first place and eventually rejecting all but one. This is what you are doing when you investigate classes (remember that today's Smalltalks contain thousands), read and experiment with their methods, or create your own throwaway classes and methods. Struggling over naming classes and selectors, or wordsmithing comments, counts too. Working in Smalltalk can be a form of design, but it is not the only form.

21.2 Where projects go awry: borders

Spectacular project overruns occur when development teams underestimate the difficulty in connecting their applications to other critical computing systems. These systems may be off-the-shelf database products or homegrown systems that are de facto standards for the business. Crossing the borders between the Smalltalk application and each of these systems requires thoughtful design. Smalltalk objects are on one side of each border, and something quite different is on the other. Development teams rarely invest enough time or talent to resolve this mismatch.

The classic system border is the relational-to-object interface that occurs in most of today's client/server applications. The database server may be on a local LAN, but if it is at a remote or mainframe computer the number of conceivable techniques for crossing the border multiplies considerably. Culling the solutions that cannot handle the size or flux of traffic, or cost too much to implement, or are difficult to test, takes seasoned developers. Clean, efficient translations result from intimate familiarity with both sides of the border.

The hurdles proliferate when other kinds of "servers" enter the picture. The requirements of projects I've worked on include borders with other corporate systems—the payments system, the global customer database, the workflow system, and so on. These borders can be treacherous, for these reasons:

- The other system isn't working yet.
- The other system was never designed to have an interface with our new client application.
- The interface exists, but new programs will have to be written on the other system to process our client's requests.
- The system is written in another language, and so we must entrust the work to an entirely different organization.
- The physical connection to the other system is unreliable.
- The cost of testing the border crossing skyrockets.

A small failure at one of these system borders stops the application cold; this kind of failure is more critical and costly than a bug in a user interface or model object. Experienced project planners allot more than half (60 percent—see page 266) of a project's resources to the border problem. Turnkey, black-box solutions rarely match your problem and are difficult to adapt. Workable solutions involve frameworks on one side and perhaps foreign languages on the other.

System borders may be the most spectacular failure points, but all borders are opportunities for missteps. Chapter 13 concerns the treacherous human–computer border. That border dovetails with what is traditionally called requirements gathering, which is the border between the problem-domain expert and the analyst. Ill-defined requirements acquired at this border are at the heart of many disappointing projects. But every human-to-human border in software development exacts some toll for the inefficiency of handing off ideas.

The ultimate, fine-grained border is the public interface of a programming object. Each object is supposed to have an understandable outside, consisting of its public method selectors, so that people will know how to use it. Getting these object borders right is the programmer's core obligation. The lesson of individual objects coincides with the lesson of large-scale software development: borders, or interfaces, matter most. Peter Deutsch, one of the eminences from Smalltalk's heyday at Xerox PARC, summarized it thus: "Interface design and functional factoring constitutes the key intellectual content of software and is far more difficult to recreate than code" [Deutsch 1991].

21.3   Characteristics of successful projects

If we are going to cross our borders efficiently, we will have to understand them. The first guideline is therefore readability.

Readability

You sometimes encounter software in which, as soon as a bug appears and it becomes necessary to peer into the code, you discover a fragile labyrinth of object-oriented spaghetti. You have no hope of fixing the bug, let alone extending the software, without introducing new errors. Working software isn't impressive unless it is also a joy to read: it should hold no mysteries.

Readability plainly involves comments; style; names of methods, classes, and instance variables; and so on. (See [Skublics et al. 1996].) But it includes broader considerations, like window classes weighed down by too many methods, or complicated behavior that ought to have been reified, or code that could be re-factored into patterns or abstract classes, or.... Readability is almost synonymous with good design, and is more of an art than a measurable commodity.

Motivation to write clear code can come from unusual sources. One project, suffering in the wake of client/server code left behind by some eager but inexperienced framework developers, sponsored a contest for "The Method from Hell." To win, you had to find the most hopelessly incomprehensible method in the framework. As a by-product of this friendly competition, developers thought twice before writing methods of their own that might be eligible for future honors.

Reading samples of code is like taking someone's temperature: a project with muddy code, like a person with a fever, cannot be healthy. The code is where all other factors come together; if it is unreadable you have a problem somewhere. You may not know immediately if the root of the problem is faulty analysis, crude design, or slipshod implementation, or even haphazard organizational structures or processes. But you know you must begin the investigation.

Names

Clear names are an essential element of readability: names of methods, names of instance variables, names of classes. The first thing a Smalltalk programmer does when looking at a class is browse through the class's method selectors. Well-named selectors are signposts; poorly named ones confuse programmers and hinder understanding. Bad names haunt a project forever; good names trumpet the software's design.

Names are especially significant in object-oriented software. The name someone gives a class is supposed to clearly and immediately evoke the nature of that class to everyone else—analysts, developers, testers. Effective names connote the right idea *and* act as handles for conversations between developers. Here are some examples of the consequences of names—a good, mediocre, and bad choice, respectively:

- Nicknames for ideas help developers communicate. After deciding to use **Skinny-Customer** for the name of a class of ghosts (page 226), we referred to instances as "skinnies." This nickname expedited countless rapid-fire conceptual discussions.[2]

- Precise names can be too cumbersome for day-to-day thinking and conversation. **MutualFundAccountTelephoneExchangeRole** may be precisely right, but it is a mouthful that takes a while for the brain to process. Sometimes it is worth sacrificing a little precision for the sake of a simpler name and to trust the context of a project to supplement everyone's understanding.

- At the other extreme, a name like **SmartGuy** is too vague. Explanations of this unfortunate name dragged on through weeks of meetings because it evoked disparate ideas in the minds of different people. Here, the choice of names impeded rather than enhanced design. (In this project, the behavior of **SmartGuy** encompassed ideas that could have been identified by several specific names, including **TaskMonitor** and **WorkflowServer**.)

Bad names waste time and money. We expend mental energy reconstructing what they mean. If a project names the yellow-rumped warbler a "red-winged blackbird," then whenever someone says "red-winged blackbird" we start to imagine a chunky dark bird in the reeds instead of the tiny flitty bird overhead that we are supposed to imagine. Our brains start down the wrong track, processing excess, irrelevant thoughts.

---

[2] We rejected several alternatives: **SummaryCustomer** (connotes collapsing and paraphrasing rather than simple subsetting); **LiteCustomer** (too trendy to stand the test of time); **DietCustomer** (pointlessly humorous); and **SynopsisCustomer** (difficult to repeat quickly during a spirited design conversation).

Understanding the problem

Nothing is more disgraceful than paying expensive Smalltalk programmers to produce what they think an organization needs. If they don't understand the problem they've been asked to solve, be it how bankers finance international trade or geneticists infer the locations of genes on chromosomes, the project's outlook is grim. The remedy, whether you call it requirements gathering or object-oriented analysis, is a sizable investment of time and work with someone who *does* understand the problem. The border between developers and users must be crossed.

Understanding object-orientation

This is the obvious factor. Until you are comfortable with containers, abstract classes, polymorphism, and all the rest, your designs are bound to be crude. And until you have written a sizable body of Smalltalk code, you can benefit from an experienced Smalltalk programmer who reviews your work and suggests ways of cleaning it up.

Leadership

Leaders may be managers, or team leaders, or programmers. The title matters less than the qualities. Effective leaders understand the problem and have firsthand experience with the power and limitations of their object-oriented tools. They also have political savvy: they are familiar enough with the surrounding organization to secure the support and resources the project needs. When any of these elements is missing, a project founders. It acquires the wrong tools and frameworks at the wrong times, and misapplies whatever it acquires. Something will work and delight the team or its customers, but no culture or discipline moves the effort toward an industrial-strength product. In the saddest scenarios, programmers and designers run amok formulating grand abstractions and trying to solve general problems. (If they knew the adage, "The devil is in the details," they would know that there are plenty of challenges in basic, concrete problems, and that until they overcome those challenges, any attempt to solve general problems is futile.)

I once heard it suggested that software development proceeds like the universe unfolding from the Big Bang. What happens at a key moment can shape the whole course of the future. The hiring of an unusual developer or manager, an insinuation about an architecture or tool, the fateful throwaway remark—any of these can lead eventually to products with entirely different looks and feels, performance, or durability. Each decision influences the next decision, and the next, and the next. Software development is a chaotic phenomenon like the weather, whose outcome in New York can pivot on how a butterfly happened to flap its wings one month earlier in Beijing. No one is prescient enough to forecast the precise shape of the future. We only hope that our leaders' hunches—their flapping wings—will save us from the costliest blunders.

Involving prospective users, continuously

A parable: A partnership was formed late in the 1980s to build a 14-mile road. The partners planned to reap a profit by charging motorists $1.75 for driving on it. The road would serve a high-income area with a rapidly growing population. In 1995 the road opened, toll booths and all. But the partnership landed immediately in financial trouble because few motorists were willing to pay $1.75 for the privilege of using the road. It turns out that no one ever asked any motorists how much such a road would be worth to them.[3]

Had this been a software project, the developers might have surveyed prospective users before the project began, and several more times while construction proceeded. As often as practical, the developers would even show the users what they hoped to deliver. This is the best way to prevent unwelcome surprises at the end of the project. The developers might even have decided that the project wasn't worth doing.

Humility

Unless you've done it before, whether it's delivering industrial-strength software or running a marathon, it's going to hurt more than you think. Make the first milestone modest. You will learn object-oriented design and programming, how to make objects persist in a database across a network, and how to tune the application so that it performs acceptably.

21.4   An optimistic conclusion

You know by now that the overall difficulty of software development has not changed much from the days before objects. Design, leadership, technology, and so on were important then too. Producing high-quality software has always been difficult, and always will be difficult. Better tools and technologies help, but mostly to simplify the tasks that we have come to understand well enough to build tools for. The hard work is understanding new kinds of problems and designing solutions for them. No matter how good our tools get, the next generation of problems will tax our ingenuity.

---

[3] You can find this story documented in the *Washington Post*, December 26, 1995.

Objects present the opportunity for creating elegant software solutions by applying polymorphism and patterns and frameworks and the like. But amid the hoopla over these buzzwords we should not overlook the underlying benefit of objects. It is what we began with (page 7): objects equip programmers with the same cognitive tools, the same mental processes and metaphors, which the rest of the human population enjoys. Objects therefore reduce the cost of translating ideas from one mind to another. They reduce the occasions for misunderstanding throughout the software enterprise, from requirements analysis through final testing.

We don't know how to quantify the price of these misunderstandings, or the savings from preventing them. Misunderstandings are not as measurable as methodologies, tools, and schedules, or method size, numbers of abstract classes, depths of inheritance hierarchies, or numbers of patterns. We therefore scarcely appreciate the essential economic value of objects: they reduce misunderstandings, so that we can deliver better software.

Some differences between dialects

The table below outlines some of the differences among major Smalltalk dialects. It is neither detailed nor complete and therefore is not meant for the faint of heart. But for readers with an investigative bent it hints at discrepancies that are likely to arise between this book, written for IBM Smalltalk, and other dialects. It also points to a few areas not discussed in this book where the dialects are based on fundamentally different precepts. Note that ParcPlace-Digitalk is working to converge the VisualSmalltalk and Visual-Works products into one offering, which will reconcile the differences between the last two columns in the table.

	VisualAge **(IBM Smalltalk)**	**VisualSmalltalk** **(Smalltalk/V)**	**VisualWorks** **(Smalltalk-80)**
Image name (default)	image	v.exe v.image (Macintosh)	visual.im
	Execute	Do It	do it
	Display	Show It	print it
Transcript's class	**EtTranscript**	**TextWindow**	**TextCollector**
Global variables (use sparingly)	Must be explicitly declared	Prompts you on first attempt to use one	Prompts you on first attempt to use one
Class instance variables	Yes	Yes—literally instance variables of the class's class (absent in older versions)	Yes—literally instance variables of the class's class
Dispatching the message **aMsg**	aMsg sendTo: anObject	aMsg perform	anObject perform: aMsg selector withArguments: aMsg arguments

	VisualAge (IBM Smalltalk)	VisualSmalltalk (Smalltalk/V)	VisualWorks (Smalltalk-80)
Pure virtual (abstract, deferred) method	subclassResponsibility	implementedBySubclass	subclassResponsibility
Opening a text window	EtWorkspace new show: 'Hello, world'	TextWindow new openOn: 'Hello, world'	ComposedTextView open: 'Hello, world' asComposedText
Collection hierarchy is subtyped	No	No	No
Finalization and weak references	Yes	Yes (absent in older versions)	Yes
Look and feel governed by platform's window manager	Yes	Yes	No
Literal strings may be modified	No	Yes	Yes
Literal arrays may be modified	No	Yes	Yes
Block temporary variables [lxl ...]	Yes	No	Yes
Pool dictionary class	EsPoolDictionary	Dictionary	Dictionary
Pool dictionary keys	String	String	Symbol
Subclasses inherit pool dictionaries	Yes	No	Yes
SmallInteger range (on 32-bit platforms)	-2^{30} to $2^{30}-1$	-2^{30} to $2^{30}-1$	-2^{29} to $2^{29}-1$
Broadcaster	AbtObservableObject [a]	EventManager [b]	Model [c]
Exceptions	Instance hierarchy	Class hierachy	Instance hierarcy

[a] Also, the same protocol, but less efficient and less encapsulated, is available for any **Object**. A third protocol is the traditional one using the class variable **Dependents** in **Object**.

[b] Also, the same protocol, but less efficient and less encapsulated, is available for any **Object**. Older versions supported the traditional protocol using the class variable **Dependents** in **Object**.

[c] This class supports the traditional (original MVC) protocol. Also, the same protocol, but less efficient and using the class variable **Dependents**, is available for any **Object**. ParcPlace-Digitalk intends to add **EventManager** broadcasting, as in VisualSmalltalk.

References

[Agha et al. 1989] Gul Agha, Peter Wegner, Akinori Yonezawa, editors. *ACM SIGPLAN Notices* (Proceedings of the ACM SIGPLAN Workshop on Object-Based Concurrent Programming, September 26–27, 1988), vol. 24, no. 4 (April 1989).

[Agha et al. 1991] Gul Agha, Carl Hewitt, Peter Wegner, Akinori Yonezawa, editors. *ACM OOPS Messenger* (Proceedings of the ECOOP-OOPSLA Workshop on Object-Based Concurrent Programming, October 21–22, 1990), vol. 2, no. 2 (April 1991).

[Alexander 1979] Christopher Alexander. *The Timeless Way of Building.* New York: Oxford University Press, 1979. The first of Alexander's twelve volumes (eight published, four to appear) discusses the "quality without a name."

[Alexander et al. 1977] Christopher Alexander, Sara Ishikawa, Murray Silverstein, with Max Jacobson, Ingrid Fiksdahl-King, Shlomo Angel. *A Pattern Language.* New York: Oxford University Press, 1977. The highly readable catalog of 253 patterns for building living spaces.

[America 1991] Pierre America. "Designing an Object-Oriented Programming Language with Behavioural Subtyping," *Foundations of Object-Oriented Languages: REX School/Workshop,* Noordwijkerhout, The Netherlands, May 28–June 1, 1990, Proceedings. Berlin: Springer-Verlag, 1991, pp. 60–90.

[Aristotle 330BC] Aristotle. "Parts of Animals," *A New Aristotle Reader.* J. L. Ackrill, editor. Princeton: Princeton University Press, 1987.

[Baker 1978] Henry G. Baker, Jr. "List Processing in Real time on a Serial Computer," *Communications of the ACM,* vol. 21, no. 4 (April 1978), pp. 280–294. Baker credits the idea of semispaces all the way back to work by Marvin Minsky in 1963; this paper hones the algorithm for real-time applications.

[Beck and Cunningham 1989] Kent Beck, Ward Cunningham, "A Laboratory for Teaching Object-Oriented Thinking," *ACM SIGPLAN Notices* (OOPSLA '89 Conference Proceedings), vol. 24, no. 10 (October 1989), pp. 1–6. The article that introduced CRC cards.

[Black et al. 1986] Andrew Black, Norman Hutchinson, Eric Jul, Henry Levy. "Object Structure in the Emerald System," *ACM SIGPLAN Notices* (OOPSLA '86 Conference Proceedings) vol. 21, no. 11 (November 1986), pp. 78–86.

[Booch 1994] Grady Booch. *Object Oriented Analysis and Design with Applications,* 2nd ed. Redwood City, CA: Benjamin/Cummings, 1994. Probably the most popular object-oriented design methodology.

[Briot 1992] Jean-Pierre Briot. *Tutorial 5: Object-Oriented Concurrent Programming*, OOPSLA '92. Ottawa, Canada, 1992.

[Buhr and Casselman 1992] Raymond J. A. Buhr, Ronald S. Casselman. "Architectures with Pictures," *ACM SIGPLAN Notices* (OOPSLA '92 Conference Proceedings), vol. 27, no. 10 (October 1992), pp. 466–483.

[CACM 1993] *Communications of the ACM* (Special Issue: Concurrent Object-Oriented Programming), vol. 36, no. 9 (September 1993).

[Cardelli et al. 1992] Luca Cardelli, James Donahue, Lucille Glassman, Mick Jordan, Bill Kalsow, Greg Nelson. "Modula-3 Language Definition," *ACM SIGPLAN Notices,* vol. 27, no. 8 (August 1992), pp. 15–42.

[Chambers 1989] Craig Chambers, David Ungar, Elgin Lee. "An Efficient Implementation of SELF, a Dynamically Typed Object-Oriented Language Based on Prototypes," *ACM SIGPLAN Notices* (OOPSLA '89 Conference Proceedings), vol. 24, no. 10 (October 1989), pp. 49–70.

[de Champeaux et al. 1993] Dennis de Champeaux, Douglas Lea, Penelope Faure. *Object-Oriented System Development.* Reading, MA: Addison-Wesley, 1993.

[Civello 1993] Franco Civello. "Roles for composite objects in object-oriented analysis and design," *ACM SIGPLAN Notices* (OOPSLA 1993 Conference Proceedings), vol. 28, no. 10 (October 1993), pp. 376–393.

[Coad 1992] Peter Coad. "Object-oriented patterns," *Communications of the ACM,* vol. 35, no. 9 (September 1992), pp. 152–159.

[Coad et al. 1995] Peter Coad, David North, Mark Mayfield. *Object Models: Strategies, Patterns, and Applications.* Englewood Cliffs, NJ: Prentice-Hall, 1995.

[Coad and Yourdon 1991] Peter Coad, Edward Yourdon. *Object-Oriented Analysis*, 2nd ed. Englewood Cliffs, NJ: Prentice-Hall, 1991.

[Collins 1995] Dave Collins. *Designing Object-Oriented User Interfaces.* Redwood City, CA: Benjamin/Cummings, 1995. The broadest and deepest resource relating user interfaces to object-oriented programming.

[Cook 1989] W. R. Cook. "A Proposal for Making Eiffel Type-safe," *ECOOP '89* (Proceedings of the 1989 European Conference on Object-Oriented Programming). Cambridge, UK: Cambridge University Press, 1989, pp. 57–70. Part of the subtyping debate; this paper supports contravariance of argument types.

[Cook 1992] William Cook. "Interfaces and Specifications for the Smalltalk-80 Collection Classes," *ACM SIGPLAN Notices* (OOPSLA '92 Conference Proceedings), vol. 27, no. 10 (October 1992), pp. 1–15. The definitive analysis of types versus classes in Smalltalk-80's collection classes.

[Coplien and Schmidt 1995] James Coplien, Doug Schmidt, editors. *Pattern Languages of Program Design.* Reading, MA: Addison-Wesley, 1995.

[Crick 1988] Francis Crick. *What Mad Pursuit: A Personal View of Scientific Discovery.* New York: Basic Books, 1988.

[Cunningham and Beck 1986] Ward Cunningham, Kent Beck. "A Diagram for Object-Oriented Programs," *ACM SIGPLAN Notices* (OOPSLA '86 Conference Proceedings), vol. 21, no. 11 (November 1986), pp. 361–367.

[Davis and Morgan 1993] John Davis, Tom Morgan. "Object-Oriented Development at Brooklyn Union Gas," *IEEE Software*, vol. 10, no. 1 (January 1993). Describes an early object-oriented tour de force.

[Deutsch 1991] L. Peter Deutsch. "Objects: Just Another Technology?" Presentation at *Symposium on Object-Oriented Computing*. Thornwood, NY: IBM, 1991.

[Dijkstra et al. 1989] Edsger Dijkstra. "On the Cruelty of Really Teaching Computing Science," *Communications of the ACM*, vol. 32, no. 12 (December 1989), pp. 1398–1404. Rejoinders follow by David Parnas, W. L. Scherlis, M. H. van Emden, Jacques Cohen, R. W. Hamming, Richard Karp, Terry Winograd, pp. 1405–1414.

[Eggenschwiler and Gamma 1992] Thomas Eggenschwiler, Erich Gamma. "ET++ Swaps Manager: Using Object Technology in the Financial Engineering Domain," *ACM SIGPLAN Notices* (OOPSLA '92 Conference Proceedings), vol. 27, no. 10 (October 1992), pp. 166–177. Terse descriptions of some patterns that have since entered the object-oriented vernacular.

[Feynman 1967] Richard Feynman. *The Character of Physical Law.* Cambridge, MA: MIT Press, 1967. Illuminating lectures aimed at the non-specialist.

[Gabriel 1993–1994] Richard Gabriel. (5 articles) "The quality without a name"; "Pattern languages"; "The failure of pattern languages"; "The bead game, rugs, and beauty, parts I and II"; *Journal of Object-Oriented Programming*, vol. 6, no. 5 (September 1993), pp. 86–89; vol. 6, no. 8 (January 1994), pp. 72–75; vol. 6, no. 9 (February 1994), pp. 84–88; vol. 7, no. 3 (June 1994), pp. 74–78; vol. 7, no. 5 (September 1994), pp. 44–49. A retelling of the architectural odyssey of Christopher Alexander, with attempts to link it to software.

[Gamma et al. 1995] Erich Gamma, Richard Helm, Ralph Johnson, John Vlissides. *Design Patterns: Elements of Reusable Object-Oriented Software.* Reading, MA: Addison-Wesley, 1995. The standard reference on patterns, written by the so-called Gang of Four.

[Gibson 1990] Elizabeth L. Gibson. "Objects—Born and Bred," *BYTE Magazine* (October 1990), pp. 245–254. The first description of the Object Behavior Analysis (OBA) design methodology.

[Goldberg and Robson 1983] Adele Goldberg, David Robson. *Smalltalk-80: The Language and its Implementation.* Reading, MA: Addison-Wesley, 1983 (Reprinted with corrections, July 1985). The classic Smalltalk sourcebook, now, sadly, out of print.

[Hadamard 1954] Jacques Hadamard. *An Essay on the Psychology of Invention in the Mathematical Field.* Reprint of 1949 Princeton University Press edition, New York: Dover, 1954.

[IBM 1995] *IBM Smalltalk Programmer's Reference: Version 3, Release 0.* SC34-4493-02. IBM Corporation, 1995. Clear exposition of Motif widget support, as well as other facets of IBM Smalltalk.

[Ingalls 1986] Daniel H. H. Ingalls. "A Simple Technique for Handling Multiple Polymorphism." *ACM SIGPLAN Notices* (OOPSLA '86 Conference Proceedings) vol. 21, no. 11 (November 1986), pp. 347–349. The original discussion of double dispatch, succinct and lucid.

[Jacobson 1987] Ivar Jacobson. "Object Oriented Development in an Industrial Environment," *ACM SIGPLAN Notices* (OOPSLA '87 Conference Proceedings), vol. 22, no. 12 (December 1987), pp. 183–191.

[Jacobson et al. 1992] Ivar Jacobson, Magnus Christerson, Patrik Jonsson, Gunnar Overgaard. *Object-Oriented Software Engineering: A Use Case Driven Approach.* Reading, MA: Addison-Wesley, 1992.

[Johnson 1992] Ralph E. Johnson. "Documenting Frameworks Using Patterns," *ACM SIGPLAN Notices* (OOPSLA '92 Conference Proceedings), vol. 27, no. 10 (October 1992), pp. 63–76. Patterns for understanding the HotDraw framework.

[Johnson 1995] Ralph E. Johnson. "Accounts: A framework for business transaction processing," http://st-www.cs.uiuc.edu/users/johnson/Accounts.html.

[Johnson and Russo 1991] Ralph E. Johnson and Vincent F. Russo. "Reusing Object-Oriented Designs," *University of Illinois Technical Report* UIUCDCS 91-1696.

[Kay 1988] Alan Kay. Presentation at IBM symposium, *Directions in Object-Oriented Computing*. Thornwood, NY: IBM, 1988.

[Kay 1990] Alan Kay. "User Interface: A Personal View," *The Art of Human-Computer Interface Design*. Brenda Laurel, editor. Reading, MA: Addison-Wesley, 1990, pp. 191–207.

[Kay 1993] Alan Kay. "The Early History of Smalltalk," *ACM SIGPLAN Notices (History of Programming Languages–II)* vol. 28, no. 3 (March 1993), pp. 69–95. The lore of how Smalltalk came to be, told by its creator.

[Krasner 1984] Glenn Krasner, editor. *Smalltalk-80: Bits of history, words of advice*. Reading, MA: Addison-Wesley, 1984.

[Lakoff and Johnson 1980] George Lakoff, Mark Johnson. *Metaphors We Live By*. Chicago: University of Chicago Press, 1980.

[Lalonde et al. 1986] Wilf LaLonde, Dave Thomas, John Pugh. "An Exemplar-Based Smalltalk," *SIGPLAN Notices* (OOPSLA '86 Conference Proceedings) vol. 21, no. 11 (November 1986), pp. 322–340. An early attempt to resolve the type versus class conflict in Smalltalk.

[Laurel 1990] Brenda Laurel, editor. *The Art of Human-Computer Interface Design*. Reading, MA: Addison-Wesley, 1990.

[Lea 1992] Doug Lea. "Run-Time Type Information and Class Design," *USENIX C++ Technical Conference Proceedings 1992*. Usenix Association, 1992, pp. 341–347. Practical advice for using the recent RTTI feature of C++.

[Lewis et al. 1995] Ted Lewis, Glenn Andert, Paul Calder, Erich Gamma, Wolfgang Pree, Larry Rosenstein, Kurt Schmucker, André Weinand, John M. Vlissides. *Object-Oriented Application Frameworks*. Greenwich, CT: Manning Publications, 1995. Summaries of several notable frameworks.

[Lieberman 1986] Henry Lieberman. "Using Prototypical Objects to Implement Shared Behavior in Object Oriented Systems," *SIGPLAN Notices* (OOPSLA '86 Conference Proceedings), vol. 21, no. 11 (November 1986), pp. 214–223.

[Lieberman and Hewitt 1983] Henry Lieberman, Carl Hewitt. "A Real-Time Garbage Collector Based on the Lifetimes of Objects," *Communications of the ACM*, vol. 26, no. 6 (June 1983), pp. 419–429.

[Linnaeus 1753] Carl Linnaeus. *Species Plantarum, A Facsimile of the first edition 1753, with an introduction by W. T. Stearn*. London: the Ray Society, 1957 (vol. 1) 1959 (vol. 2).

[Meyer 1988] Bertrand Meyer. *Object-Oriented Software Construction*. Hertfordshire, UK: Prentice Hall International, 1988.

[Meyer 1992] Bertrand Meyer. *Eiffel: The Language*. Hertfordshire, UK: Prentice-Hall International, 1992.

[Muir ca. 1880] John Muir. *The Wilderness World of John Muir.* Edwin Way Teale, editor. Boston: Houghton Mifflin, 1954. The passage on page 147 comes at the climax of the adventure of the singular mutt Stickeen.

[Nelson 1990] Theodor Holm Nelson. "The Right Way to Think About Software Design," *The Art of Human-Computer Interface Design.* Brenda Laurel, editor. Reading, MA: Addison-Wesley, 1990, pp. 235–244.

[Objectshare 1995] *WindowBuilder Pro 3.0 Tutorial and Reference Guide.* Edition for IBM Smalltalk and VisualAge. Objectshare Systems, Inc., 1995. Includes excellent discussion of Motif widget programming.

[Orfali et al. 1994] Robert Orfali, Dan Harkey, Jeri Edwards. *Essential Client/Server Survival Guide.* New York: John Wiley & Sons, 1994. A comparative approach to the concepts and implementation alternatives of client/server computing.

[Petroski 1985] Henry Petroski. *To Engineer Is Human: The Role of Failure in Successful Design.* New York: St. Martin's Press, 1985. Failure has always been intertwined with progress, and always will be.

[Pirsig 1974] Robert Pirsig. *Zen and the Art of Motorcycle Maintenance.* New York: Bantam, 1974. A study of quality and the hopelessness of describing it.

[Plato 375BC] Plato. *The Republic.* London, UK: Penguin rev. ed., 1987. The date is approximate; the famous dialogue on beds begins Book X.

[Power 1988] Leigh Power. "Specification and Design of Objects," *ACM SIGPLAN Notices* (OOPSLA '87 Addendum to the Proceedings), vol. 23, no. 5 (May 1988), pp. 7–16. Kent Beck discusses a tiny pattern language for user interfaces that is as relevant today as then.

[Reenskaug 1996] Trygve Reenskaug, with Per Wold, Odd Arild Lehne. *Working with Objects: The OOram Software Engineering Method.* Greenwich, CT: Manning Publications, 1996. Peppered with wisdom on the human role.

[Rubin and Goldberg 1992] Kenneth S. Rubin, Adele Goldberg. "Object Behavior Analysis," *Communications of the ACM,* vol. 35, no. 9 (September 1992), pp. 48–62.

[Rumbaugh et al. 1991] James Rumbaugh, Michael Blaha, William Premerlani, Frederick Eddy, William Lorensen. *Object-Oriented Modeling and Design.* Englewood Cliffs, NJ: Prentice-Hall, 1991. A standard reference on object design, slanted toward entity-relationship modeling.

[Sacks 1985] Oliver Sacks. *The Man Who Mistook His Wife for a Hat, and Other Clinical Tales.* HarperCollins, 1985. Revealing tales of neurological irregularities.

[Sakkinen 1989] M. Sakkinen. "Disciplined Inheritance," *ECOOP '89* (Proceedings of the 1989 European Conference on Object-Oriented Programming). Cambridge, UK: Cambridge University Press, 1989, pp. 39–56.

[Samples et al. 1986] A. Dain Samples, David Ungar, Paul Hilfinger. "SOAR: Smalltalk Without Bytecodes," *ACM SIGPLAN Notices* (OOPSLA '86 Conference Proceedings), vol. 21, no. 11 (November 1986), pp. 107–118.

[Sarkela 1989] John Sarkela. Presentation at IBM workshop, *Management Implications of Object-Oriented Programming.* Westlake, TX: IBM, ca. 1989.

[Schmucker 1986] Kurt J. Schmucker. *Object-Oriented Programming for the Macintosh.* Hasbrouck Heights, NJ: Hayden, 1986. The MacApp framework, plus an appendix on Macintosh UI standards.

[Shakespeare 1609] William Shakespeare. "Sonnet 18," *The Riverside Shakespeare*. Boston, MA: Houghton Mifflin, 1974.

[Shoch 1979] John F. Shoch. "An Overview of the Programming Language Smalltalk-72," *ACM SIGPLAN Notices,* vol. 14, no. 9 (September 1979), pp. 64–73.

[Skublics et al. 1996] Suzanne Skublics, Edward J. Klimas, David A. Thomas. *Smalltalk with Style*. Englewood Cliffs, NJ: Prentice-Hall, 1996. One hundred and twenty-six guidelines worth considering.

[Snyder 1986] Alan Snyder. "Encapsulation and Inheritance in Object-Oriented Programming Languages," *ACM SIGPLAN Notices* (OOPSLA '86 Conference Proceedings), vol. 21, no. 11 (November 1986), pp. 38–45.

[Stroustrup 1991] Bjarne Stroustrup. *The C++ Programming Language,* 2nd ed. Reading, MA: Addison-Wesley, 1991.

[Stroustrup 1994] Bjarne Stroustrup. *The Design and Evolution of C++*. Reading, MA: Addison-Wesley, 1994. The story of where C++ has been and where it might go, by its chief inventor.

[Sun 1995] *The Java Language Specification, Release 1.0 Alpha*. Sun Microsystems Computer Corporation, 1995.

[de Troyes 1190] Chrétien de Troyes. "The Story of the Grail," *Arthurian Romances*. New York: Penguin, 1991. The earliest known telling of Arthurian tales.

[Ungar and Jackson 1988] David Ungar, Frank Jackson. "Tenuring Policies for Generation-Based Storage Reclamation," *ACM SIGPLAN Notices* (OOPSLA '88 Conference Proceedings), vol. 23, no. 11 (November 1988), pp. 1–17.

[Wegner 1987] Peter Wegner. "Dimensions of Object-Based Language Design," *ACM SIGPLAN Notices* (OOPSLA '87 Conference Proceedings), vol. 22, no. 12 (December 1987), pp. 168–182.

[Wegner and Zdonik 1988] Peter Wegner, Stanley Zdonik. "Inheritance as an Incremental Modification Mechanism or What Like Is and Isn't Like," *ECOOP '88* (Proceedings of the 1988 European Conference on Object Oriented Programming). Berlin: Springer-Verlag, 1988, pp. 55–77.

[Wirfs-Brock et al. 1990] Rebecca Wirfs-Brock, Brian Wilkerson, Lauren Wiener. *Designing Object-Oriented Software*. Englewood Cliffs, NJ: Prentice-Hall, 1990. Focus first on the responsibilities of objects.

[Wolf and Liu 1995] Kirk Wolf, Chamond Liu. "New Clients with Old Servers: A Pattern Language for Client/Server Frameworks," *Pattern Languages of Program Design*. James Coplien, Doug Schmidt, editors. Reading, MA: Addison-Wesley, 1995, ch. 4.

[Yonezawa and Tokoro 1987] Akinori Yonezawa, Mario Tokoro, editors. *Object-Oriented Concurrent Programming*. Cambridge: MIT Press, 1987.

Index

Printed in the United States
1036600001B